Sister Helen Marie OSF

may be kept

DICTIONARY OF SCHOLASTIC PHILOSOPHY

DICTIONARY
OF
Scholastic Philosophy

BERNARD WUELLNER, S.J.
JOHN CARROLL UNIVERSITY, CLEVELAND

THE BRUCE PUBLISHING COMPANY
MILWAUKEE

IMPRIMI POTEST:

> LEO D. SULLIVAN, S.J.,
> *Praepositus Provincialis*
> *Regionis Ohio-Michiganensis*

NIHIL OBSTAT:

> JOHN A. SCHULIEN, S.T.D.,
> *Censor librorum*

IMPRIMATUR:

> ✠ ALBERT G. MEYER,
> *Archiepiscopus Milwauchiensis*
> October 27, 1955

PREFACE

A dictionary of the language of scholastic philosophy fitted to the needs of beginners and of undergraduate students of the subject is not available in English. The usual manuals supply indices of terms used and sometimes even a glossary of the terms of the particular branch which is treated in a course. But a dictionary combining the usage in all parts of the scholastic system is also needed. Surely, the beginner must master the language of philosophy before he can conquer the thought of the scholastic philosophers.

The scholastic philosopher is interested in definitions for a different reason than the lexicographer and linguist. The philosopher is trying to learn things. He defines, after investigating reality, in an attempt to describe reality clearly and to sum up some aspect of his understanding of reality. Hence, we find our scholastic philosophers adopting as a main feature of their method this insistence on defining, on precise and detailed explanation of their definitions, and on proving that their definitions do correctly express what a nature or activity is.

In this DICTIONARY, references to some texts of the great philosophers are often given. These will help the alert student to find the descriptions, analyses, divisions, debates, or proofs on these definitions in some of the great scholastic writers. Yet this is not meant to be an historical catalogue of the usage of scholastic terms even in the principal scholastic writers. Such a project is not the answer to the undergraduate's need. It would require a large team of experts in the history of scholastic philosophy working together for a long period of years to achieve such a dictionary; and it might open up as many debates on shades of meaning and usage as it would definitively settle the preferred usage among the classical writers on the subject.

This maze of diverse historical usages is a good field for scholarly study, and some of this has been done, particularly by our French writers. The practical way out of the maze has been chosen for the undergraduate's benefit by preferring the meanings and descriptions used by Aristotle or St. Thomas or the commoner usage of the better written modern textbooks.

At the same time it is recognized that the discoveries of the right definitions have been important landmarks in the history of philosophical ideas. Of this sort are a number of Aristotle's definitions, e.g., those of art, change, judgment, life, nature, potency, prime matter, soul, time, and virtue. Add to these Boethius' honored definitions of eternity, freedom, and person; and Augustine's on eternal law, peace, and virtue; and St. Thomas' contributions on analogy, law, substance, and many others.

A particular need of the undergraduate is help in defining the incidental and compound terms so often used in scholasticism. Even very good dic-

v

tionaries seldom supply this assistance to the student, though it seems to be one of his needs. To this end, such incidental terms in their bearing on principal terms have been given considerable attention in this DICTIONARY. They follow in alphabetical order after the main term to which they are applied.

Some lists, charts, and diagrams have been included to help the student see the relationships between the members of a family of terms. Some of the divisions and groupings given are certainly debatable, especially as divisions sometimes can be only approximate, sometimes must include analogous members, and sometimes show the result of some historical confusion in the meaning of terms and in the selection of a principle of division of the related meanings. Multiple combinations of the terms are usually omitted in these charts and lists as they seldom occur in that way in any one philosophical context.

A word of attention must be given to some omissions other than mere oversights. First, few terms of specifically theological content have been given, for they can be found in accessible dictionaries of theology and they are useful to the philosopher chiefly by way of contrast to philosophical meanings of the same term. Second, few philosophical systems, doctrines, and opinions are listed, partly because these belong to the general historical study of philosophy rather than to the corpus of scholasticism, and partly because their many varieties need extended and often debatable description rather than crisp definition. Third, the historical variations of usage among scholastics have been rather minimized; and as a consequence, criticism of definitions has not been given in the text, though no doubt a constant criticism of usage was going on in the compiler's mind while selecting from the varieties of opinion and of expression about the same term and thing. Fourth, no attempt has been made to include all the new shades of meaning and even the new coinage of terms by recent scholastic writers. For both the task of collating such novelties would be impracticable, and undergraduates still learning common scholastic language would find slight use in these burdensome details. Finally, many terms which are seldom studied in undergraduate courses are omitted; many of the potential and integral virtues and their opposite vices are examples of such terms.

It was further judged to be unnecessary to follow the practice of full dictionaries in listing the various terms formed from the same root. For example, *knowledge* is listed in this DICTIONARY; but *know, knowable, knower, known* are not listed.

After these explanations for teachers and scholars of scholasticism, a comment for students in our schools is merited. The student should note that a small special dictionary of a subject cannot substitute for his intelligent interpretation of the meaning of a term in context. A dictionary lists usages; but context gives the full-bodied meaning of a word. The student must also recognize that the meaning of the terms listed, not the literal phrasing of a definition, is the point for his attention. Many alternative statements of a definition are often possible. Teachers and textbooks often give such alternative phrasings; so, too, does this DICTIONARY in an effort to explain a term better or in a way that may strike a familiar association in the student's mind. But the mind never can escape its task of judging which phrasing exactly describes the thing, discriminates it from all other terms, and meets the meaning of the context which one is studying. Finally, the student should observe that no special dictionary is a substitute for regular use of a general dictionary of sufficient size, for understanding even of philosophical language often requires good grasp of the meanings of other non-philosophical words that appear in texts, books, and articles that one is reading.

Pope Pius XII in his encyclical, *Humani Generis,* adverted to certain needs and dangers in modern theological and philosophical studies. He called attention to the advantage of understanding and using the tried language of the schoolmen. It is our hope that this dictionary may help the student to find in scholasticism a fair land of light and truth.

ACKNOWLEDGMENTS

After a few years of assembling a file of definitions, in the first instance for one's own use in teaching, a compiler has faded memories of the teachers and students whose inquiries and comments have focused attention on many problems. One remembers better the books, articles, philosophical dictionaries, and footnotes which proved disappointing. The help of Aristotle, of St. Thomas, and of numerous English dictionaries used on many occasions has, of course, been exceptional. Students have begged for relief in annoying problems of terminology. Staff members have not only sponsored this DICTIONARY but have given basic and much appreciated suggestions. Of these suggestions those from two Jesuit priests at John Carroll University, Joseph O. Schell and T. F. Hecht, have been worthy of special thanks. The friendly editor of *The Modern Schoolman,* Reverend George P. Klubertanz, S.J., has helped with advice on abbreviations of scholastic works. The keen eyes and mind of Miss Jane Thompson, also of John Carroll University, have seen to the final polishing of many details. To each of them let me wish the deepest joys of philosophy.

GUIDE TO ENTRIES

1. *Order of Entries*

Entries have been made in alphabetical order. Abbreviations sometimes are not separately listed but are included with the term abbreviated when the abbreviation's spelling begins in exactly the same way as the term and is used as an abbreviation for only one term.

Entries have been made according to the principal term. The modifying incidental terms combining with the principal term follow in alphabetical order after the set of meanings of the principal terms. One result is that most entries in this DICTIONARY are nouns. But a few of the widely used adjectives or incidental terms are also listed alphabetically. The alphabetical order of incidental terms makes them easy to find, but the order has the disadvantage of not pairing opposite terms. Cross references and charts help the locating of opposite incidental terms.

Within an entry this sequence is used as far as it is pertinent to the term being discussed: term or phrase; its part of speech; its meanings; cross references to antonyms, synonyms, and related terms; abbreviation of the term; uses, particularly of adjectival terms; divisions or incidental terms and phrases using the main term; references; charts or diagrams.

2. *Order of Meanings*

If a term has several meanings, the more generalized meaning is given first; then meanings for particular fields of philosophy are given, with an appropriate label for the field. In a few instances, the meaning of a term in several different philosophies is given in order to help understanding and comparison of usage. No attempt has been made to arrange the meanings in an etymological or historical order, as etymology is not the philosopher's province and history of usage descends from popular usage in the case of most scholastic words.

Distinct meanings are separated from each other by a period and number. Meanings or definitions that are approximately the same are separated from each other only by a semicolon. The Arabic numeral and the letters **a, b, c** are sometimes used for clearer grouping of meanings within a field.

3. *Variants and Alternatives*

Variant spellings of the same word are usually given together.

Alternatives of the same main or the same incidental term are usually given in parentheses immediately after the term cited. The definition of the alternatives is usually given only once, but ordinarily with a cross reference from the alternative to the entry under which the definition is fully given.

Some variants and alternatives are listed in standard English dictionaries as obsolete or obsolescent. But as some of these still lead a lively existence in current scholastic writing, they have been included in this DICTIONARY, usually without the notation of their desuetude.

4. *Latin Phrases*

Latin terms and phrases which are not recognized by standard dictionaries as Anglicized have been indicated by the symbol ‡ in main entries and by italics elsewhere. Anglicized phrases are entered just as ordinarily is done for native words.

5. *Abbreviations*

Abbreviations used in this DICTIONARY are listed on a separate page.

Abbreviations for philosophical words are those recognized by several dictionaries of the English and American language.

Standard abbreviations of philosophical classics seem to be non-existent. This DICTIONARY has adopted usage that is accepted in carefully edited books and in footnotes in learned scholastic journals. But no usage seems to be quite general and regulatory in this matter.

6. *References*

References have been entered in historical order of the authors cited. Not all passages in which the term is defined or proved in an author are given, but one or more important passages are given. As it is so much a matter of individual judgment which passage among a number is the most important, no effort was made to indicate the preferred reference.

GUIDE TO ABBREVIATIONS USED

a., aa. — article, articles

Abbr. — abbreviation

ad — reply to objection (by number or numbers)

adj. — adjective

adv. — adverb

Ant. — antonym, antonyms

c. — corpus (body of the article)

C., CC. — chapter, chapters

Cat. — Aristotle's *Categories,* cited by chapters

C.G. — St. Thomas' *Summa contra Gentiles,* cited by books (Roman numerals) and chapters (Arabic numerals)

Comm. in Met. — St. Thomas' *Commentary on Aristotle's "Metaphysics,"* cited by books and lectures

Consolation — Boethius' *Consolation of Philosophy,* cited by books and sections

e.g. — for example

esp. — especially

Generation — Aristotle's *On Generation and Corruption,* cited by books and chapters

i.e. — that is

In Boeth. de Trin. — St. Thomas' *Commentary on the Books of Boethius "On the Trinity,"* cited by questions and articles

lect. — lecture, lesson

Met. — Aristotle's *Metaphysics,* cited by books and chapters, and arranged so that Ia is Book II

n. — noun

N. Eth. — Aristotle's *Nicomachaean Ethics,* cited by books and chapters

no. — number

On the Soul — Aristotle's *De Anima,* cited by books and chapters

part. — participle

pl. — plural

Post. Anal. — Aristotle's *Posterior Analytics,* cited by books and chapters

Power — St. Thomas' *On the Power of God,* cited by questions and articles

Prior Anal. — Aristotle's *Prior Analytics,* cited by books and chapters

q., qq. — question, questions

q.v. — *quod vide,* consult, see

Ref. — reference, references

S.T. — St. Thomas' *Summa Theologiae,* cited by parts in Roman numeral, questions in the first Arabic numeral, and articles, preceded by *a*

s.v. — *sub voce, sub verbo;* see under the word (named)

Syn. — synonym, synonyms, synonymies

Truth — St. Thomas' *On Truth* (*De Veritate*), cited by questions and articles

v. — verb

‡ — symbol indicating Latin terms and phrases which are not recognized by standard dictionaries as Anglicized

? — disputed classification; disputed interpretation; uncertain date

Other references to authors and to works are given by full name and title.

CONTENTS

DIAGRAMS AND CHARTS

DICTIONARY OF SCHOLASTIC PHILOSOPHY

A

A, the symbol for a universal affirmative proposition.

absolute, *adj.* **1.** *chiefly metaphysical senses.* **a.** self-sufficient in being and needing no other; independent of or altogether free from all external causes and conditions and external limitations and having the reason for its being and perfection entirely within itself. **b.** perfect, whole, or complete in itself. **2.** *chiefly logical and epistemological senses.* **a.** considered or conceived in itself, independently of its relations; not thought of as referred to something else. **b.** unqualified; unrestricted; unconditional; simple; categorical. ABBR. – *abs.* USES – *absolute* being, justice, nature, norm, necessity, obligation, perfection, power, supposition, supremacy, or authority. Compare RELATIVE.

absolutely, *adj.* **1.** without condition, limit, exception, or any other qualification, relationship, or attendant circumstance. **2.** in itself alone; in its substance or nature. **3.** abstractly or in separation from all that is not itself. ABBR. – *abs.*

absolutism, *n.* **1.** the doctrine that civil sovereignty or the civil sovereign is unrestricted in authority. **2.** the practical application of such a theory in governing.

abstract, *adj.* **1.** being apart from or considered apart from the actual subject of being. **2.** expressing an essence, property, quality, or other attribute apart from a concrete subject or thing; e.g., sweetness, humanity, patience. ABBR. – *abs., abstr.* ANT. – *concrete.* It is not properly contrasted with *realistic.* In scholasticism it is seldom synonymous with *universal.* USES – *abstract* idea, noun, term, etc.

in the abstract, absolutely; in a condition of mental separation from other concrete relationships and circumstances.

abstracted, *part. as adj.* removed or separated from something, usually by some mental act.

abstraction, *n.* **1.** *in general.* a mental act apprehending some note or formal object of a thing in which the mind attends to this note and does not attend to other notes naturally present in the same concrete object of perception. Abstraction thus has first a negative aspect of detaching or leaving out something as well as a second positive aspect of concentration on some object considered apart from other aspects actually present in the particular real thing. **2.** abstraction *by the senses* in which a sense attends to one sensible property and not to others in the sensible object; as the eye attends only to the color and not to the temperature or taste of an apple. **3.** abstraction *by the imagination* in which the imagination considers a material object or some features of it, but does not attend to the presence or absence of that object. **4.** abstraction *by the intellect* or *reason* in which the intellect considers the nature or a form apprehended in a material object or in the image (phantasm). Compare ANALYSIS; DISTINCTION; INTENTION; MATTER; PRESCISSION; SEPARATION; UNIVERSAL. This intellectual abstraction, to which reference is usually made in philosophical writing, can be of several kinds:

abstraction of first intention, the mental act which results in a direct universal concept or which apprehends an essence which is common to many things.

abstraction of second intention, an act of judgment following the abstraction of first intention and which results in a reflex universal (or transcendental) concept wherein the mind recognizes the universal nature represented as being common to many and predicable of many.

abstractive abstraction, the mental act forming an abstract concept which represents the object attended to as com-

1

pletely detached from its concrete object; e.g., sweetness, roundness, courage are thus abstracted.

first mode (first degree) of abstraction, the abstraction, proper to the philosophy of nature, in which the mind disregards individual (signate) matter, but retains sensible matter while attaining to the universal nature of the material reality so known. Examples are the abstractions which form our first concepts of water as such, of color as such.

formal abstraction, an intellectual separation of a form from sensible matter, without attending to the matter or other forms present at the same time in the object; e.g., abstraction of mathematical objects from physical objects.

second mode (second degree) of abstraction, the abstraction, proper to mathematics (at least to arithmetic and Euclidean geometry), in which the mind disregards both signate and sensible matter, but retains intelligible matter while attaining to the concept of abstract quantity. Examples are the abstractions which form our concepts of circle, plane, etc.

third mode (third degree) of abstraction, the abstraction, more properly called a separation or judgment, peculiar to metaphysics, in which the mind disregards all matter and grasps its object without any necessary relation to matter. Examples are the mind's knowledge of being, existence, substance, unity, etc.

total abstraction, the intellectual representation of the universal or absolute nature taken from the particulars in which the nature exists; the abstraction of the whole nature or essence from all accidental elements in the concrete object. REF. – *On the Soul,* I, C. 1, near end. *S.T.,* I, 40, a. 3; 85, a. 1 ad 1, 2. *Truth,* q. 2, a. 6. *In Boeth. de Trin.,* q. 5, a. 3. This last text is that principally followed in the foregoing expositions, some of which are differently explained by other scholastic writers. See also A. Maurer, C.S.B., *The Division and Methods of the Sciences.*

abstruse, *adj.* difficult to understand;

hidden. It should not be misused for *abstract.*

accident, *n.* 1. *metaphysics.* something whose essence requires naturally that it exist in another being; a being of a being; a mere modification or attribute of another being; being in a qualified sense; being inhering in another being as in a subject of existence; one of the nine modes in which substance is determined in its being; *ens entis.* In the plural, accidents are often referred to as appearances, phenomena, or species. ANT. – *substance.* See the chart on CATEGORIES OF BEING.

absolute accident, a. one that is really distinct from the subject in which it inheres, as opposed to a modal accident. **b.** one that immediately affects the substance to which it belongs as opposed to a modal accident that immediately affects another accident; thus, quantity as distinguished from shape.

intrinsic accident, one that really modifies a subject, and so is not merely an extrinsic change or name; an accidental form.

metaphysical accident, any accident in the nine categories of accidental being.

modal accident, a. a state affecting the substance, but which is thought of by some scholastic philosophers as not really distinct from the substance or other accidents in the being; e.g., sitting, standing. **b.** one that immediately inheres in or affects other accidents. **c.** a mode of being. See MODE.

physical accident, an absolute accident.

accident, *n.* 2. *causal sense.* what is unforeseen or unintended; the result of chance. 3. *ethics.* a circumstance of a human act. See CIRCUMSTANCE.

accident, *n.* 4. *logic.* an attribute belonging to some nature but not constituting its essence or a part of its essence. It is sometimes called a logical accident.

contingent (logical) accident, an attribute that is not characteristic of or essential to a nature, but may be present or absent in different members of the same species; e.g., white color in human skin.

proper accident, a characteristic or distinctive accident essentially belonging to or necessarily resulting from some essence, and so found in all members of the species; a property or *proprium*. See PREDICABLE.
REF. – *Topics*, I, C. 5. *S.T.*, I–II, 7, a. 1; 17, a. 9 ad 2; 53, a. 2 ad 3; 110, a. 2 ad 3; III, 77, a. 1 ad 2.

accidental, *adj.* **1.** non-essential; not necessary; not always nor usually connected with another. **2.** merely associated with or concomitant. **3.** unforeseen; unintended; beside the intention of the agent or even contrary to intention; marked by chance. **4.** *per accidens*, q.v. **5.** pertaining to the accidents, not to the substance. USES – *accidental* cause, change, difference, event, form, result, sensible, unit.

acquired, *part. as adj.* **1.** received in some way after birth. **2.** gained by one's own activity. **3.** obtained by effort, search, or exchange. Compare CONNATURAL; INFUSED; INNATE. USES – *acquired* property, rights, titles, virtues.

act, *n.* **1.** perfection or a perfection; what is fully real, finished, or fulfilling; an actuality. **2.** *thought of as influencing potency in some way.* a determining principle; the intrinsic principle which confers a definite perfection on a being; hence, a form. **3.** the perfection resulting from an action. **4.** activity, operation, action, or second act of a power. ANT. – *potency.* See the chart on page 4.

act of the imperfect, a real change; the gaining of a new act and the privation of an old form.

act of the perfect, 1. an immanent activity, living action. **2.** especially, an intentional change.

complete act, an end or an operation that is an end; the ultimate act of a being.

entitative act, existence; the act of being; *esse*. Compare FORMAL ACT, *below*.

first act, 1. the intrinsic fundamental perfection of a being in any order. **2.** the first actuality (in a series) that determines any passive potency to be or to be something specific. Hence, the same

being may have several first acts, but each in different orders; existence will be first act in the order of being, substantial form will be first in the order of essence or nature, the power will be first in the order of activity.

first proximate act, the power considered together with all the concrete factors for action. Second act follows as the activity of the prepared power.

first remote act, the power considered all alone.

formal act, substantial form in an essence that is composed of matter and form.

incomplete act, a movement or change going on; an actualizing of a potency that has not yet reached the term of its action.

mixed act, a being or perfection which is united in some way with potency or limitation.

pure act, 1. simple perfection (of any kind) without imperfection; mere perfection free of potency. **2.** *strictest sense.* unqualified perfection of existence, which is neither present in nor united with nor limited by any passive potency.

received act, a perfection of any order combined with and present in a potential subject. *Unreceived act* is not so combined with and present in a subject.

second act, a determination or perfection added to a being which already possesses the first act, whether of existence or of form or of a particular power; e.g., intellect and will with respect to the soul itself; acts of the will with respect to the will itself; accidents of a substance. Hence, a second act presupposes and perfects another act, and is usually an accident.

ultimate act, the last in a series of acts by which a being obtains its proper fullness of being; a complete act.
REF. *Met.*, IX, CC. 6, 8; XI, C. 9. *Power*, q. 1, a. 1.

act, *v.* **1.** to do or to make something. **2.** to cause something to be in act, whether by way of efficient, final, or formal causality.

DIVISIONS OF ACT AND POTENCY

Act (Actual Being)

1. Entitative act (act of being, existence, *esse*)

 Formal act

  a) Whole essence or nature
   Form or determining part of a nature

  b) First act (substantial form)
    Subsistent
    Non-subsistent

   Second act (accidental form)
    Essential (proper)
    Contingent

  c) First act (the power)
    Remote
    Próximate

   Second act (activities of the power)

2. Pure act
 Mixed act

3. Complete act
 Incomplete act

4. Act of the perfect
 Act of the imperfect

5. Unreceived
  Of existence (God)
  Of form (angel's nature)
 Received act

Potency (Potential Being)

Active (is an act, either a nature or a power)

Passive

 Subjective

  1. Pure potency (prime matter)

   Mixed with act
    Substantial (to be other substance)
    Accidental

  2. Natural
    Essential (non-contradictory)
    Existential (producible)

   Obediential

 Objective
  Intrinsic (absolute, metaphysical)
  Extrinsic (relative to a cause)

---

action, *n.* **1.** the category of accident whereby a cause is constituted as actually causing something. **2.** the influence as proceeding from the cause; change or movement considered as proceeding from an agent; hence: **3.** activity; operation; exercise of efficient power. See meaning 4 of ACT. **4.** the actuality of an active potency or virtue. ANT. – *passion.*

action at a distance, action supposedly performed through an absolute vacuum of being so that agent and effect have no immediate or mediate contact.

formal action, what a form does; the

communication of a formal effect to a being. It is also called *improper* causal action.

immanent and **transeunt action,** see ACTIVITY.

proper causal action, the activity of an efficient cause.
REF. – *Generation,* 323b, 18 ff. *S.T.,* I, 41, a. 1 ad 2; 54, a. 1. *C.G.,* II, C. 9. *De Malo,* q. 2, a. 11; q. 5, a. 5.

activity, *n.* the operation or use of a power. In God's case the activity is only virtually distinct from the nature of God.
formally immanent, virtually transeunt activity, God's activity causing creatures, which is at the same time a living divine activity and one which results in something outside God without any passage of being or power from God.
immanent activity, activity which has its principle and term within the agent and which is a perfection of the agent itself, not of an external patient. See LIFE.

transeunt (transitive) activity, activity which has its term outside the cause in another distinct being that is changed by the agent.
REF. – *Met.,* VIII, C. 8; XII, C. 16. *S.T.,* I, 18, a. 3, esp. ad 1; 54, a. 2. *Truth,* q. 8, a. 6.

act of man, *phrase.* an action performed by a human being, but not performed freely or in a specifically human way; e.g., digesting food, hearing loud noises. A *human act* is one proceeding from man's deliberate reason and free will. See HUMAN; VOLUNTARY.

actuality, *n.* **1.** act. **2.** act thought of abstractly. **3.** the state of being in act or of being real and complete.

actualize, *v.* **1.** to impart a new form or actuality to a being, or even to create a being from nothing; to realize the potency of something; to make perfect. **2.** to improve something by giving it a better substantial or accidental form. **3.** to move some power to its proper activity.

adaptation, *n.* the fitting of one thing to another, as of means to end, of part to whole, organs to stimuli or to functions, organisms or environment.

adequate, *adj.* complete, relatively to the topic or problem or nature of which adequacy is predicated; sufficient.

adoration, *n.* the honor and reverence due to another. Today, though not in older literature, the word is commonly reserved for the honor and reverence specially due to God, *latria.*

‡**ad rem,** *Latin phrase.* **1.** to the point; relevant; connected with the topic or thing. **2.** *jus ad rem,* the right to the thing which is not in one's possession, but over which one has a just claim.

adventitious, *adj.* acquired; accruing to a being already complete in essence and in proper accidents.

aesthetics, *n.* the study of the nature and causes of beauty, of the modes of its perception, and of the modes of its realization in artistic products. In strict scholastic usage, aesthetics is not the same as philosophy of art. It is also spelled *aesthetic, esthetics, esthetic.*

aeviternity, *n.* duration with periodic or irregular intervals of change; a mean between the changeless duration of eternity and the constant change of time. The period between change and change in such beings is an *aevum,* i.e., a long period or stage of its existence.
REF. – *S.T.,* I, 10, a. 5.

affection, *n.* **1.** *logic, metaphysics.* an accident, attribute, or modification. **2.** *psychology.* either an agreeable or an unpleasant condition or reaction of the appetite to a stimulus.

affective quality, *phrase.* that class of qualities which are capable of causing agreeable or unpleasant reactions in a perceiving subject; e.g., heat, cold, colors, sweet.
REF. – *Cat.,* C. 8. *Met.,* V, C. 21.

affirmation, *n.* a judgment or proposition that asserts some objective identity between subject and predicate or between antecedent and consequent. See the chart on PROPOSITIONS.

a fortiori, *adjectival phrase.* "for a stronger reason"; all the more so. It is said of a conclusion that is even more logically cogent than a conclusion already accepted.

agent, *n.* an efficient cause. See EFFICIENT CAUSE.

agent intellect, *phrase.* the intellect which abstracts from matter in the phantasms and acts on the possible intellect. See INTELLECT.

aggregate, *n.* a sum, mass, heap, or collection of things not having one nature; an accidental unity composed of many things either like or unlike each other. An aggregate is usually something less organized than a tool, machine, or deliberate product of art.

‡**agibilia,** *n. pl., Latin.* things to be done within the agent and which perfect the agent when they have been done. These are the objects of prudence, while *factibilia,* things to be made, are the objects of art.

agnosticism, *n.* the general view that knowledge or certitude about ultimates is impossible. It especially stresses uncertainty about essence or substance, the existence of the soul, the origin of the universe, the existence or perfections of God, and final causes.

alteration, *n.* **1.** change in regard to the quality or qualities of a thing; otherness in quality. **2.** especially, qualitative change in sensible things.
REF. – *Physics,* VII, C. 3. *Generation,* I, C. 4.

ambiguous, *adj.* capable of being understood in more than one sense; equivocal; uncertain in meaning.

amphiboly, *n.* **1.** a fallacy due to ambiguously selected language. **2.** in reasoning, a fallacy of four terms under the appearance of three terms in a syllogism.

anal., abbreviation for *analogous, analogy, analysis, analytic, analytical.*

analogate, *n.* an analogue, q.v.

analogical, *adj.* somewhat like and somewhat unlike another; intermediate between the univocal and equivocal.

analogues, *n., pl.* the things, attributes, concepts, or terms which bear an imperfect resemblance to each other.

principal (primary) analogue, the one which chiefly and more perfectly has the compared perfection.

secondary (subordinate) analogue, the one which is referred to the principal, or named from the principal, and which is less perfect and posterior in a set of analogues.

analogy, *n.* **1.** *logic.* a form of probable argumentation in which we reason from a known relation between two things to a suspected similar relation between other things that partly resemble the known things; an argument based on similarities, but not on identities, between different things or pairs or groups of things. ABBR. – *anal.*

false analogy, the fallacy of ignoring significant differences in observing and especially in reasoning about imperfectly like things or like relations.

analogy, *n.* **2.** *metaphysics.* resemblance without identity; any imperfect likeness between two or more beings that are compared with each other. ABBR. – *anal.* USES – *analogy* of being, of kinds of knowledge, of kinds of goodness, of life, of predication, of substance and accidents, of various perfections or names.

analogy of attribution, an imperfect resemblance of two or more because of a simple relation or connection of the secondary analogues with the principal analogue. Some property of the principal is attributed to the secondaries because of a real or imagined connection between them; e.g., health belongs to a living body primarily, but only by attribution to medicine, climate, vacation. It is disputed whether or not all analogies of attribution are extrinsic analogies.

analogy of inequality, a univocal likeness of nature with unlikeness in perfection in which that nature or its fullness of attributes is possessed.

analogy of proportionality, an imperfect resemblance between analogues because of a complex set of relations (or a complex relation of proportions) between them; an imperfect resemblance of sets of distinct relations; e.g., goodness in a grape and goodness in an act of kindness. Extrinsic proportionalities are all metaphors; e.g., the flowers *smiled* their welcome. The intrinsic proportionality of being is defended by Thomists, but not all scholastics.

extrinsic analogy, a resemblance or comparison in which the analogous note is truly (intrinsically, properly, or formally) present only in the principal analogue, but is outside the other analogues and is said of them only because of some relation (or reference) to the primary analogue; e.g., metaphors, relations of signs, relations between analogical causes and connected effects.

intrinsic analogy, a resemblance in which the analogous note is truly (intrinsically, properly, formally) present in all the analogues which are being compared. It is occasionally called a *natural* analogy.

REF. – *Met.,* V, C. 7; VII, CC. 1, 4. *S.T.,* I, 4, a. 3; 13, aa. 5, 6, 9, 10. *C.G.,* I, C. 34. *Truth,* q. 2, a. 3 ad 4, 16, 18; a. 11. *Power,* q. 7, a. 7. Cajetan, T., *The Analogy of Names.*

analysis, *n.* **1.** the breaking down of any composite thing into smaller parts, components, or units. **2.** the breaking down of any complex object of thought into simpler concepts and implied judgments. **3.** the mental division of an object and the detailed study of the divided parts or notes one after another. Abstraction attends to only one nature or note, but does not attend to all in turn, as analysis does. **4.** the analytic method. ABBR. – *anal.* See METHOD.

analytic, *adj.* **1.** verifiable by mental inspection of the objects compared without need of experience. See JUDGMENT; PRINCIPLE. **2.** pertaining to mental division.

angel, *n.* an incorporeal substance or creature; a separated intelligence or substance.

anger, *n.* the passion of the irascible appetite which desires revenge for hurt or injury.

animal, *n.* a sentient corporeal substance. Brutes are mere animals, sentient but irrational. Men are both sentient and rational and are known as rational animals. Philosophy does not use the term "animal" in any connotation of disrespect or blame in regard to persons.

animate, *adj.* living; having a soul.

animism, *n.* **1.** the attribution of human powers to material beings and animals. **2.** the confusion of the powers of living things with divine powers: a variety of anthropomorphism. **3.** any theory of vitalism.

annihilation, *n.* the hypothetical reduction of the whole substance of a being to nothingness; the supposed act of God by which He would cease to conserve a creature in existence. Compare CORRUPTION; CREATION.

annulment, *n.* an official declaration by competent authority for lawful reasons that an act or contract is invalid, nonexisting (null), and therefore not binding, or even not allowing performance of its terms.

antecedent, *adj.* going before; preceding; prior. ANT. – *consequent.* USES – *antecedent* concupiscence, necessity, passion.

antecedent, *n. logic.* **1.** that upon which something else is based. **2.** in a syllogism, the premises taken together. **3.** the condition in a conditional proposition.

anthropomorphism, *n.* the practice of thinking of and describing the non-human and particularly the divine merely in terms that are properly applicable only to human nature and human traits.

antinomy, *n.* some self-contradiction of laws or rules; irreconcilable conclusions. The word is particularly famous in Kant's philosophy in reference to the antinomies of pure reason and the supposed antinomies of divine attributes. Compare CONTRADICTION; MYSTERY.

apart, *adj.* separated; not in contact; *adv.* in a different place.

REF. – *Physics,* V, C. 3. *Met.,* XI, C. 12.

apodictic, *adj.* certain; conclusive. Compare DIALECTICAL; PROBABLE.

apodosis, *n.* the consequent or conditioned clause in a conditional proposition; the clause correlative to the protasis.

apologetics, *n.* the historical-philosophical explanation and defense of the presuppositions of the Christian religion, its existence, and its divine origin. Though apologetics is nowadays usually treated as a subordinate science in theology, it has been classified also as a branch of philosophy or as a part of the philosophy of religion because of its large dependence on philosophical truths and on the meaning of historical facts pertinent to religion.

a posteriori, *adj. phrase* (*lit.,* "from the later," "from the back," "from what is after"). **1.** proceeding from facts to principles or from effects to cause. **2.** generalizing from particulars to the universal; inductive. **3.** based on observation and experience and leading thence to theoretical interpretations; empirical in method or reasoning. ANT. – *a priori.* USES – *a posteriori* judgment, method, proof, reasoning.

apperceive, *v.* to interpret and judge new experiences and knowledge by the help of one's past experience or background.

appetency, *n.* an act or movement of an appetite to or away from an object; elicited appetite; appetition.

appetite, *n.* **1.** *commoner sense.* a form and especially a power that has an inclination toward an object suitable to itself or away from an unsuitable object. **2.** *less often.* a movement of the faculty to its good, as in desire or choice; appetency; appetition. In this sense, appetite is contrasted with dislike, indifference to the object, etc.

concupiscible appetite, the sensitive appetite which seeks what is suitable to the senses and flees what is evil to the senses; concupiscence.

irascible appetite. the sentitive appetite by which the sentient being resists the attacks that hinder its good or inflict harm on it. See ANGER; PASSION.

natural appetite, 1. the spontaneous, habitual, and unvarying tendency or inclination of a natural body or natural power to a good naturally suitable to itself or away from something evil to it; the direction of a non-cognitive thing according to its specific nature to its proper operation, proper end, or natural perfection. Sometimes reference is made to a *legal* tendency in inanimate natures and a *plastic* tendency in plants. See FINALITY, NATURAL; LAW, NATURAL PHYSICAL. **2.** any spontaneous, indeliberate, and habitual act of any appetite toward its proper object or end. ANT. – *controlled, deliberate, elicited* appetite. Men, for instance, have natural movements to happiness and deliberate pursuit of happiness.

rational appetite, the power or tendency to a good that has been perceived by the intellect or away from an evil perceived by reason; the will.

sensitive appetite, an inclination in a sentient being to a sensible good that has been known by the senses and the correlative tendency away from known sensible evils; sensuality. REF. – *On the Soul,* III, CC. 9, 10. *S.T.,* I, 59, a. 1; 80, aa. 1, 2; 81, aa. 1, 2.

application, *n.* the exercise or use of causal power or the direction of an instrument to a specific work at a particular time.

apprehension, *n.* an act of the intellect seizing upon the essence of a thing; the intellectual grasp of an object or meaning; the mental act representing an object without affirmation or negation. *Simple apprehension* is the same as apprehension, and is contrasted particularly with the more complex act of judging. REF. – *S.T.,* I, 85, a. 5.

DIVISIONS OF THE APPETITES IN SENSE 1

Natural or non-cognitive	{ Legal in lifeless natural objects { Plastic in plants	
Cognitive or dependent on knowledge	{ Sensitive { Rational { Intellectual (in a pure spirit or in God)	{ Concupiscible { Irascible

---

approbation, knowledge of, *phrase.* an expression descriptive especially of God's knowledge of the good and of the elect connoting satisfaction of His will in this knowledge. ANT. – *reprobation.*

appropriate, *v.* 1. to make what is common proper; to limit something common to one. 2. to transfer unowned material things to one's own ownership.

a priori, *adjectival phrase* (*lit.,* "from the earlier," "from the front," "from what is before"). 1. *logic.* proceeding from cause to effect or from assumption to implicit conclusion; reasoning from cause to effect. 2. *epistemology.* prior to, and thus independent of, experience; proceeding from principle, from analysis of what is already known, from insight into the content of experience, rather than from experience of the object of the judgment; not established or verified empirically. USES – *a priori* judgments, principles, proof.

a priori forms, *in Kant's philosophy.* ideas, principles, presuppositions which are antecedent to our experience and not obtained from experience, but which are necessary to make experience intelligible; categories and modes of thought which by psychological necessity we attribute to phenomena or objects of experience, but which are beyond our objective perception of reality; e.g., the forms of space, time, universality, necessity, cause.

‡**a quo,** *Latin phrase.* 1. from which, as in the expression, *terminus a quo,* i.e., the term from which. 2. by which, expressing agency by a person.

archetype, *n.* the original form, actual or mental, according to which existing things are made. It is especially used of the divine ideas of the Creator, of providence, of the eternal law, and of Platonic forms.

argument, *n.* the reason, proof, or evidence offered for or against something; the middle term of a proof. See DEMONSTRATION; REASONING.

metaphysical argument, a proof based on the nature of things, on necessity, or on a universal or nearly universal characteristic of beings.

moral argument, a proof based on concrete characteristics of moral beings, i.e., of persons.

ontological argument, a proof or attempt at proof for the existence of God which is drawn from our idea of being, of perfect being, or of some divine attribute.

physical argument, a proof based on concrete facts in material nature, such as order or beauty.

psychological argument, a proof based on the data of consciousness.

argumentation, *n.* the verbal expression of a reasoning process; a declaration which draws one statement from others.

aristocracy, *n.* 1. government by the best citizens usually without popular consent to such rule by the reputed leaders in virtue, experience, wisdom, etc. 2. a constitution based on government by the best citizens. REF. – *Politics,* IV, CC. 7, 8.

art, *n.* correct knowledge joined to skill in making things; deliberate skill in making things; right reason in regard to the making of things; a form or plan in the artist's intellect that gives sure direction in producing a definite product by suitable means. See VIRTUE, INTELLECTUAL.

architectonic (master) art, that art in a related group that guides the others and controls them to the purpose of the master art.

fine art, an art whose object of production is an end in itself, not a useful good. Thus, a portrait is an object of fine art, a billboard sign is not.

liberal art, an art which is directed to knowledge, and whose result is not in a material subject; e.g., the arts of logic, of teaching.

practical art, one which uses objects for the agent's purpose, e.g., sailing.

productive art, one which makes its objects by changing matter, e.g., shipbuilding.

servile art, an art directed to a useful product and whose immediate purpose is production of a change in matter. REF. – *N. Eth.,* I, CC. 1, 2; VI, C. 4. *Politics,* I, C. 11. *Poetics. Physics,* II, C. 2. *S.T.,* I–II, 57, aa. 3–5.

artefact, *n.* any object made by human

work or art, but not by nature alone. It is also spelled *artifact*.

‡**a se,** *Latin phrase.* from himself or from itself; the mode of uncaused being. It is especially used in the expressions *ens a se,* the *a se* being.

aseity, *n.* the divine attribute of uncaused existence.

assent, *n.* **1.** the judgment; the perception of the relation between subject and predicate; mental acceptance of the judgment as true. **2.** *loosely.* consent.

external assent, performing some external act or making a declaration as a sign of internal acceptance of a proposition.

internal assent, the mind's (and will's) acceptance of a judgment or proposition as true. See CONSENT, INTERNAL.

REF.—*S.T.,* I–II, 15, a. 2 ad 3. *Truth,* q. 14, a. 1. John Henry Cardinal Newman, *An Essay in Aid of a Grammar of Assent,* for the psychological differences of notional assent, real assent, complex assent, simple assent, etc.

assimilate, *v.* **1.** to make something like to another; to cause a resemblance. **2.** specifically, to take in and absorb food, making it like the living body that uses it. **3.** *philosophy of man, epistemology.* to conform the mind to things; to make the mind intentionally like things; to unite new knowledge with previous experiences and interpret the new according to this experience. See LIKENESS.

association, *n.* **1.** *social sense.* a union or combination for a common purpose, especially if it is unchartered. **2.** *psychological and epistemological senses.* **a.** connection of ideas in thought. **b.** the power and the process of making such mental combinations. **c.** recall of past experiences through some connection with a present state of mind. **3.** *physiological sense.* correlation of nervous functions.

assumption, *n.* **1.** something taken for granted or posited. **2.** a minor premise.

atheism, *n.* the view that God does not exist.

practical atheism, acting and living as though God did not exist or did not rule human life, whether or not one has an opinion of God's non-existence.

speculative (dogmatic) atheism, an opinion or system claiming that God does not exist. It occurs in the form of *negative atheism,* when the person thinks that there are no arguments to prove God's existence; in the form of *positive atheism,* when someone asserts that God's existence has been disproved.

attention, *n.* **1.** *general sense.* close or earnest awareness of something; concentrated looking, or listening, or reflecting. **2.** *logic and epistemology.* the turning of the mind to one object out of many simultaneously in the field of perception; the voluntary application of the mind to one thing to the exclusion of others. **3.** *ethics.* practical care.

external attention, physical attitudes suitable to or indicative of *internal (true, mental)* attention; e.g., external and internal attention in prayer.

attribute, *n.* **1.** any act or perfection or quality which belongs to a thing and is predicated of a thing. It is usually an accident. **2.** a logical attribute or predicate which is declared to belong to some subject or to be caused by it, or to be due to it, or to be in some way referred to it. **3.** *grammar.* an adjective.

divine attribute, 1. a perfection or name of God. **2.** *restricted sense.* a perfection thought of as flowing from the essence of God. See PERFECTION.

essential attribute, some perfection or predicate necessary to the nature of a thing.

incommunicable attribute, a perfection that is and can be possessed by only one, as God's possession of infinity. Perfections that can be formally shared by many are *communicable attributes;* e.g., life.

negative attribute, a perfection that is known as a denial of some imperfection or limitation, though it is altogether actual and positive; e.g., immortality.

proper attribute, a characteristic or specific attribute. See PROPERTY.

transcendental attribute, a predicate that belongs to all beings and is formally distinct from the concept of being; as one, true, good.

attribution, *n.* **1.** predication. **2.** analogy of attribution. See ANALOGY.

augmentation, *n.* material change by way of increase of quantity or volume. See CHANGE.

authority, *n.* **1.** *ethics.* the right to command and enforce obedience. See JURISDICTION. **2.** *epistemology.* knowledge and truthfulness.

argument from authority, an argument or proof based on statements or approvals or authentic citations from others, but not on intrinsic evidence or the direct discoveries of one's experience or of one's reason.

authority of a witness, the right of the witness to command assent to what he narrates or to command belief because of his knowledge and truthfulness.

civil authority, social authority in the state over the members for the true proper good of the state; political authority; legitimate power in the state or its rulers to direct and compel the mem-

bers to co-operate in using common means for the common good.

moral authority, the right granted by moral law to impose obligation on the human acts of others.

social authority, the right to oblige and compel the members of a society to seek by their co-operative activity the specific end of that society.

sovereign authority, supreme authority in a perfect community (state or church or universe).

automatism, *n.* an action or regular way of acting resembling a habit but existing in the sensitive or motor powers and not controlled by intellect and will. See HABIT.

awareness, *n.* consciousness.

axiom, *n.* a self-evident, primary truth; also called a "dignity"; a proposition which states a universal and immediately evident truth and whose self-evidence leads us to legitimately assume its truth in any inquiry.

REF. – *Post Anal.*, I, C. 2.

B

Bannezianism, *n.* a doctrine named from Domingo Bañez (or Bannez or Vañez), O.P. (1528–1604), who teaches that God foresees futuribles and free futures in His predetermining decrees and physically premoves the free created will to one course of action. This physical premotion is natural concurrence with the will's natural acts and in the supernatural order is actual efficacious grace for the will. Without this premotion the will cannot act in this way. Hence, omissions and sins are also known in the predetermining decrees. The main rival theory is known as *Molinism.*

be, *n.* the act of being; existence. Some writers refer to it as the *"to be."*

be, *v.* the copula of a proposition, meaning the union of a predicate with a subject by an act of judgment.
REF. – *S.T.,* I, 3, a. 4 ad 2.

beatitude, *n.* 1. *ethics.* happiness, and especially perfect happiness; blessedness; the full and enduring possession of supreme (perfect) good. 2. *theology.* the eight blessings or beatitudes of Christ, which are supernatural acts and supernatural rewards.

accidental beatitude, all the gifts possessed by the beatified over and above the spiritual possession of the perfect good. Hence, it includes consequent beatitude.

adequate beatitude, perfect happiness including both essential (formal) and accidental beatitude.

antecedent beatitude, happiness preparatory to formal beatitude, as the temporal happiness of a good life on earth.

consequent beatitude, the happiness that flows from the state of formal beatitude. Thus, if formal beatitude is in the intellect, joy belongs to consequent beatitude.

essential (formal) beatitude, that particular activity in which perfect happiness is achieved; perfect knowledge (or knowledge and love) of the necessary good.

imperfect beatitude, any state of happiness which is less than or merely preparatory to essential beatitude.

natural beatitude, perfect happiness in as far as the nature of man without the light of glory can possess the perfect good. It connotes an analogical knowledge of God, hence, some writers say it remains imperfect.

objective beatitude, the object of perfect happiness; the necessary and sufficient beatifying object.

perfect beatitude, essential beatitude completely fulfilling human capacities for the perfect good.

subjective beatitude, the general indefinite state of being happy or perfectly happy.

supernatural beatitude, the perfect happiness belonging to nature elevated by sanctifying grace and the light of glory to the eternal vision of God.
REF. – *N. Eth.,* I, CC. 4, 11; X, CC. 6–8; *Rhetoric,* I, C. 15. Boethius, *Consolation of Philosophy,* III, prose 2, 10. St. Augustine, *Confessions,* X, C. 23. *S.T.,* I, 26, a. 3; I–II, 2, a. 8; 3, aa. 3, 6; 5, a. 3; 62, a. 1; 69.

BEATITUDE, SENSE 1

1. Antecedent Formal Consequent Adequate (formal together with consequent)	3. Natural { Imperfect / Perfect Supernatural (Perfect)
2. Subjective Objective Formal	4. Temporal Eternal 5. Essential Accidental

---

12

beauty, *n.* that which gives pleasure upon being seen; that whose disinterested contemplation delights the mind; that property of being whereby it can please upon being intuited because of its integrity, due proportion, and brightness or splendor.
REF. – *S.T.*, I, 5, a. 5 ad 1; I–II, 27, a. 1 ad 3; II–II, 145, a. 2; 180, a. 2 ad 3; III, 87, a. 2 ad 3.

becoming, *n.* any passing from potency to act; any coming into being. Hence, it includes creation and all forms of change. See CHANGE.

begging the question, *phrase.* the fallacy of assuming the very point or principle to be proved. It is committed by assuming the conclusion, by substituting in the premises a mere paraphrase of the conclusion, or by assuming as premise something derived from the certainty of the conclusion.
REF. – *Prior Anal.*, II, C. 16.

beginning, *n.* a principle that has temporal, positional, or serial priority over something else, but has no other bearing or influence on other members in that same set or series of things, propositions, or numbers; the start or first point in a set or series, upon which the other members do not depend for their being, but only for their position in a given set or series. See chart on PRINCIPLES.
REF. – *Met.*, V, C. 1.

behavior, *n.* **1.** manner of acting, especially in the presence of others; observable actions. **2.** the observable reactions of a sentient organism when stimulated. See CONDUCT.

being, *n.* **1.** *very general sense.* that which in any way is (whether in the state of existence, in potency, in the power of its cause, in the mind, in the imagination, or in mere statement). **2.** *logic.* the affirmation in a proposition; the being that belongs to the copula "is" or "are." **3.** *metaphysics.* the real; that to which existence belongs; that whose act is existence; an existing thing or some real principle or state, such as subjective potency, in an existing thing. Some scholastics prefer to describe being as the same as essence or thing. Some describe it as that which is or can be at any time. Some restrict being to the existent and occasionally to the act of existence. This last is referred to as the participial sense of being.

Note. The purpose here is not to give an historical sketch of the shades of meaning and description which different scholastic writers have given to being. Nor is this the place to criticize such descriptions, nor to discuss the proper object of metaphysics, the type of abstraction of being, and such metaphysical questions. It seems to be enough to list here frequent usages of St. Thomas and modern scholastics.

analogy of being, the imperfect likeness of things in being or in existence. See ANALOGY.

being as such, the being that belongs to any and all beings. See BEING-IN-GENERAL.

being-from-another, caused being; creature.

being-from-itself, uncaused being; being with uncaused existence; God.

being-in-act, actual or existing being. See ACT.

being-in-another, accident, q.v.

being-in-general, that characteristic which is found in all real beings and by reason of which they are beings. This transcendental characteristic, abstracted from all individual differences between beings, is usually regarded as the object of the science of metaphysics.

being-in-itself, substance, q.v.

being-in-potency, **1.** a possible being. See POSSIBLE. **2.** a potency or potential principle in a real being.

being of reason, a being that can exist only as an object of thought, but lacks potency for real existence; logical being; being of the mind. See List B in appended chart of usages of BEING.

common being, being-in-general, q.v.

contingent being, **1.** contingent in existence, i.e., a being whose essence is not of itself determined to be existing or non-existing; a being whose existence is indifferent in itself or non-necessary. **2.**

USAGE IN REGARD TO BEINGS

A. Real Being

1. God (being-from-Himself, *ens a se,* unparticipated being, absolute being)
   Creature (being from another, *ens ab alio,* participated being, relative being)

2. Substance (being-in-itself, *ens per se*)
   Accident (being-in-another, *ens in alio*)   Subdivisions under categories

3. Act (actual being)
   Potency (potential being, being in potency)   Subdivisions under act

4. Complete being (a being, a whole, suppositum, *ens quod*)
   Incomplete being (an intrinsic principle or part or power of a being, *ens quo*)

5. Existence (*esse,*   ⎧ Self-subsistent (uncaused, *Ipsum Esse*)
   the "to be")   ⎨ Subsistent (caused, existing in an essence)
   ⎩ Non-subsistent

Essence
⎧ Divine: identified with God's existence
⎨ Finite (distinct from existence)
  ⎧ Specific
    ⎧ Actuated individual
      ⎧ Whole essence ⎨ Completely actuated / Mutable
      ⎨ Formal part of essence
      ⎩ Abstracted (logical beings?) ⎨ In absolute state (the direct universal) / In reflex state
    ⎩ Merely possible essence (objectively possible) (logical beings?) ⎨ As an individual (this possible) / In absolute state (such a possible)

6. Necessary being ⎧ In its existence (God)
   ⎨ In its essence
   ⎪ In its operation (not free)
   ⎩ In its truth (necessity of principles and of fact)

Contingent being ⎧ In existence
   ⎨ In essence or nature
   ⎪ In objects of its choice
   ⎩ In accidental attributes

7. Absolute being ⎧ God, "Ipsum Esse" (strict sense of absolute)
   ⎨ Substance (in extended sense)
   ⎩ Anything actual or existing (occasional usage)

Relative being ⎧ Relative to existence and its extrinsic causes; potency
   ⎪ Relative to subject of inherence; accidents
   ⎨ Relative to other parts of itself
   ⎪ Relative to other finite beings
   ⎪ Relative to mind as knowable or true
   ⎩ Relative to will and desire as good

8. Simple being   Subdivisions under *categories,* s.v. "substance," and under
   Composite being   *unity,* s.v. "natural"

USAGE IN REGARD TO BEINGS (Continued)

B. Beings of Reason (Logical Beings)

(All in Group I are certainly unreal and are logical beings. The merely logical character of those in Group II is disputed, for some writers place these in real being and some place absolute natures as intermediate between real and logical being.)

I. 1. Negations
    2. Privations
    3. Contradictions; chimeras; impossibles
    4. Logical relations
    5. Mental constructs such as abstractions and reflex universals
    6. Enuntiables of erroneous judgments

II. 7. Mere possibles
    8. Mere futuribles or conditioned futures
    9. Beings that used to exist; the perished
   10. Absolute natures (direct universals)

C. Intentional Being Can Include

1. All that is certainly real
2. The mere possibles and futuribles
3. The unreal or merely logical beings

---

contingent in essence; changeable, especially in its substantial form. See CONTINGENT.

ideal being, intentional being, q.v.

incomplete being, a part, mere form, potency or substrate, accident, etc., of a suppositum or whole being.

intentional being, the being of an object as known; the being belonging to any object, real or logical insofar as it is an object of thought; ideal being; representative form. See FORM; INTENTION.

logical being, being of reason, q.v.

necessary being, that being which of its own nature must exist and cannot be non-existing nor existing in any way other than as it is; that which essentially exists. See NECESSARY for less common meanings.

participated being, an imperfect being, lacking the fullness of being or of perfection of its order or type, univocally like others of its own class, and caused.

possible being, 1. a mere possible. See POSSIBLE. **2.** potency. See POTENCY.

real being, see sense 3 under BEING. Real being is directly opposed to intentional being and to beings of reason. Some writers may also oppose it to merely possible being, so that real being is that which is distinct from knowledge and from extrinsic causes of its existence.

REF. – *Met.,* V, C. 7; VI, C. 4. *On Being and Essence,* CC. 1, 3. *S.T.,* I, 3, a. 4 ad 2; 4, a. 1 ad 3; 5, a. 1 ad 1; 48, a. 2 ad 2; 104, a. 4; I–II, 2, a. 5 ad 2; III, 10, a. 3. *C.G.,* II, C. 54.

belief, *n.* faith.

benevolence, *n.* willing good to another; loving another for his own sake. See LOVE.

best, *adj.* the highest or fullest good of which a nature, act, or object is capable. It is distinguished as best in itself and best relatively to circumstances. USES – *best* state of man or beatitude, civil state, laws, virtue, world, etc.

REF. – *Politics,* IV, C. 1.

bilocation, *n.* the simultaneous presence of one body in two places.

blessedness, *n.* beatitude; perfect happiness.

body, *n.* **1.** *philosophy of nature.* an individual material thing; a real material unit. **2.** *specifically.* the human body.

artificial body, a material thing produced by art, composed of many distinct things, but usually having one common function, place, or some unifying bond extrinsic to the nature of the component things; e.g., tools, machines, houses.

mathematical body, a material thing considered only according to its quantitative or its numerical properties and independent of physical change and physical influences. See charts on CATEGORIES and UNITY.

mixed body, a natural body which contains more than one of the (four) elements. The Thomistic view considers the forms of the elementary bodies to be only virtually present in the mixed body.

natural body, one material substance with one nature; or a single material unit complete in the order of being and of operation.

REF. – *On Being and Essence,* C. 2.

bond, *n.* 1. *in general.* that which binds or holds together. 2. *ethics.* an obligation. 3. *metaphysics.* the foundation of a relation or of a union; a mode of being or a mode of union.

bond of marriage, the duty of exclusive and lifelong union with only one spouse. The *primary* bond is the duty of chaste fidelity to the spouse. The *secondary* bond is common life, mutual support, etc.

brute, *n.* a merely sentient living substance; the species (not the genus), animal.

C

canon, *n.* a norm; a rule.

canon law, *n.* Church law; the code of Church laws, especially the *Codex Juris Canonici* of the Catholic Church. Each separate principle or rule in the Code is known as a canon. See LAW.

capacity, *n.* aptitude; power or faculty; potency to act or to be acted on.

capital, *n. or* capital goods, *phrase.* productive property or finances available for securing or controlling productive property.

capitalism, *n.* a system of private ownership which is characterized by concentrated private ownership and control of capital goods, large-scale production, the dominance of the profit motive, substantial freedom of enterprise with a minimum of public or social regulation of ownership, labor relations, trade, and profit. Capitalism often connotes undue emphasis on owners' rights, control, and profit.

Cartesianism, *n.* the system of Descartes or of one of his followers; any doctrine characteristic of Descartes or of his followers; any logical consequence from a characteristic view of Descartes. Examples are his views of substance, of innate ideas, of dualism in man.

casuistry, *n.* applied ethical science or applied moral theology, dealing with the correct and prudent application of moral principles to particular facts, instances, or cases.

categorematic, *adj.* capable of standing alone as a completely meaningful subject or predicate of a proposition; e.g., the terms "man," "ship."

categorical, *adj.* absolute; free from conditions. See PROPOSITION; SYLLOGISM.

categorical imperative, an absolute command or prohibition of the law or of one's conscience. It is chiefly used in Kantian ethical theory.

category, *n.* 1. *metaphysics.* one of the ten primary ways or modes in which finite being can exist. 2. *logic.* any one of the ten supreme genera to which all predicates of a subject can be referred or be reduced; a predicament; the ultimate logical classification of all genera, species, and finite individuals. See chart on page 18.
REF. – Aristotle, *Categories.* Simplicius, *Commentary on the Categories of Aristotle.*

catharsis, *n.* purification and relief of the emotions and emotional tensions by artistic contemplation and participation.
REF. – Aristotle, *Poetics.*

causality, *n.* the influence of a cause being actually exercised on a being. The modes of causality are efficacy for the efficient cause; finality or attraction for the final cause; guidance for the exemplar; and communication of its being for both the formal and material causes.

principle of causality, the main principle on efficient causality, namely: "Every contingent being requires a cause distinct from itself to explain its existence." There are a number of variants of the principle.

causation, *n.* the act of causing; causality. ABBR. – *caus.*

cause, *n.* 1. *general definition applying to all types of causes.* a principle from which something originates with dependence; a being which in some way directly influences the being or change of something else; that which in some way gives existence to another; the reason for the existence of another being. For the types of causes, see CAUSE, *sense 2;* END; FORM; MATTER; MODEL.

constituent causes, those causes which together make up the internal nature of a being; hence, matter and form.

17

CATEGORIES OF BEING

1. Substance

- *a*) First (singular; *hoc aliquid;* natural substance)
  - Second (universal)
    - Genus
    - Species
  - Multiple (collective; artificial substance; a group)
- *b*) Simple (subsistent; spiritual; pure form)
  - Compound of substantial parts
    - Of spiritual form and matter
    - Of material form and matter
- *c*) Living (five grades: divine, angelic, human, sentient, vegetative)
  - Non-living
    - Element
    - Compound
- *d*) Complete (a whole)
  - Nature
  - Suppositum
    - Mere thing
    - Person
  - Incomplete
    - Essential part
    - Organic part (of a living corporeal substance)
    - Integral part (of a material body)
      - Prime matter
      - Disposed matter
      - Substantial form
        - In matter
        - Separated from matter

ACCIDENTS

2. Quantity
- *a*) Adjacent
  - Discrete
  - Continuous
    - Simultaneous or dimensive
    - Successive or mobile
- *b*) Separate

3. Quality
- *a*) Entitative and operative
- *b*) Disposition and habits, good or bad; see VIRTUES
  - Active powers and incapacities
  - Affective qualities
  - Passions (passive powers) and passible qualities
  - External shape and mathematical figure
  - Immanent (living) acts

4. Relation
- *a*) Real
  - Predicamental (contingent)
  - Transcendental (essential, absolute, necessary)
  - Internal divine
  - Moral (rights and duties)
  - Logical
    - Purely logical (without foundation in reality)
    - With foundation in reality (virtual distinctions)
- *b*) Mutual and mixed

5. Action (transeunt)
6. Passion (received)
7. Place: proper and common

8. Time
9. Posture (position, situs, attitude)
10. Habitus or natural adjuncts

extrinsic causes, those causes which are outside the effect; hence, efficient, final, and exemplary causes.

intrinsic causes, causes inside the effect; hence, matter and form.
REF. – *Physics,* II, CC. 3, 7. *Met.,* V. C. 2. *Comm. in Met.,* V, lect. 1–3.

cause, *n.* 2. the efficient cause; the agent; that which by its activity or exercise of power produces existence or change in another. Both in popular and philosophical use, the term "cause," without modifier, often means efficient cause.

accidental cause, some attribute of the cause or some feature accompanying the effect which however has no influence in the causal process nor in the origin of the effect; something incidental to the cause or effect or coincidental. Thus, Michelangelo carved the *Pietà* as a sculptor, not as someone who spoke Italian. His Italian speech is an accidental cause of the *Pietà.*

analogous cause, a cause that produces an effect of a nature specifically different from its own nature. Sometimes it is called an equivocal cause.

cause *in esse,* the cause productive of the very existence of a being.

cause *in fieri,* the cause productive of becoming or change in a being already existing.

common cause, 1. a universal cause. 2. a cause not determined to one effect or one kind of effect.

co-operating cause, one that acts together with another cause in producing an effect. The co-operation may be immediate, mediate, or remote. See CO-OPERATION.

equivocal cause, analogous cause.

essential cause, a proper cause.

first cause, 1. The first in any series of causes. 2. God as first cause of all things, and as immediately operating in all finite causality.

free cause, an agent acting with deliberate purpose.

immediate cause, that one in a set of causes which is directly connected with the effect.

instrumental cause, an instrument or tool serving as a subordinate cause; a cause without initiative in the start of action, but applied and directed as a help to its efforts and purpose by a principal agent, and influencing the product chiefly according to the form and intention of the principal; e.g., a hammer used by a carpenter, an automobile used by a driver.

moral cause, 1. a free cause. 2. an occasion favoring action of a free cause. 3. a motive for the action of a free cause.

natural cause, 1. a thing acting according to the innate tendencies of its nature or according to uniform necessary natural laws. 2. a cause contained in the natural order and acting without special help of grace or supernatural special intervention.

necessary cause, a cause that acts according to the compulsory tendencies of its nature or not under the influence of free will; a naturally determined agent.

per accidens cause, accidental cause, *above.*

per se cause, proper cause, *below.*

physical cause, a natural or necessary cause, as distinguished from a moral cause.

principal cause, a cause which works by the power of its own form and makes the effect in some way like itself. If it be an intelligent cause, it also intends the effect, acts by its own initiative, and controls the instruments to its own purposes.

proper cause, the precise cause which is required for producing this particular type of effect; a cause which has its own special, distinctive, and natural connection with this kind of effect. Thus, God is the proper cause of existence; a human being is the proper cause of meaningful speech; a camera and photographic plate is the proper cause of a snapshot. The proper cause prescinds from accidental or causally non-relevant associations with either the cause or the effect.

second (secondary) cause, a cause under and dependent upon the first cause; a created cause; a cause that can only specify the kind, but not the being of the effect.

subordinate cause, in a set of causes,

DIVISIONS OF EFFICIENT CAUSE

1. First cause (cause of being, its origin or continuance)
   Second cause (cause of change)

2. Principal cause

   Subordinate cause
   - a) Instrumental cause
     Secondary principal cause (co-operator)
   - b) Essentially subordinate
     Accidentally subordinate

3. Cause as being (cause in potency to cause; cause *in actu primo*)
   Cause as causing (cause in act; cause *in actu secundo*)

4. Univocal cause
   Analogous cause (sometimes called equivocal)

5. Proper cause (essential; *per se*)

   Accidental (*per accidens*) cause
   - Having accidental connection with the cause
   - Having accidental connection with the effect
     - Removing impediments
     - By chance related to the effect
     - Incidentally or coincidentally related to the effect, but not influencing effect

6. Immanent (living) cause
   Transeunt (transitive) cause
   Formally immanent, virtually transeunt

7. Immediate cause
   Mediate (intermediate, mean) cause
   Remote cause
   Ultimate (first) cause

8. Adequate cause
   - One total cause
   - Concurring causes
     - Immediate co-operator
     - Mediate co-operator

   Partial (inadequate) cause
   Exciting cause or stimulus (partial cause)

9. Metaphysical cause
   Physical (natural, necessary) cause

   Moral cause
   - Free agent
   - Human act
   - Occasion
   - Motive

10. Natural cause
    Supernatural cause

11. Common cause
    - Universal
    - Generic

    Particular cause

one that follows another, or depends on another, or is controlled by another cause. **accidentally subordinate cause,** a cause whose exercise of causality is marked by one or more of these characteristics: it does not depend here and now on the prior cause in the set, though it may have formerly depended on it; it is univocal in nature with the prior cause; it is merely by chance or by unneeded association working after or under the prior cause.

essentially subordinate cause, one whose present exercise of causal influence naturally and necessarily needs the simultaneous action of another prior cause analogical in nature to itself.

universal cause, a cause influencing all or very many effects, even though these are of different species; e.g., God, the sun, air currents.

univocal cause, a cause that produces an effect specifically like itself. Living generation is of this type.

voluntary in cause, culpable in cause, indirectly voluntary, q.v.

REF. – *Physics,* II, C. 3; VIII, C. 4. *S.T.,* I, 104, a. 1; 114, a. 3; I–II, 85, a. 5; III, 43, a. 4 ad 3; 47, a. 1. *C.G.,* III, CC. 10, 14. *Comm. in Met.,* V, lect. 3.

cause, *n.* 3. the purpose of action; the sufficient good justifying action; e.g., we made *common cause;* self-defense was the *cause* of his action.

celibacy, *n.* the state of being and remaining unmarried.

certainty, *n.* 1. certitude; the quality or state of being certain. 2. an evident truth.

certitude, *n.* 1. the firm assent of the mind to a proposition or enunciable without fear of error; certainty. 2. the sure connection of cause with effect or of any events with each other because of their direction by an unchanging intelligence. This is called *certitude by participation.*

formal certitude, the firm assent to a proposition together with clear knowledge that the evidence for the assent excludes error and the possibility of error; the known infallibility of the judgment.

a. metaphysical (perfect, absolute) certitude, infallible assent from a motive which the mind recognizes as unqualifiedly necessary so that any opposite true judgment is metaphysically impossible.

b. physical certitude, a certain assent concerning objects in physical nature which act necessarily. This certitude is conditional insofar as (1) miracles remain possible; (2) chance interferences in nature are possible, or man does not know all the conditions which may modify natural action in particular combinations of natural objects and forces.

c. moral certitude, certain assent concerning human conduct based on men's evident and usual responses to their needs, abilities, and motivations.

d. prudential certitude, an assent based on evidence sufficient to justify the ordinary prudent person in acting concerning his own or other's welfare; high probability based on reasonable diligence in evaluating the evidence and motivated by good will in practical affairs; good practical judgment. Such certitude is also called *moral certitude in the wide sense, ethical certitude, relative certitude.* It is often all that is available to man in contingent matters.

natural (direct, common) certitude,

CHIEF DIVISIONS OF CERTITUDE

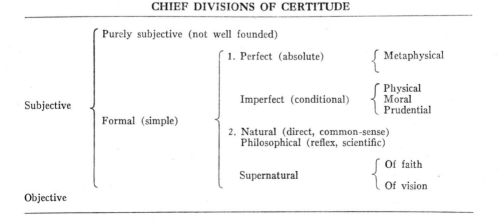

formal certitude without critical and explicit reflection on the motives for certitude and their degree of necessity.

objective certitude, the necessary ontological truth of the object of the judgment; objective evidence.

philosophical (reflex, scientific) certitude, formal certitude with explicit (critical) consideration of the weight of the motives for assent, their exclusion of the possibility of error, and the proportion of the motives to the quality of the mind's firmness in assent.

subjective certitude, firm assent of the mind. In this use of the word, the justification of the firm assent is not considered. A person may be subjectively certain yet be wrong because of insufficient evidence, prejudice, etc. But also subjective certitude may have the same quality as formal certitude.
REF. – *Post. Anal.,* I, C. 2. *N. Eth.,* I, C. 3. *S.T.,* II–II, 18, a. 4; 70, aa. 2, 3. *Truth,* q. 6, a. 3; 14, a. 1 ad 7.

chance, *n. and adj.* **1.** the unforeseen, the unintended. **2.** the seeming absence of cause or design. **3.** that which is said to happen without a deliberate purpose. **4.** the accidental, the irregular, or the unusual in nature's course. **5.** that whose cause is indeterminable. Chance is not properly ascribed to the absence of efficient cause. ANT. – *end, intention.*

absolute chance, that which is not planned nor foreseen and permitted by any agent. Scholasticism denies this kind of chance occurrence.

contract of chance, see CONTRACT.

relative chance, that which is unforeseen by certain agents, especially by the immediate ones; coincidence; e.g., a chance meeting, a chance discovery of an object when one is looking for something else.
REF. – *Physics,* II, CC. 5, 6. *Rhetoric,* I, C. 10, 1369a 31.

change, *n.* **1.** *proper sense.* the actualization of a being in potency inasmuch as it is in potency; the movement of a movable being inasmuch as it is movable; the passing from (subjective) potency to act. **2.** *improper and extended sense.*

any newness in a being; any origin of a difference. In the proper sense, change is always from something and into something, and so requires a term from which and a term to which; and it involves the gaining of a new form and the privation of an old form.

accidental change, real change in the accidents of a being.

apparent (seeming *or* extrinsic) change, a difference in a being but without any change in the substance, substantial parts, or intrinsic accidents of a being.

change of law, see LAW.

extrinsic change, apparent change.

intentional change, the change in the knower whereby he gains new knowledge without producing any physical change in the object known and without losing any form in his own knowing powers.

intrinsic change, real change or change in the reality or being of a thing; a gain and loss of substantial or real accidental form.

local change, change of place. See MOTION.

mechanical change, movement as in a machine; hence, quantitative and local and positional changes of the parts of something without any intrinsic change.

nominal change, change of names; an extrinsic change in the one who gives the name but not in the thing itself; e.g., the shift from naming in one language or in another, or in synonyms in the same language.

physical change, a change in which there is gain or loss of some real form. This is particularly contrasted with *intentional* change.

real change, intrinsic change.

substantial change, change in the substance of a thing because of change of its substantial form; generation of a new substance or of a new substantial form; the actualization of a new substantial form in a subject and the perishing of the previous substantial form or its return to the potency of matter.
REF. – *Cat.,* C. 14. *Physics,* III, CC. 1, 2. *Generation,* I, CC. 3, 4. *Met.,* XI, C. 12;

XII, C. 2. St. Thomas' *Commentary on the Physics of Aristotle,* Bk. III: see J. A. McWilliams, S.J., *Physics and Philosophy: A Study of St. Thomas' Commentary on the Physics of Aristotle.*

CHANGE AND BECOMING

A. Reduction to Categories

In the order of substance
1. Creation — origin from non-being
2. Transubstantiation — complete change of substance
3. Transformation — substantial change properly so called
   a) Generation
   b) Conversion
   c) Perishing (corruption, decay)

In the order of accidents
4. Change of place (locomotion, local change) — motion in the proper sense
5. Change of quantity (extensive change)
   a) Increase (expansion)
   b) Decrease
   c) Union with other bodies without substantial change
   d) Division into parts of itself without substantial change
6. Change of quality (alteration)
   a) Qualities gained or lost
   b) Change of intensity in qualities possessed
7. Intentional change — gaining new knowledge with no loss of form (qualitative)
8. Change in relationships
   a) Change of predicamental relationships
   b) Change in external relationships while the object itself remains the same: as, to become known
   c) Change in name without any change in the object changed
9. Change in position
   a) Change in internal position of parts of things; change of posture; internal rearrangement of parts
   b) Change of relative position because of local change in other objects; external rearrangement: as from right to left of an object

B. Divisions of Real and Apparent Change

Intrinsic changes: Nos. 3, 6, and probably also 8a
Extrinsic changes: Nos. 4, 5, 8, 9
Mechanical changes: Nos. 4, 5, 9
Change in an improper sense: Nos. 1, 2, 7
Motion in the proper sense: No. 4

---

character, *n.* the habitual virtues and vices of a person, founded on his temperament and distinguishing his moral personality; integration of a person's nature and nurture in his habits and the expression of these in living.

charity, *n.* 1. the will to do good to another by giving him of our own; the habitual will to desire and advance another person's good by giving him more than is his due in justice; spiritual love for another or others for his or their sake. 2. a thought, word, deed, or act of will prompted by such spiritual good will to another. 3. *theological virtue.* the infused supernatural virtue whereby man loves God above all things for His own sake and his neighbors for the sake of God. See LOVE.
REF. – *S.T.,* II–II, 23.

chastity, *n.* the moral virtue which controls the use of one's sexual powers and desires in accordance with right reason (i.e., in accordance with their natural purpose in the married state). There are three modes of chastity: virginity, conjugal chastity, and widowhood.
REF. – *S.T.,* II–II, 151.

choice, *n.* a free act; "a free judgment arising from reason"; an act of the will selecting means to an end. See FREEDOM; HUMAN ACT; WILL.

Christian, *adj.* of, from, or in some way pertaining to Christ; as taught by Christ; flowing from Christ's teaching; patterned after Christ or His teaching; traditional among Christians. ABBR. – *Chr.* See LAW, CHRISTIAN NATURAL; NORM OF MORALITY; PHILOSOPHY; VIRTUE; etc.

church, *n.* 1. an organized religious society. 2. a building used for worship of God, particularly if it is a large and separate structure, as distinguished from a chapel or oratory.

Catholic Church, the society (congregation) of all those who profess the faith of Christ, partake of the same sacraments, and are governed spiritually by their lawful pastors under the one visible head, the Pope.

circumstance, *n. particularly used in regard to the circumstances of a human act.*

something that at times accompanies and at times is missing from some moral object or from some moral intention; the third of the moral determinants. An intrinsic circumstance modifies or changes the species of the moral act; an extrinsic circumstance makes no moral difference in the quality of the object or intention. REF. – *N. Eth.*, II, C. 3. *S.T.*, I–II, 18, aa. 3, 10, 11.

citizen, *n.* one who has a right to participate in some way in the government of his state, at least by voting or by jury service. REF. – *Politics*, III, CC. 1, 2, 5, 12.

class, *n.* 1. a genus or a species. 2. a universal or collective concept representing a nature. 3. a set. 4. a number of persons, objects, facts, activities, events, etc., having common essential or common accidental properties or interests.

clemency, *n.* the moral virtue disposing one to moderation in inflicting punishment on the guilty. REF. – *S.T.*, II–II, 157.

coactivity, *n.* that property of a perfect right which morally justifies a person or community in using force in defense of that right. *Coaction* is the use of force. See RIGHT, PERFECT.

cogitative power, *phrase.* the estimative sense; the particular reason. REF. – *S.T.*, I, 78, a. 4; 81, a. 3.

cognition, *n.* knowledge; awareness and representation, whether sentient or intellectual; the power or act of apprehending or knowing.

cognoscible, *adj.* knowable; that can be known or perceived; in potency to be known.

coll., abbreviation for *collective.*

com., abbreviation for *common; communicate; communicated; community.*

come from, *phrase.* to arise or proceed from in some way. Aristotle indicates four varying senses of the phrase: 1. to come after (time); 2. to come from the pre-existing (matter); 3. to come from the maker (efficacy). 4. to be an exciting occasion from which action starts. REF. – *Met.*, V, C. 24. *Generation of Animals*, I, C. 18.

command, *n.* 1. *in general.* a rational order, direction, or dictate. 2. an act of the reason, prompted by the will, directing oneself in human activity or in the carrying out of one's decisions and choices. 3. an act of the reason of the lawgiver or superior requiring subjects to take definite action to an end. 4. *infrequent.* an order imposed on a subject for his private good, either by private or public authority. See IMPERIUM. REF. – *S.T.*, I–II, 17, esp. a. 1; 90, aa. 2, 3.

commanded act, *phrase.* an act of some one of the powers of man, directed by the will and act of command. The commanded act as such is not free and not in itself a human act. The commanded act is sometimes called *imperated* act. REF. – *S.T.*, I–II, 6, a. 3; 17, aa. 5–9.

common, *adj.* 1. pertaining to, connected with, applicable to, or shared in by two or more persons, things, concepts, terms, or members of any class. What is common is not always universal, since it may be analogously common to two or more. ANT. – *singular, exclusive, incommunicable.* 2. public; general. ANT. – *private.* 3. frequent, ordinary, usual. ANT. – *exceptional, rare, unusual.* ABBR. – *com.*

communicate, *v.* 1. to share with. 2. to have in common with another; to participate in (as one out of many). 3. to share its being with another; to unite its being with another; to cause formally. 4. *somewhat improperly in scholasticism.* to give being to another as an efficient cause. ABBR. – *com.*

community, *n.* 1. a group of persons having common interests; the public; a social or political body. ABBR. – *com.* See SOCIETY. 2. participation.

perfect community, a perfect society, q.v.

comparison, *n.* an act of the mind attending to the relations (especially of likeness, unlikeness, and implication) between things or objective concepts. ABBR. – *comp., compar.*

complete, *adj.* whole; perfect. REF. – *Met.*, V, C. 16.

composite, *adj. and n.* 1. constituted of

the natural union of two or more parts, principles, or elements; something compound. See SIMPLICITY; BODY, MIXED; SEPARATION. 2. something conceived as having parts. 3. something joined with another in thought. See chart on UNITY.

composition, *n.* 1. presence and possession of parts; constitution or formation of a unity out of a plurality. 2. the affirmative judgment or act of combining the concepts of subject and predicate in one declaration, signified by the copula *is* or *are.* 3. any mental joining together, as that of associating ideas, forming arbitrary ideas (as golden steel), or uniting a concept with its differences. The last mentioned is called metaphysical composition or contraction, q.v.

composition and division, *phrase.* affirmative and negative judgment.

compound, *adj. and n.* composite. ABBR. – *comp., cpd.*

comprehend, *v.* 1. *strict sense.* to possess and include another. 2. to know a thing as perfectly as it itself is knowable; to know it with complete thoroughness. 3. to possess an end.
REF. – *S.T.*, I, 12, a. 7, c. and ad 1; 16, a. 3, c. and ad 1; I–II, 4, a. 3 ad 1.

comprehension, *n.* 1. the essence represented in a concept; the sum total of notes actually represented in the concept. 2. intension of a term. ANT. OF SENSES 1 AND 2 – *extension.* 3. understanding.

compulsion, *n.* the fact or state of being forced or necessitated, especially contrary to one's natural inclination or contrary to one's choice.
REF. – *N. Eth.*, III, C. 1; V, C. 8.

con., abbreviation for *conclusion; connection; contra.*

conation, *n.* 1. a faculty of desire, exertion, or impulse as distinguished from cognition and passive states in an animal or man. 2. the active aspect of effort and energy in any conscious activity.

concept, *n.* 1. the intellect's representation in itself of the form or essence of a thing; the intellectual likeness of a thing or form; the result of apprehension of an object; expressed intelligible species; internal word; mental term. 2. the intel-

lectual activity of forming such a representation; conception. Note that *idea* is loosely but very frequently used when concept is the proper philosophical term. SYN. – *intelligible species, mental word.*

abstract concept, a concept which represents an attribute of a real subject as though separated and subsistent apart from that subject; as, honesty from an honest man.

analogous concept, 1. an indistinct representation of a form that is imperfectly common to two or more objects or natures. 2. a concept that represents a nature that is known not immediately but by an incomplete comparison or imperfect likeness with some better known nature that is only partially like the object of this analogous concept.

clear concept, 1. a concept that so represents its object that it can be distinguished from other objects. 2. *loosely.* a distinct concept. 3. *loosely.* an object well understood.

   a. a distinct concept, a concept that is so clear a representation of the object that the mind perceives various attributes within the object and thus well discriminates it from other objects. An *adequate* or *complete concept* represents to a greater or less degree all the attributes of an object.

   b. an indistinct *or* **confused concept,** a concept that distinguishes the known object from other different objects, but does not explicitly represent its internal notes.

collective concept, a concept that applies to all individuals as a group, but not to the single members of the group if taken separately.

concrete concept, a concept which expresses a nature or attribute as actually belonging in a subject.

derived (mediate, indirect) concept, a concept formed either by mental union of immediate (original, primitive) concepts, or by analysis of these into components, or by reasoning to the objective concept provided by other immediate concepts; a construct.

immediate (direct, intuitive, primi-

DIVISIONS OF CONCEPTS OR IDEAS
(Basis of Division in Parentheses)

1. (Being of the concept)

   Subjective or formal concept
   Objective concept

2. (Origin of concepts)

   Innate
   Primitive

   Derived (construct) { Reasoned / Arbitrary / Mixed
   Infused

3. (Comprehension of the concept)

   a) Simple
      Compound
      Collective

   b) Concrete
      Abstract

4. (Extension of the concept)

   Singular
   Particular
   Universal { Direct (the ten categories) / Reflex (the five predicables)
   Transcendental

5. (Degree of representation of the object)

   a)
      Clear { Distinct { Complete { Scientifically complete / Comprehensive / Incomplete } / Indistinct (confused) }
      Obscure

   b)
      Proper { Primitive / Derived { From other proper concepts / From analogous concepts }
      Analogous

6. (Relations between objects represented in objective concepts)

   Identical { Intrinsically (formally) the same / Objectively (materially) united

   Different { Intrinsically (formally opposed) { Contradictories / Contraries / Relatives (correlatives) / Privatives } / Objectively (materially) { Associated / Sociable (compatible) / Opposites (the same as intrinsically different) / Disparate }

tive, original) concept, a concept formed by the object's direct presence to the knower without the medium of concepts of other objects already known.

initial concept, the concept of a topic at the beginning of the effort to study it or define it or scientifically understand it. As knowledge progresses, the initial concept is refined into the *discursive, reasoned,* or *scientific* concept.

objective concept, the essence, form, or object represented in the intellect; the object considered as known or present in the knower; the formal object of the subjective concept.

obscure concept, a concept that so poorly represents its object that it cannot be distinguished from other unlike objects.

particular concept, a concept that represents a part of a class, and usually an indeterminate part of a class.

proper concept, a concept which represents an object according to its own special nature, and not by imperfect likeness to better known natures.

singular concept, a concept which represents one single object or single group, but is not representing a class.

subjective *or* formal concept, the act of the intellect representing a form or essence.

universal concept, the intellectual representation of a species or genus or of a common form or attribute that can be in many individuals in specifically (or generically) the same perfection and can be predicated of many individuals in exactly the same (a univocal) sense. It need not be present in equal perfection in the members of the class.

a. the direct universal concept, a concept which represents something which can belong to many. See ESSENCE, ABSOLUTE.

b. the reflex universal concept, a concept which represents a common nature or attribute insofar as it is explicitly recognized to be common to many, to be a class nature or form or attribute, and to be predicable of many individuals in the class in exactly the same (a univocal) sense.

REF. – C. Bittle, O.F.M.Cap., *Science of Correct Thinking,* C. 2, for divisions.

conceptualism, *n.* any of the varieties of the theory that universal concepts are pure concepts with no objective foundation in things other than the reality of a collection of individuals; the admission of the existence of universal concepts together with the denial of their objectivity or realism.

conclusion, *n.* the last judgment or proposition in a chain of reasoning; the consequent proposition in a syllogism. ABBR. – *con.*

concrete, *adj.* 1. the individual or that found actually in the individual. 2. what can be immediately experienced; hence, the singular and usually the material sensible thing. 3. belonging to something actual. 4. named or known as it is in existing objects; not named or represented as separated from these objects and as detached or subsistent. ANT. – *abstract.* 5. definite, detailed. USES – *concrete* concept, individual, term, universal, etc.

concupiscence, *n.* 1. the sensitive appetite that seeks pleasure in an object that it does not possess; the concupiscible appetite. 2. any actual movement of this sensitive appetite, usually accompanied by physiological reactions in other powers of the animal or man. Secondary movements of this appetite are away from unpleasant objects.

antecedent concupiscence, a movement of the appetite for pleasure (or of any sensitive appetite) prior to premeditation or incitement by the will.

consequent concupiscence, a movement of the appetite for pleasure stimulated or increased by the will; hence, such a movement subsequent to and at least partly dependent on volition.

REF. – *S.T.,* I–II, 30, aa. 1, 3; 77, a. 5.

concurrence, *n.* co-operation or the working together of two or more agents in the performance of some activity or the production of some effect. See CO-OPERATION.

concursus, *n.* co-operation; concurrence. It is especially said of God's co-operation with creatures.

condition, *n.* 1. *logic.* any proposition or

clause which when posited necessarily involves positing another proposition or clause; the antecedent or protasis. **2.** *metaphysics.* that real principle or circumstance or set of circumstances which removes impediments to a cause (agent, form, or end) or lessens difficulties, and thus negatively helps the beginning of causal influence. See the chart on PRINCIPLES. **3.** *ethics.* one of the requisite factors in a complex moral principle, as the *conditions* for just warfare.

‡**conditio sine qua non,** an indispensable or even a unique condition, for which there is no substitute, and whose absence would prevent causal influence.

conduct, *n.* human acts; volitional acts as distinguished from mere behavior.

conformity, *n.* the quality or fact of agreement with a standard or ideal form of thought, truth, conduct, perfection, etc.

conjugal, *adj.* pertaining to spouses or the married; as *conjugal* duties, *conjugal* society.

conscience, *n.* **1.** *in general.* the act or trained ability of judging between right and wrong in conduct. **2.** *proper sense.* *antecedent* conscience, i.e., the last practical judgment concerning the moral lawfulness of one's human act here and now to be performed, knowing this act to be either commanded, forbidden, or permitted. **3.** *consequent* conscience, i.e., the judgment after a human act that one has or has not followed one's antecedent conscience when one acted; judgment of the conformity or difformity of one's past acts to one's knowledge of the moral law.

certain conscience, prudentially certain antecedent conscience.

doubtful conscience, a probable conscience. *Speculative* doubt concerns the theoretical reasons for and against a certain way of acting, if I should ever be required to act or not act in such a type of situation; *practical* doubt concerns action here and now proposed to me or urgent upon my decision. See DOUBT.

REF. – *S.T.,* I, 79, a. 13. *Truth,* q. 17, a. 1.

consciousness, *n.* immediate awareness; internal experience here and now of something either internally or externally present to the perceiver. See AWARENESS; EXPERIENCE.

intellectual consciousness, immediate intellectual knowledge of a present object or of one's own cognitive or appetitive act.

self-consciousness, immediate awareness of one's own acts or one's own being as here and now present to the mind; internal self-experience.

sensitive consciousness, sensory knowledge of sensible objects or sensible acts immediately present to the sensory knowing power.

consent, *n.* **1.** a free act in which one agrees to do, accept, or reject something; the free acceptance or rejection of some motive or good proposed. Usually, however, the word is reserved for the acceptance. **2.** *loosely.* the assent of the mind.

external consent, the use of external signs, as words or signatures, to express the *internal* consent of the will.

mutual consent, the agreement of two or more persons to a common object, as in any contract.

REF. – *S.T.,* I–II, 15, esp. a. 4, c. and ad 1; 16, a. 2; 74, a. 7.

consequence, *n.* **1.** the objective bond or connection between antecedent and consequent judgments. **2.** *especially.* the connection between premises and conclusion as usually signified by "therefore."

consequent, *adj.* that which follows from or happens after something else. USES – *consequent* concupiscence, necessity, truth, will, etc.

consequent, *n.* **1.** the judgment or proposition derived from another, and especially the conclusion in syllogistic reasoning. **2.** the second or dependent member of a conditional proposition which follows upon the statement of the condition or hypothesis; the apodosis; the conditioned clause in a conditional proposition.

conservation, *n.* the act of preserving something in being, activity, beauty, goodness, or any other perfection or state.

divine conservation, God's act of preserving existence and perfections in creatures.

negative (accidental, indirect) conser-

vation, the act of aiding the continuance of some being by removing obstacles to its continuation and by refraining from any hindering action of one's own.

positive (essential, direct) conservation, the act of maintaining the causal action which is necessary for the being of something.

REF. – *S.T.,* I, 104, a. 1.

consistency, *n.* **1.** *logic.* correctness of mental relations; concordance or non-contradiction; coherence. **2.** *ethics.* agreement of conduct with principles; especially, the sustained steadiness of character.

constitution, *n.* **1.** *metaphysics, philosophy of nature.* the internal structure, make-up, organization, or composition of a being or essence. **2.** *political philosophy.* the fundamental law of a state setting up its system of government, of offices, officials, and other institutions and guarantees. ABBR. – *cons., const.*

REF. – *Politics,* III, CC. 6, 7; IV, CC. 1, 3.

constitutive, *adj.* belonging to the constitution of something; aiding in the formation of some nature; essential; internal.

contact, *n.* a touching or other union of two substances.

contact of power (virtual or intrinsic contact), the union of two substances by the causal action of one touching the substance of the other.

contact of quantity (corporeal, physical or extrinsic contact), the touching or joining together of the outside parts or surfaces of two bodies.

REF. – *Physics,* V, C. 3. *Generation,* C. 6. *Met.,* XI, C. 12. *S.T.,* I, 75, a. 1 ad 3; 105, a. 2 ad 1. *C.G.,* II, C. 56.

contemplation, *n.* **1.** the pursuit of truth for truth's own sake rather than for action and use. **2.** the contemplative life; the life of prayer, study, and thought.

REF. – *S.T.,* II–II, 180, a. 3, replies.

contiguous, *adj.* adjacent. See QUANTITY.

continence, *n.* **1.** *general sense.* resistance to evil desires. **2.** *specifically.* abstention from venereal use and pleasure.

REF. – *N. Eth.,* VII, C. 7. *S.T.,* II–II, 155.

contingent, *adj.* **1.** that which can be or

not be or be other than it is; that which happens to be actual. **2.** that which is changeable or perishable in being, disposition, or operation. **3.** that which is an indifferent or non-necessary means; hence, the object of a free judgment. **4.** that which can fail in its proper or intended effect. **5.** that which is not necessarily or essentially true; that which is only historically real and true. ANT. – *necessary.* See table on uses and kinds of BEING.

REF. – *C.G.,* III, CC. 67, 94.

continuity, *n.* **1.** the state of beings or natures which are arranged in an unbroken series of progressively greater perfection with no gaps between the members of the series. **2.** the law of such arrangement of natures. Thus, every form of life is found in the degrees of life: vegetative, sentient, rational, angelic, and divine.

continuum, *n.* any quantity or series whose parts or members are adjacent to each other and whose limits coincide. See chart on CATEGORIES OF BEING, under "quantity."

dimensive continuum, a quantity, extension, or series whose parts are simultaneous.

mobile or successive continuum, a continuum whose parts follow upon one another, one at a time, not simultaneously; e.g., as in time or movement.

REF. – *Physics,* V, C. 3; VI, C. 2. *Met.,* XI, C. 12.

contraception, *n.* any act or method of sexual intercourse from which conception of a human being cannot result; birth limitation in mode or time of intercourse.

artificial contraception, any method or means or action which deliberately interferes with the natural sexual act and so makes conception impossible, during either the fertile or infertile period; birth prevention; popularly, birth control.

natural contraception, natural performance of sexual intercourse during the infertile period and especially if deliberately limited to this period.

contract, *n.* a free and mutual agreement between two or more competent parties concerning the transfer of a right; the consent of two or more juridically capable persons to the same juridical effect. See the chart on titles of OWNERSHIP.

contract of chance (aleatory contract), the mutual agreement concerning burdens and advantages which will come to the contracting parties, depending upon the outcome of an event that is uncertain to both (all) parties to the contract. Some main forms of such contracts are life insurance, fire insurance, wagers in games of chance, betting on uncertain future events, and lottery.

contraction, *n.* the mental act of restricting the extension of a transcendental or universal concept or term to a class or member of the wider concept or term. The methods are spoken of as (1) *explicitation* or adding a clearer note or term already indistinctly included in the transcendental or generic concept; and (2) *metaphysical composition,* which adds a new metaphysical grade or a new and distinct specific difference to the broader term. Explicitation is also called imperfect contraction; metaphysical composition is called perfect composition.

contradiction, *n.* **1.** the absolute denial or the complete exclusion of the opposite. **2.** inconsistency. **3.** the relation of contradiction: (*a*) the opposition between absolute natures or concepts which cannot simultaneously both be or both not be in the same being; (*b*) the opposition between judgments or propositions that cannot be simultaneously both true or both false; the opposition between propositions on the same subject matter which have neither the quantity nor quality of the propositions in common; therefore, the oppositions of the A-O and E-I types; (*c*) the opposition between concepts and terms which have nothing in common and exclude each other.

principle of contradiction, the law of being and of thought that a thing cannot be and not be at the same time in the same respect.

REF. – *Interpretation,* CC. 6, 7. *Post. Anal.,* I, C. 2. *Met.,* IV.

contraposition, *n.* an immediate inference in which the subject of the inferred proposition is the contradictory of the original proposition; a conversion of the obverse of the original proposition.

contrariety, *n.* the type of opposition that exists between contrary things or judgments or propositions.

contrary, *adj.* altogether opposite or completely different in the same series or genus of things; opposed in such a way that the extremes cannot exist or be true at the same time, but either one of the extremes or a mean partaking of some measure of the characteristics of both extremes may exist and be true. ABBR. – *contr.*

contrary to nature, altogether opposite to the being, activities, mode of action, order, or end of a particular nature or of nature generally. See MIRACLE; NATURAL; UNNATURAL; VIOLENT.

contrary opposition of propositions, the difference between two propositions having the same quantity but opposite to each other in quality, and dealing with the same terms. Such an opposition of quality between two *particular* propositions about the same terms is sometimes called *subcontrary opposition.*

REF. – *Interpretation,* CC. 7, 14. *Met.,* V, C. 10; X, C. 3, end, and C. 4.

conventional, *adj.* set up by agreement, precedent, custom, general consent, or mere contract, but not by nature or natural tendencies. USES – *conventional* laws, morals, rules, signs, societies, etc.

conversion, *n.* **1.** *philosophy of nature.* substantial change, especially in inorganic things. See chart on CHANGE. **2.** *logic.* an immediate inference in which the subject and predicate change places in such a way that the proposition in its transposed (converse, changed) form is legitimately derived from the original proposition. Three types are distinguished: **contraposition,** a conversion of the obverse of the original proposition.

conversion by limitation or *per accidens,* transposition of the terms in such a way that the quantity of the proposition is changed from universal to particular while the quality remains unchanged.

simple conversion, transposition of the terms of the original proposition without changing the quantity of the proposition.

conversion to the phantasm, *phrase.* the turning of the possible intellect to the image in the process of moving from knowledge of the universal nature to definite knowledge of the singular material thing(s) possessing that nature. REF. – *S.T.,* I, 84, a. 7.

co-operation, *n.* deliberately doing or omitting something by which one assists another agent.

divine co-operation, God's causal help given to the action of creatures.

formal co-operation, intending the good or evil which the other (principal) agent intends when giving him help in his activities or omissions.

immediate co-operation, taking part in the very act of another; being in some way the direct cause of the action, good or evil, that another performs or of the result he produces; e.g., two oarsmen stroking together.

indifferent co-operation, aiding another agent in such a way that the helper does not compel action of the agent in only one direction or to only one effect; help offered and given according to the agent's choice.

material co-operation, rendering assistance to another but not joining in the other's good or evil intention. ANT. – *formal co-operation.*

mediate co-operation, taking part in preparations for some act or omission or in concealment or protection after the act of another. Mediate co-operation is remote or proximate as it comes closer and closer to direct participation in the act of another.

moral co-operation, influence brought to bear on the mind or will of another agent inducing him to act because of the persuasion, advice, command, example, ridicule, promise of protection, or other such influence; scandal, when the influence is toward evil.

necessary co-operation, some form of help given to another without which the other's act could not take place and for which there is no substitute.

physical co-operation, immediate or mediate partnership in another's act or omission by giving external help or omitting external prevention of his act.

simultaneous co-operation (concurrence, concursus), help given at the moment of acting, not a prior physical or moral compulsion on the agent who is helped. Molina's theory of God's concurrence with free acts of creatures is that God's help is indifferent and simultaneous.

universal co-operation, help given in all the activities of all other agents.

co-ordination, *n.* a form of order among similars or especially among equals; harmonious and mutual relation especially of beings in the same order, rank, or class; parallel co-operative activity.

co-principle of being, *phrase.* a principle, element, or any part in a being which unites with some other internal principle, element, or part to constitute the reality of some whole.

copula, *n.* 1. *logic.* the connection between the subject and predicate of a proposition; the affirmative or negative sign by which identity or difference of subject and predicate is either stated or denied in a proposition. 2. *ethics.* the physical act of sexual union.

corollary, *n.* a proposition or truth that follows easily from one that has been proved. ABBR. – *corol., coroll.*

corporative society, *phrase.* an occupational, vocational, or functional group. See SOCIETY.

corporeity, *n.* the so-called form of the living body by which it is a body, and different from the soul by which it is a living thing. This is chiefly a Scotistic usage. See diagram on FORM. REF. – *C.G.,* IV, C. 81.

correspondence theory, *phrase.* the view that truth consists in (some) conformity of mind with reality as it is in itself.

corruption, *n.* 1. the breaking up or dis-

solution of a nature or thing into parts.
2. the perishing of the substantial form
upon the generation of the new form.
ABBR. – *cor., corr.* ANT. – *generation.* Also
see IMMORTALITY.

direct (essential, *per se,* **proper,
simple) corruption,** the decay of a
thing from within by the separation of
its essential natural constituents from each
other; perishing because of internal breaking up of its parts.

indirect (accidental, *per accidens,* **relative) corruption,** the decay of a thing
because of the destruction or removal
of something on which it intrinsically depends for its being.
REF. – *S.T.,* I, 89, a. 5. *C.G.,* II, C. 55.

cosmogony, *n.* **1.** the origin of the universe. **2.** the study or theory of the
origin of the universe or of the development of its present order and variety.

cosmological, *adj.* pertaining to the order
or especially to ordered causality in the
universe.

cosmology, *n.* in the Wolffian division of
philosophy, that branch which treats of
the ultimate reasons and universal characteristics of the merely material universe.
This is not the equivalent of philosophy
of nature, though there is some coincidence of topics treated in cosmology and
in the philosophy of nature.

cosmos, *n.* the ordered universe; world
order. See MACROCOSM.

counsel, *n.* **1.** inquiry concerning the right
choice of means. **2.** a direction, recom-
mendation, or advisory opinion of a
superior which does not bind to its observance as a law or precept does. **3.** the
better course of action.
REF. – *S.T.,* I–II, 14, aa. 1–4; 108, a. 4.
C.G., III, C. 130.

courage, *n.* the virtue of bravery in facing

difficulties in doing good, especially in
overcoming the fear of death or related
dangers; fortitude.
REF. – *N. Eth.,* III, CC. 6–9.

covetousness, *n.* immoderate love of acquiring and of keeping possessions;
avarice.
REF. – *S.T.,* I–II, 84, a. 1.

created, *part. as adj.* produced from
nothing. ABBR. – *cr.*

creation, *n.* **1.** *active or causal sense.* an
act whereby the entire substance of a
thing is brought from non-existence to
existence; the production of all things
in their entirety; the production of something from absolutely nothing pre-existing.
2. *passive sense, from the viewpoint of
the effect.* created things; beings produced entirely from nothingness; newness
of being together with a relation to God.
REF. – *S.T.,* I, 41, a. 3; 45, aa. 1–4, 8.
Power, q. 3, a. 3.

Creator, *n.* God considered as Maker of
all things from nothingness.

criterion, *n., pl.* **-ia** *or* **-ions.** a norm;
standard of judgment or of values.

criticism, *n.* **1.** the act of judging the
truth, goodness, or beauty of some thing,
person, act, or product. **2.** critical philosophy, esp. Kantian; theory of knowledge; epistemology. ABBR. – *crit.*

cult, *n.* worship; a definite form of worship or of religious observance.

custom, *n.* **1.** an ordinary or uniform
performance of the same act in the
same circumstances by a group of people, and originally for a definite reason
and not as a mechanical routine. **2.** common usage; old and general usage. **3.** a
uniform way of acting which has become
socially binding and has the force of
law.
REF. – *S.T.,* I–II, 97, a. 3.

D

datum, *n., pl.* data. 1. what is given in experience; the object of direct experience; phenomenon. 2. a fact assumed or premise granted.

debt, *n.* what is due to another in justice; the just object or act.

marital debt, the act of sexual union due to the married partner.

decree, *n.* 1. an authoritative application of a general law to a particular case. 2. a decision of a superior's will; e.g., a divine decree to help the prayerful. REF. – *N. Eth.*, V, C. 7. *S.T.*, I–II, 96, a. 1 ad 1.

deduction, *n.* an argument which moves from a more universal premise to a less universal (or occasionally, equally universal) conclusion; reasoning from principle or law to instance. See the chart on REASONING.

‡de facto, *Latin, adjectival phrase.* in fact; actual, whether moral, lawful, or not.

definition, *n.* 1. *logical and philosophical senses.* a proposition either stating the meaning of a term or explaining what an essence is. ABBR. – *def.*

accidental definition, tells what a thing is by giving its characteristic accidents or properties.

causal definition, tells what a thing is by naming its external causes or principles, i.e., its agent, purposes, model, or some combination of these.

essential definition, tells what the essence is or of what it is composed. An essential definition is (*a*) *metaphysical,* when it explains a thing by giving its metaphysical parts or grades, namely, its genus and specific difference. (*b*) *physical,* when it tells what a thing is by giving its ultimate essential parts, namely, its matter and form or intrinsic causes.

initial definition, a definition stated, assumed, or conceded at the opening of a discussion for purposes of identification or exploration of matters referred to.

nominal definition, an explanation of the meaning of a word or of its roots or sources; verbal definition by synonym.

real definition, an explanation of what the thing represented by a concept or word is; the statement of what a nature is. REF. – *Post. Anal.*, I, C. 2; II, CC. 3, 10. *Topics*, I, CC. 5, 8. *Met.*, IV, C. 8.

definition, *n.* 2. *theological sense.* a declaration of religious doctrine or a condemnation of heresy made solemnly by supreme religious authority. Thus, Pope Pius XII defined the doctrine of the Assumption of the Blessed Virgin Mary.

deformity, *n.* lack of conformity to a standard.

deformity of a human act, the evil of a human act because of its opposition to the norm or law for human conduct or to the will of God. REF. – *S.T.*, I–II, 18, a. 5; II–II, 6, a. 2 ad 2.

degree, *n.* 1. one member in a sequence of steps or grades of perfection. 2. relative rank in any series, order, or chain of relationships. 3. comparative measure of intensity of a quality. 4. comparative excellence of power or authority. ABBR. – *d., deg.*

deism, *n.* a view that accepts God's existence on rational grounds as the supreme being and usually also as author of nature, but denies God's omnipresence, conservation and co-operation, personal providence and love of men; and hence, it also denies miracles, the supernatural order, and all divine revelation.

‡**de jure,** *Latin, adjectival phrase.* by right; in accordance with natural or positive law; juridical. Compare "DE FACTO."

deliberate, *adj.* done after reflection on motives for acting or after inquiry and advice; opposed to the merely passionate, thoughtless, and hasty.

deliberate, *v.* to consider reasons; to take counsel by inquiry, seeking advice, and weighing the worth of reasons. See PRUDENCE.

delight, *n.* 1. pleasure. 2. joy in the possession of some good.

demerit, *n.* 1. a voluntary misdeed which offends another and is of itself deserving of some penalty. 2. the liability to such a penalty. 3. the penalty inflicted for voluntary misdeeds that have offended another.
REF. – *S.T.,* I–II, 21, aa. 3, 4.

demonstration, *n.* a legitimate or valid argument from evident premises; a proof or syllogism that yields a certain or scientific conclusion; an inference from certain and necessary premises whose predicates are essential attributes. See the chart on REASONING.

a posteriori demonstration, a legitimate argument from evident a posteriori premises, i.e., from premises better known than the conclusion, though the premises are effects posterior in being or in time to the cause in the conclusion; e.g., demonstrations of the existence of God.

a priori demonstration, a legitimate argument from evident a priori premises, i.e., from something prior in nature or in time to the being in the conclusion; e.g., demonstrations from cause to effect, from form to properties.

direct (proper) demonstration, a proof drawn from truths or facts accepted by all parties interested in the proof.

indirect (negative) demonstration, (*a*) a proof drawn from the meaning, assumption made, or conclusion accepted by another person and arguing from this to false or absurd consequences that necessarily follow from that position and which the other person is unwilling to accept; or (*b*) a refutation of another's position by an indirect attack on the reasons for his position, showing that it is supported by wrong reason, unnecessary hypotheses, or misunderstandings.

proof *propter quid* **or proof by means of causes,** a demonstration that gives the reasons for the truth of the conclusion and not merely of the fact of the true conclusion because it proceeds from knowledge of causes to consequences of those causes; proof of the reasoned fact.

proof *quia* **or proof of the fact,** a demonstration of a fact but not of the intrinsic reasons or necessity of the fact; a demonstration that does not proceed from knowledge of causes to knowledge of things dependent on those causes.
REF. – *Post Anal.,* I, CC. 2, 4, 6. *Met.,* IV, C. 4.

denial, *n.* a negative proposition or judgment; the judgment of division.

denominate, *v.* to name.

denominated, *adj.* named after or named from, as a commanded act is said to be or is named free because of its close dependence on the elicited free act, though it is not free in itself.

denotation, *n.* the extension of a term, especially referring to the singular objects to which the term refers rather than to the classes of things to which it refers.

dependent, *adj.* 1. needing something other than itself for its being or its activity. 2. controlled by something exterior to itself. 3. subordinate to another, as to its cause or to an authority. See INDEPENDENCE; SPIRITUAL.

extrinsically dependent on matter, in action using or depending on matter as upon a condition outside its own being which helps action by way of preparation, removal of obstacles, supplying data for knowledge, etc.

intrinsically dependent on matter, 1. in essence needing union with matter or control by something material. 2. in action needing the help of some material part or agent as participant of its action. Thus, sentient acts of touching material things are intrinsically dependent on the material organ of touch.

description, *n.* exposition which enables us to recognize a thing by citing some of its features, but lacks the full explanation which a definition would provide.

design, *n.* **1.** an arrangement; pattern; plan; artistic exemplar. **2.** a fixed purpose or intention. **3.** adaptation of means to end.

desire, *n.* tendency; inclination.

desire, *v.* to wish or long for the possession or enjoyment of something which the appetite does not presently possess.

determinant, *n.* one of the factors which influences the concrete goodness or evil of a human act. Object, end, intrinsic circumstance are the three determinants.

determination, *n.* **1.** *logic.* a definite, limiting, specifying note which makes a general concept or class name more definite or particular. **2.** *metaphysics, philosophy of nature.* a perfection or attribute added to a nature; a modification of another being, as an accident; an act or form removing the indetermination of a potency. **3.** *philosophy of man, ethics.* **a.** self-determination; the act of decision, choice, resolution. **b.** firm intention.

determine, *v.* to cause a definite perfection. It is said of both efficient and formal causes.

determinism, *n.* the opinion that every effect occurs necessarily and nothing is the result of free causes; the denial of free will.

intellectual determinism, the view that every act of will necessarily follows the mind's judgment of what is better.

natural determinism, a. the view that the human will is completely determined by nature or environment or that the human will is no more free than are physical bodies. **b.** the view that the whole universe arose necessarily, not by the free decision and free creative act of God.

devotion, *n.* the act of the will to do promptly what concerns the service of God.

dialectic, *n.* **1.** discussion and reasoning about matters of general or expert opinion. **2.** method of arguing and defending with probability and consistency on open questions. Senses 1 and 2 may be ascribed to Aristotle. **3.** critical argument or disputation. **4.** the science or art of logic. **5.** *Plato.* dialogue discussion as a scientific method of investigation; analytic investigation; the science of ideas (Forms) and of being. **6.** *Kant.* the logic or epistemology of appearances or illusions. **7.** *Hegel.* the process of development of thought and of history from thesis through antithesis to synthesis. **8.** *Marx.* the physical and political evolution of matter. ABBR. – *dial.*

REF. – J. Isaac, "La notion de dialectique chez saint Thomas," in *Revue des sciences philosophiques et théologiques,* 1950:481–506.

difference, *n.* **1.** *in general.* otherness; a lack of sameness or identity between two or more. **2.** *logic.* a concept or predicable or determination which distinctively characterizes one species and distinguishes it from all others in the same genus; the specific difference. ABBR. – *dif., diff.*

accidental difference, diversity among things only in some contingent accident; also, difference in the mere degree or amount of some perfection without any difference in species or proper accidents. ANT. – *essential difference.*

analogical difference, unlikeness in some perfection that is partly alike and partly unlike the other perfection with which it is compared.

essential difference, unlikeness in kind or species of being when a certain perfection is in no way found in another type of being with which it is compared. ANT. – *accidental difference.* See SUPERIORITY.

generic difference, unlikeness in genus; difference between things not contained under the same proximate genus.

numerical difference, the individual difference of units within the same species or class.

specific difference, the ultimate essential characteristic distinguishing species from species in the same proximate genus; the

distinguishing part of an essential definition; the predicable that distinguishes the classes of beings within the same proximate genus.
REF. – *Met.*, V, C. 9; X, CC. 3, 8. *On Being and Essence*, C. 2. *Power*, q. 7, a. 3 ad 2.

dignity, *n.* the excellence of a thing; the superior goodness or value of something when compared with some other.

dilemma, *n.* a complex argument in which one premise is a compound conditional proposition and the other premise is a disjunctive proposition and so arranged that either (*a*) false, absurd, or unacceptable consequences are shown to flow from each disjunction in the minor or (*b*) in a second type, something true is deduced from each member of the disjunction. It is particularly effective as a form of refutation.

dimensive, *adj.* having extension, dimensions, and capacity to be measured.

direct, *adj.* 1. straight or on a straight course toward something. 2. free from intervening steps, agencies, conditions, obstacles, etc.; hence, immediate. 3. nearest. 4. knowingly sought; hence, intentional, as opposed to accidental. See INDIRECT; INVOLUNTARY; MEDIATE; PROXIMATE.

discursive, *adj.* inferential; proceeding by or resulting from reasoning from step to step. ANT. – *immediately known.*

discursive power, see SENSE, COGITATIVE.

dispensation, *n.* the act of a lawful superior for a sufficient reason releasing a subject from the observance of a law, precept, oath, or vow in particular circumstances; official permission to act contrary to the letter of the law while the law itself retains general force for other subjects, places, and times.
REF. – *S.T.*, I–II, 97, a. 4.

dispose of, *v.* to deal with property in any way that ownership can be exercised, such as use, consumption, gift, exchange, rental.

disposition, *n.* 1. the state of a substance or power ready to receive form; e.g., bodily *disposition, disposed* matter, *disposed* faculty. 2. a variable or unstable quality modifying or perfecting some

power; e.g., health, opinion. See the chart on CATEGORIES OF BEING under "quality." 3. a putting in order. 4. some right or power to control or manage property. See OWNERSHIP.
REF. – *Cat.*, C. 8. *Met.*, V, C. 19. *S.T.*, I–II, 50, a. 1, c. and replies; III, 9, a. 3 ad 2.

disprove, *n.* to present evidence that some proposed statement is false, incorrect, unsure, or invalidly drawn; to refute.

disputation, *n.* a formal scholastic debate on a given subject or group of related subjects conducted according to a traditional or accepted procedure.

disteleology, *n.* lack of purpose, design, or order; disorder.

distinction, *n.* the lack of identity between things, parts, concepts, or terms; difference. ANT. – *identity, sameness.* See the chart on UNITY, IDENTITY, AND DISTINCTIONS.

conceptual distinction, logical distinction.

distinction of reason, logical distinction, whether purely mental or virtual.

‡**distinctio rationis ratiocinantis,** *lit.,* a distinction of the reason of the reasoner; i.e., a purely mental distinction.

‡**distinctio rationis ratiocinatae,** *lit.,* a distinction of the *ratio* (intelligible object) as thought about; i.e., a virtual distinction.

essential distinction, essential difference, q.v.

formal distinction, *used chiefly by Scotists.* a distinction between a thing and its formality or between formalities of a thing.

logical distinction, a difference dependent on thought, but not found in the thing itself because of no real plurality in the thing thought about. It may be either a nominal (purely mental) distinction or a virtual distinction.

metaphysical distinction, Suaresian terminology for virtual distinction.

modal distinction, distinction between a thing and its modes.

nominal distinction, a distinction only between words or terms describing the same object without any distinction in the thing to correspond to these differences of names.

real distinction, a true lack of identity between things, or between their parts and principles, or between objective concepts antecedently to and independently of the mind's distinguishing activity. A *major* real distinction exists between two separate or complete wholes; a *minor* real distinction between parts, between whole and part, or between substance and its absolute accidents.

virtual distinction, a logical (mental) distinction between different aspects of only one essence or perfection where the being is actually one and indivisible but is rich enough to present various aspects of its reality to the mind; e.g., the distinction between the divine attributes or between the several transcendental concepts. It is sometimes called a metaphysical distinction or, again, a logical distinction with a foundation in reality. REF. – *S.T.*, I, 41, a. 4 ad 3. *Truth*, q. 1, a. 1. Suarez-Vollert, *On Distinctions* (from Suarez' *Disputationes Metaphysicae*).

distributed, *adj.* used according to its whole extension; used universally. The middle term of a syllogism is distributed when it is used universally at least once; and the predicate of a proposition is distributed when used in common supposition. ABBR. – *distr.*

div., abbreviation for *divine, division.*

division, *n.* 1. separation into parts. 2. a negative judgment. Judgment itself was called by Aristotle a composition (affirmation) and division (negation). ABBR. – *div.*

dichotomous division, division of things by specific differences contradictorily opposed to each other; therefore, division by two differences, as in the Porphyrian tree. ABBR. – *div.*

logical division, division only in the mind or between objects in their status of existence in the mind.

real division, actual separation of real things or of parts of real things.

essential division, division of the es-

sence, i.e., separation of form from matter.

quantitative division, separation of integral parts from each other.

divorce, *n.* 1. the dissolution of a true marriage. 2. legal or illegal separation of husband and wife or release from any one or more of the bonds of matrimony between them.

imperfect divorce, separation of the married parties so that the duty of common life and sometimes of support is relaxed, without any right to remarry; separation from "bed and board," but not from the primary bond of exclusive, lifelong fidelity in use of marital rights.

perfect (complete) divorce, the total dissolution of all the bonds of marriage so that both parties are free of all obligations to each other and free to remarry.

do, *v.* to act immediately. To *make* is to produce or act transeuntly. REF. – *Met.*, VI, C. 1. *N. Eth.*, VI, C. 4.

doctrine, *n.* some proposition that is taught or some teaching, especially by a specific philosophical school. Cf. dictionaries for synonymies of belief, doctrine, dogma, principle, tenet, etc.

dogma, *n.* 1. *strictly.* a doctrine defined and binding. 2. *loosely.* anything taught or believed as immutably certain, such as the principle of contradiction.

domain, eminent, *phrase.* the right of the state as the superior to regulate or appropriate private property for public use in accordance with the demands of the common good.

dominative power, *phrase.* the right of authority over acts of persons in private societies. See the chart on forms of OWNERSHIP.

dominion, *n.* ownership of material goods. ABBR. – *dom.* See OWNERSHIP.

doubt, *n.* hesitation of mind in regard to both sides of contradictory views; a movement of reason in regard to both sides of opposed views, accompanied by a fear of error.

methodical doubt, in a state of certainty, one abstracts from his certitude in order critically or scientifically to examine the truth of some matter. ANT. – *real doubt.*

practical doubt, uncertainty of mind concerning the prudent course of action or concerning the moral rectitude of something to be done here and now. See CONSCIENCE, DOUBTFUL. ANT. – *speculative doubt.*

real doubt, suspension of assent or judgment because of lack of sufficient motive or evidence to one or other side of opposed opinions.

speculative doubt, uncertainty of mind concerning (*a*) the mere truth or error of something or (*b*) the mere abstract goodness or evil or prudence of something, but which does not presently concern one's own action.

universal doubt, 1. the state of suspended assent to any and every truth, usually as a methodical type of doubt. **2.** real general doubt of the skeptic.

voluntary doubt, uncertainty of mind because the will withholds assent even in the presence of sufficient or prudentially adequate evidence.
REF. – *Truth,* q. 14, a. 1.

dualism, *n.* any view of reality which recognizes two fundamental irreducibly different types of beings or of operations.
psychological dualism, the view that exaggerates the difference of soul and body in man and makes man two beings, a spirit and a body, not a natural unit. Plato, Descartes, and others have held this or a cognate view.

due, *n.* **1.** debt; the object of justice; an objective right or service payable to another; the legal *debitum.* **2.** a proper good of a nature; something needed by a nature and sufficient for it either in its constitution, powers, end, or means to its end. In this sense it is contrasted with the gratuitous character of the supernatural.

dulia, *n.* **1.** reverence of a servant for a lord. **2.** honor given to the servants of God, the saints and angels, for the sake of God.
REF. – *S.T.,* II–II, 103, aa. 3, 4.

duration, *n.* continuing existence; persistence in existence.

duty, *n.* **1.** obligation; the moral necessity of acting or omitting some act. **2.** the act which one is morally bound to do or omit. Compare PERMISSION; RIGHT.

ethical duty, a moral, but non-juridical duty; a true obligation but not binding under the virtue of justice. It is said to be merely ethical.

juridical duty, an obligation between equals and binding in justice, especially under justice of the natural law and natural commutative justice; a duty corresponding to a perfect right.

legal duty, 1. a duty to obey a law, especially a positive law, but not a duty arising from the nature of man. **2.** a duty binding in legal justice only.
REF. – *N. Eth.,* V, C. 7. *S.T.,* I–II, 99, a. 5.

dynamics, *n.* **1.** the forces producing or governing activity or change of any kind. **2.** the methods of such activities or movements.

dynamism, *n.* any philosophical theory of nature that tries to explain phenomena in the universe chiefly or wholly in terms of force, especially material force or energy, and denies the reality of extension.

E

E, symbol for a universal negative proposition.

education, *n.* **1.** *active sense.* application by the educator of the means by which any or all aspects of the life and personality of another person are developed. **2.** *passive sense.* complete and habitual development in the recipient of nurture, teaching, training, and formation by another. ABBR. – *educ.* Note the corresponding difference between the right to give education or to teach and the right to receive an education.

eduction, *n.* **1.** *logic.* the mental act of drawing out the immediate implications of a previous judgment; an immediate inference. **2.** *philosophy of nature.* the actualization of a form out of a subject in which it had been only potentially; the developmental aspect of change.

effect, *n.* result; product; end attained.

formal effect, see under FORM.

proper effect, the immediate and particular kind of effect of a proper cause; the direct and specific effect of a specific causal ability. See CAUSE, PROPER. REF. – *Power,* q. 7, a. 2. *S.T.,* I, 8, a. 1.

efficacy, *n.* the activity of an efficient cause; the specific type of causality that distinguishes efficient causes from the other main kinds of causes.

efficient cause, *phrase.* an agent; that which by its activity or its exercise of power produces existence or change in another. See CAUSE, sense 2, for divisions.

ego, *n.* the conscious and permanent subject of one's own psychical acts and experiences.

election, *n.* the act of choice or selection of means to an end made by an intelligent agent. See CHOICE.

divine election, God's choice of those whom He absolutely wills to be saved. REF. – *Truth,* q. 22, a. 15. St. Thomas Aquinas, *De Malo,* q. 6.

element, *n.* a primary physical ingredient or constituent of a body; any ultimate or fundamental constituent within a body which cannot be subdivided or analyzed into other components of the same kind. REF. – *Met.,* V, C. 3; VII, C. 17, near end. *On the Heavens,* III, C. 3.

elicited, *part. as adj.* immediately or internally pertaining to the activity of some power; the activity itself, not the power nor the preparatory stages nor the influence of that activity on other powers. See COMMANDED ACT. Some contrast *elicited* with *innate.*

emanation, *n.* **1.** the flowing forth from some source. **2.** proceeding from a material cause. **3.** the pantheistic teaching that all things arise necessarily out of the substance of God's being.

eminent domain, see DOMAIN.

eminently, *adj.* in a higher or better way, or even in a supreme or infinite way. REF. – *S.T.,* I, 6, a. 2; 108, a. 5.

emotion, *n.* **1.** a strong feeling or movement of an appetite, experienced as an agreeable or disagreeable state, and accompanied by some bodily (organic) change. **2.** *loosely.* a spiritual affection or sentiment. See LOVE; SENTIMENT.

empirical, *adj.* dependent chiefly or solely on experience or on observed experiments.

end, *n.* a good for the sake of which something is made, is done, exists, or is changed; the purpose; the final cause; the aim or objective to be attained by the agent.

end of the act, the purpose or natural result of the action performed by a moral agent, considered independently of the agent's intention or modifying circumstances. In some concrete uses it is the same as *end of the work.*

end of the agent, 1. the good which the agent, maker, or workman seeks in acting, producing, or using something. **2.** *particularly.* the good or bad intention of a moral agent when acting.

end of the work (*finis operis*), the object or good which the thing itself by its operation can achieve; the definite object of a function.

existential end, a good or goal implied in the existence of a nature and its capacities and tendencies, such as self-preservation or beatitude of man. It is contrasted with an ideal end, which depends on hypothesis or human invention or arbitrary selection.

extrinsic end, 1. a good achieved by a thing for something else. **2.** an end imposed on it by another but for which it has no special natural or mechanical destination. See FINALITY, EXTRINSIC.

formal end (*finis quo*), the act in which the person possesses and enjoys the good sought for.

intrinsic end, a good within the nature of the active being and for which its operations are naturally suited.

means-end, intermediate end; a good

DIVISIONS OF END

1. Objective end (the end which; *finis qui*)
   Personal end (the person or being for whose sake the objective end is sought; *finis cui*)
   Formal end (the activity in which the agent possesses the end; *finis quo*)

   Adequate (complete) end
   $\left\{\begin{array}{l}\text{The objective and personal ends together} \\ \text{The ultimate formal end (the agent's ultimate activity in} \\ \quad \text{possessing the objective end)}\end{array}\right.$

2.

   End of work (*finis operis*)
   $\left\{\begin{array}{l}\text{Of natural object} \\ \text{Of organ or power of a nature} \\ \text{Of an act and its normal effects} \\ \text{Of an artefact (machine, etc.)}\end{array}\right.$

   End (intention) of agent, maker, or workman (*finis operantis*)
   $\left\{\begin{array}{l} a) \ \begin{array}{l}\text{Intrinsic, same as end of work in natural objects, powers,} \\ \quad \text{and acts} \\ \text{Extrinsic, other than end of work} \\ \text{Sometimes both intrinsic and extrinsic}\end{array} \\ \\ b) \ \begin{array}{l}\text{Directly intended} \\ \text{Indirectly intended} \\ \text{Merely permitted} \\ \text{Unintended (chance)}\end{array} \quad \left\{\begin{array}{l}\text{Actually} \\ \text{Virtually} \\ \text{Habitually} \\ \text{Interpretatively}\end{array}\right.\end{array}\right.$

3. Natural end
   Voluntary (imposed) end

   Moral end (purpose)
   $\left\{\begin{array}{l}\text{End of the act} \\ \text{End of the agent}\end{array}\right.$

   Supernatural end

4. Immediate (proximate, direct) end
   Intermediate (means-end)
   Ultimate end
   Supreme end

5. End to be obtained
   End to be produced
   End to be preserved
   End to be enjoyed
   End attained (properly a result, not an end)

which in one respect is sought for itself and in another respect is a means directed to another end.

natural end, a good that fulfills the natural needs of a being and that can be achieved by the proper operations of its natural powers.

objective end (*finis qui*), the good or object which is sought. It may be a thing or an activity in regard to a thing.

personal end (*finis cui*), the person (or thing) for whose sake the object is sought.

supernatural end, a purpose or good beyond the needs, powers, and tendencies of a nature as such, and which can be realized only by special divine helps.

supreme end, the highest good which a nature is capable of attaining in its activity.

ultimate end, the last in any given series of ends. In the complete series of ends for any nature it will be the same as the supreme end.
REF. – *On the Soul,* III, C. 4. *S.T.,* I–II, 1, a. 8; 2, a. 7; 3, a. 1.

enjoyment, *n.* the delight of an appetitive power in the attainment of an end.
REF. – *S.T.,* I–II, 11; 12, a. 2 ad 3.

‡**ens,** *Latin, n.* being.

‡**ens ab alio,** being from another, i.e.. produced or caused being; a creature.

‡**ens a se,** being from itself, i.e., the uncaused being.

‡**ens entis,** being of a being, i.e., accident.

‡**ens in se,** being in itself, i.e., substance.

‡**ens per se,** being through its own nature or being in an unqualified sense, i.e., substance.

‡**ens rationis,** a being of reason; a purely logical being.

‡**ens ut sic,** being as such, the object of metaphysics.

entelechy, *n.* **1.** the internal specifying principle that actively directs a nature to its specific goo.¹ or end; hence, substantial form. **2.** that which contains or realizes an end within its nature. **3.** a directive principle, more than mechanical, and immanent in living things; hence, a vital principle.

enthymeme, *n.* **1.** a shortened syllogism in which one premise or the conclusion is not explicitly stated. **2.** *especially,* a causal proposition.

enunciable, *adj. or n.* what is capable of being definitely declared; the formal object of a judgment.

epichereme, *n.* a syllogism which has the reason for one or other or both premises added to it. It is therefore a polysyllogism with an enthymeme in at least one premise.

epikeia, *n.* equity; a liberal interpretation of law in instances not provided for by the letter of the law.

epistemological, *adj.* pertaining to knowledge, to epistemology, to the critical evaluation of knowledge.

epistemology, *n.* theory of knowledge, q.v.

equality, *n.* the state or fact of being of the same quantity, number, value, etc. as another. Equality is spoken of by the philosophers as *numerical,* as *proportional* in distributive justice, and as *practical* when giving morally the same treatment to similar persons. See JUSTICE.
REF. – *Met.,* V, C. 15. *N. Eth.,* V, C. 3. *Politics,* V, C. 1; VII, C. 14.

equipollence, *n.* obversion.

equipollent, *adj.* equivalent in meaning, force, weight, truth or falsity, etc.

equity, *n.* **1.** fairness, particularly in those matters which positive law has left unsettled. **2.** the setting aside of the letter of the law and its literal application in a particular case for the sake of preserving natural justice and the common good.
REF. – *N. Eth.,* V, C. 10. *Rhetoric,* I, C. 13. *S.T.,* I–II, 96, a. 6; 97, a. 3 ad 2; II–II, q. 120.

equivocal, *adj.* a term or proposition having two or more wholly different meanings, with mere resemblance of words or sounds employed. See AMPHIBOLY; ANALOGICAL; FALLACY; MATERIAL; UNIVOCAL.
REF. – *Cat.,* C. 1.

error, *n.* **1.** positive difformity between the mind and object; a wrong judgment. **2.** *less often.* a mistake in correctness or validity in reasoning.

substantial error, ignorance or misjudgment concerning the nature, main terms, or main motive of the object of a contract.

‡**esse,** *Latin infinitive, "to be," as noun.* the act of existence; the principle of existence in a finite being, as distinguished from the essence of such a being.

‡**in esse,** cause of being, q.v.

‡**ipsum esse,** existence itself; subsistent being; a being whose essence is existence, who essentially exists. To St. Thomas it is the proper name of God.

REF. – *S.T.,* I, q. 13, a. 11.

essence, *n.* what a thing is; the internal principle whereby a thing is *what* it is and has its specific perfections; quiddity; internal constitution of a thing. Often essence is said to be the same as being, substance, nature, or even form; yet accidents also have an essence; and existence is at least conceptually distinct from essence. See the chart on uses of BEING.

absolute essence, the essence as represented in an essential definition, abstracting from its extension; the mere representation in a direct universal concept of the perfection constitutive of this kind of being.

abstract essence, the essence represented as a form without a subject; the objective concept in an abstract idea.

actual essence, 1. an essence which exists in a real being. **2.** an individual or physical essence.

concrete essence, an essence represented as a form in a subject or as represented in a concrete concept.

divine essence, the essence or nature of God, as somehow distinguished from the persons and the attributes of God.

individual essence, a singular nature, whether actual or possible; a nature as it is independently of our knowledge of it; the constitution of one real thing.

merely possible essence, a concrete, non-existing essence.

metaphysical essence, the nature as represented in the metaphysical definition which presents its genus and specific difference; the body of notes without which *such* a thing cannot be conceived.

quasi-metaphysical essence, *said of the radical divine perfection.* that perfec-

tion of God which seems to us to be the most fundamental and most distinctive of God and which is the source from which the other divine attributes can be inferred. This is said only of a being whose simplicity and uniqueness exclude metaphysical parts which are presupposed in a properly metaphysical definition.

physical essence, a nature as it exists concretely, with its needed reality or real constituent principles or parts, and as these are independently of the mind's thinking. Thus, man's physical essence is to be a body united with a spiritual soul.

specific essence, the actuality perfecting a thing in its own species; the distinctive constitution or nature of something; all that reality whereby a thing is a being of this class or kind, distinct from all other classes.

universal essence, a species or genus; one essence or, better, a type of essence, represented as common to many in a reflex universal concept.

REF. – *On Being and Essence,* CC. 1–3.

essential, *adj.* **1.** belonging or concerning the essence or nature; constitutive. **2.** fundamental. **3.** necessary.

estimative sense, *phrase.* the sensitive power of determining what is useful or harmful for an animal.

REF. – *S.T.,* I, 78, a. 4.

eternity, *n.* **1.** *strict sense.* duration of being without beginning, succession, or ending; "the whole and perfect simultaneous possession of limitless life" (Boethius). **2.** *broad or relative sense.* immortality.

REF. – Boethius, *Consolation,* V, prose 6; III, prose 2. *S.T.,* I, 10. *C.G.,* I, C. 15.

ethical, *adj.* **1.** moral; good. **2.** pertaining to the science of ethics.

ethics, *n.* the philosophical science of the necessary good in human acts; the natural science of the first principles of obligation in human acts; the philosophy of moral conduct. See the chart on PHILOSOPHY.

‡**eubulia,** *Latinized Greek, n.* right counseling; the disposition to seek and accept good counsel; excellence in deliberation. See PRUDENCE, of which it is an integral part.

REF. – *N. Eth.*, VI, C. 9. *S.T.*, II–II, 51, aa. 1, 2; 52, a. 1.

eudaemonia, *n.* happiness or well-being. It especially refers to Aristotle's conception of happiness.

evidence, *n.* 1. any ground or reason for knowledge or certitude. 2. *especially.* adequate and objective grounds for certitude. 3. a quality of propositions whose truth is manifest to the intellect.

circumstantial evidence, convergence of facts and testimonies about a fact toward one conclusion only, but without any immediate knowledge of or testimony to the central fact or the whole fact in those circumstances that are presented in evidence.

intelligible evidence, something manifest to the mind or intelligence.

objective evidence, the reality of a thing made so manifest to the mind that it compels assent because of the object's reality (not because of subjective impression, prejudices, interpretations, etc.).

sensible evidence, something manifest to the senses through its sensible properties.

subjective evidence, the perceiver's satisfaction about the truth or clearness or certainty of some thing.
REF. – *S.T.*, II–II, 4, a. 1, obj. 5 and ad 5. *Truth*, q. 14, a. 2, ad 9, 13.

evident, *adj.* plain; manifest; clear.

immediately evident, directly manifest to the perceiver, without any intermediate aid, steps, or other knowledge; self-evident.

evident in itself (*notum quoad se*), something in its own nature so clear and fundamental that it is knowable in itself; self-evident and needing no argument to establish it.

evident to us (*notum quoad nos*), evident to the perceiver. The expression can also be attributed to what is mediately evident. Not every fact or truth evident in itself will be evident to us.

mediately evident, manifest by means of something else, as by the effects or premises or middle term; something clear but inferred.

self-evident, immediately evident.
REF. – *Truth*, q. 10, a. 12.

evil, *n.* the privation or lack of a good which naturally belongs to a nature; the absence of a good which is natural and due to a being.

metaphysical evil, anything finite, because lacking in complete goodness; any limitation even though it is natural to a being (*Leibniz;* but not accepted in scholasticism as a correct description of evil).

moral evil, privation of rectitude in human acts; a sin.

formally evil, a bad human act, performed with knowledge that it is evil and with consent.

intrinsically evil, an act or intention that of its very nature, essentially or necessarily, is not in conformity with the norm of morals and the eternal law.

materially evil, something that is objectively a moral evil, but which is in a given instance performed without knowledge of its evil or under duress without consent to the evil.

occasion of evil, a circumstance external to a person, favoring the consent to or performance of some evil. See OCCASION; SCANDAL.

physical evil, 1. privation of a natural physical good. 2. *improperly.* anything painful.

principle of evil, some being supposed to be the source of all evil. Both St. Augustine and St. Thomas repeatedly insist that there is no such being.

supreme evil, whatever is regarded as the greatest evil or as the greatest deprivation. Different writers in philosophy will regard it as sin, some species of sin, pain, death, dishonor, or a Manichaean supreme principle of evil.
REF. – St. Augustine, *Confessions,* passim. *S.T.*, I, 48, aa. 1–3; 49, a. 1; I–II, 18, a. 1; 19, a. 5. *C.G.*, III, CC. 6–8. *De Malo.*

evolution, *n.* 1. any unfolding or development. 2. change or development from a simpler stage to a more complex and complete stage, with greater differentiation of parts, specification of activities, and organization in the later stages.

excuse, *n.* **1.** a reason or an alleged reason which exempts one from the observance of a law in a given instance, even if there be no dispensation. **2.** a mitigating circumstance lessening responsibility for a human act.

execution, *n.* **1.** the use or application of physical efficient causality; production of something according to plan. **2.** any carrying out, doing, or performing. Thus, the order of execution is often contrasted with the order of intention. The means are first in the order of execution, the end is first in the order of planning.

exemplar, *n.* model, idea, or exemplary cause. See MODEL.

exercise, *n.* activity; operation; active use of a power. It is contrasted with inaction, mere capacity to act, intention, and specification.

existence, *n.* what has reality of its own and not merely in potency nor in the power of its causes; the fundamental actuality of any being insofar as it is being; the act of existence by which a substance or essence is; *esse.*

noetic existence, see INTENTION, INTENTIONAL BEING.

existentialism, *n.* *in scholasticism.* the philosophical emphasis on existence and concrete individuals rather than on essences, ideas, or abstraction. This emphasis is especially prominent in metaphysics, natural theology, and in regard to the primary sources of knowledge.

experience, *n.* **1.** any form of knowledge due to one's own immediate awareness; knowledge gained from one's own perception, action, practice, enjoyment, or suffering. **2.** accumulated practical experience about individuals of some class, as the physician's knowledge of tuberculous patients.

external experience, immediate knowledge of objects outside the perceiver.

internal experience, immediate knowledge of one's own acts or self. See CONSCIOUSNESS.

REF. – *Post. Anal.,* II, C. 19. *Met.,* I, C. 1.

experiential, *adj.* of or based on experience.

experiment, *n.* **1.** an act or operation undertaken to discover, test, or illustrate some truth, principle, fact, or hypothesis. **2.** something new and not yet well tested. Experiment is a deliberate, controlled experience or a study of others' experience.

explication, *n.* the detailed unfolding or explaining of a definition or text, term by term.

explicitation, *n.* that form of contraction of a general concept to its inferiors which consists in making more distinct what is implicitly and in a confused way contained in the general concept. This is especially true of transcendental and analogical concepts.

exponents, *n. pl.* the simple propositions implied in a complex or exponible proposition.

extension, *n.* **1.** *of a body.* the property of a body whereby it has distinct parts side by side of each other, and whereby it can occupy space, and can have one or more dimensions. ABBR. – *ext.* See QUANTITY.

aptitudinal extension, the natural requirement of quantity that the intrinsic material parts be arranged outside each other in space or that they occupy space.

extrinsic (external) extension, the position, distribution, or spread of the parts of a body outside each other in place or space; volume, size, or bulk.

intrinsic (internal) extension, the plurality and distinction of the material (integral) parts of a body; the definite position and order of the parts among themselves and in reference to the body as a whole, without regard to the place or space.

virtual extension, 1. the alleged property (in dynamist theory of matter) of unextended and indivisible points or point-forces which occupy a certain field of space through their force and motions (not through the position, distinction, and spread of their parts). **2.** virtual quantity. See QUANTITY.

extension, *n.* **2.** *of a term.* the capacity of a term to cover the classes or individuals

DIVISIONS OF EVIL

1. Relative to the being itself
   Relative to other beings (an occasion of evil)

2. Simple: formally considered is in no proper sense a good.
   Qualified: a mixed evil, especially the painful and sacrificial

3.
   Physical (evil of thing) { By excess (hyper-)
                              By defect (hypo-)

   Moral evil (voluntary,
   evil deed)

   a) By excess

   By defect

   b) Original sin

   Personal fault { Mortal sin
                    Venial sin
                    Positive imperfection
                    Vice (bad habit)

   c) In itself (in choice; { Intrinsically
        guilt)   Extrinsically (positively)

   In its consequences (evil of penalty)

   d) Directly voluntary (formally evil)
        Indirectly voluntary (permitted)
        Materially evil

   Metaphysical evil (an improper use of the term "evil")

4. Natural evil
   Supernatural evil

---

connoted by it; the objects to which the term refers. ANT. – *comprehension* or *intension*. See DENOTATION; SUPPOSITION; TERM.

extremes, *adj. and n.* the outside or most distant limits or boundaries of something; the most distant points in any series or class. USES – surface of bodies, contrary opposition, relatives, terms of a syllogism, the opposing vices between which the moral virtue is a mean, etc.

extrinsic, *adj.* **1.** external; on the outside. **2.** originating from the outside; coming into a being or affecting a being from something outside itself. **3.** hence, not inherent; not constitutive of; not essential. ANT. – *intrinsic.* USES – *extrinsic* cause, dependence, extension.

F

f., abbreviation for *form, formula.*

fact, *n.* any individual thing, event, or instance that is actual; any act, deed, or omission that has been done or is being done.

reasoned fact, a fact that is known together with its causes or with the reason why it is true.

faculty, *n.* a power, ability, or active potency to do or to make; an accident disposing a subject to operate in a specific way for a specific object. See POWER.

faith, *n.* assent of the mind to something as true on the authority of the one declaring it to be so; belief.

divine faith, assent to something as true on the authority of God revealing it; either the act or habit of assent of the mind given freely with the help of grace to whatever God has revealed.

REF.–*S.T.,* II–II, 4, aa. 1, 2. *Truth,* q. 14, a. 2.

fallacy, *n.* a violation of logical principle, disguised under a show of validity; sophism; anything illogical, misleading, or erroneous in reasoning or discussion. See also BEGGING THE QUESTION; FALSE ANALOGY; FALSE CAUSE; ILLICIT PROCESS.

fallacy of accident, illicit reasoning from what is accidental to a thing as though it were essential to it; mental confusion of material and formal identity of the attributes and the essence.

fallacy of the consequent, an illicit conclusion in a conditional syllogism, caused either by asserting the consequent or denying the antecedent.

fallacy of many questions, a presentation of several questions in the guise of a single question, when the several distinct questions contained or presupposed in the presentation require separate answers and distinctions.

formal fallacy, a sophism due to lack of logical form; faulty construction of an argument.

material fallacy, a sophism in the content of terms, propositions, or arguments.

false, *adj.* the untrue in thought, in appearance, or in speech. The untrue in thought is *logically false.* The misleading or deceptive in appearance is *ontologically false* or an occasion of error in judgment. The untrue in speech is a *lie.*

false analogy, a comparison between things which leads to misinterpretation or to erroneous conclusions based on supposed or irrelevant likenesses.

false cause, the fallacy of mistaking a mere antecedent, occasion, or condition for a true cause; the fallacy known as *post hoc, ergo propter hoc.*

falsity, *n.* positive difformity of intellect from its object; error, especially in the judgment.

family, *n.* the natural society formed by parents and their children; domestic society.

fantasm, *n.* 1. phantasm; a sense image. 2. the image in the human imagination as related to the activity of the agent intellect and the species in the possible intellect. 3. an imaginary appearance.

fate, *n.* predetermined and inevitable necessity.

REF.–Boethius, *Consolation,* IV, prose 6. *S.T.,* I, 116, aa. 1, 2.

fear, *n.* the emotion of the irascible appetite in the presence of danger.

filial fear, fear based on love and reverence for the one who is feared.

servile fear, fear based on selfish aversion to pain and penalty, but without being motivated by honor, love, or sense of duty.

REF.–*Rhetoric,* II, C. 5. *S.T.,* I–II, 42, a. 3; II–II, 7, a. 1; 19, a. 2.

feeling, *n.* an affective sensory activity

46

that involves no intellectual activity as a constituent element of itself; an act or movement of a purely sensitive appetite.

figure, *n.* **1.** *logic.* the correct arrangement or position of the terms and especially of the middle term so that a syllogism may validly lead to a conclusion. **2.** *metaphysics and mathematics.* the shape or outline of a mathematical body; "that which is enclosed by one or more boundaries" (Euclid); the species of quality which gives the external quantitative shape. This is contrasted with physical form, which is the shape of a physical body like a statue or dwelling or plant. ABBR. – *fig.*

final cause, *phrase.* end; purpose.

finality, *n.* activity directed toward an end; the direction of activity to an end; the order of means to ends; teleology.
argument from finality, the proof of God's existence which begins with the evidences of purposeful activity in the universe, particularly of internal finality.
extrinsic finality, 1. direction of a thing or activity to an end outside its own nature. **2.** extrinsic guidance of a thing to an end, and not by the natural powers and forces of its nature; direction of a mere instrument to an end of an agent other than itself.
intrinsic finality, direction of activity to an end to be achieved within the nature of a being by the activity of its own developed powers.
natural finality, the direction of a nature (*a*) to an end internal to a thing, or (*b*) to an end that can arise from the natural connection, interaction, and adaptation existing between different natural objects and forces. Hence, natural finality may be either intrinsic or extrinsic in sense 1.
principle of finality, the metaphysical truth that "every agent acts for an end."

finite, *adj.* limited in being, perfection, operations, or dimensions.

first, *adj.* preceding all others in a series; basic; elementary, earliest; ultimate. REF. – *Met.,* V, C. 1.

font, *n.* a source; that out of which something else flows or by means of which something else can be obtained.

font of knowledge, an objective principle or medium known to a mind and leading it to obtain certainty in judging.

form, *n.* **1.** formal cause, and especially the substantial form. **2.** the nature or essence of a thing (taking form, the principal part, for the whole). **3.** the internal specific principle of the special nature or special activities of any thing; the specific characteristic of a class of things. **4.** after a change, the new feature(s) in a thing. **5.** the visible or outward shape of physical bodies. See FIGURE. **6.** the original idea or model of any thing. **7.** the principle of intelligibility in a thing; the embodiment of the maker's or artist's idea in the object produced, thereby giving the being its meaningfulness, structural features, and objective capacity to awaken aesthetic pleasure. **8.** the likeness of any thing, especially the cognitive likeness of it. **9.** specific constitution or organization, as of a government. **10.** *logic, grammar.* any specifying feature or bond between parts of discourse which is analogous to form in real objects; e.g., the copula is the form of a proposition. See the chart on page 48.

accidental form, an accident considered as a secondary or added perfection that determines a nature that is already substantially complete. See ACT, SECOND.

form of the whole, the definition of a complete nature, and hence including substantial form and matter.

informing form, 1. a substantial form actuating matter. **2.** an accidental form inhering in a substance.

intelligible form, 1. a principle of intelligibility in objects due to their likeness to the maker's idea and intention; usually, the essence. **2.** a species of the intellectual order. See SPECIES.

intentional form, a species; a cognitive likeness of an object.

logical form, correct logical structure of parts in significant discourse.

Platonic form, a subsistent Idea or Model supposed to exist as one of its kind in a separate universe, and in which things in this world participate as multiple copies and degrees of the Idea's perfection.

separate form, 1. a subsistent form. **2.** an essence without matter and never substantially united to matter; a form complete in itself.

subsistent form, 1. a form that can (or does) exist and act independently of matter. **2.** a form not united with a material cause.

substantial form, the intrinsic incomplete constituent principle in a substance which actualizes the potencies of matter and together with the matter composes a definite material substance or natural body; the first or formal act in the order of essence or substance, especially of material substance; the specific differentiating factor in diverse kinds of essences; that by reason of which matter is a definite thing, a "such" rather than a "this," and by which it has its own specific powers and properties; the first (ultimate), actual (real), intrinsic, proper (specific) principle by which a natural substance is *what* it is; in other words, the formal cause.

REF. – *Met.,* VII, CC. 8, 17. *S.T.*, I, 76, a. 1; 77, a. 6. *C.G.*, II, C. 68. *Being and Essence,* CC. 1, 2. *Truth,* q. 3, a. 1.

formal, *adj.* 1. of or pertaining to the formal cause or nature. **2.** specific; definite; characteristic. **3.** done according to strict rules; precise.

formal cause, the specific element in a being which communicates itself to the indeterminate or less determinate element and together with this matter or substratum constitutes a complete being; the constituent principle that accounts for the specific perfection or the specifically new perfection of a composite being. Formal cause is said primarily of the substantial form, as in hylemorphism, and secondarily of the accidental forms which complete the substance or which occur as new determinants in the course of change.

formal effect, an immediate and necessary result within a being because of the presence or communication of the formal cause in that being. Thus, spiritual powers are formal effects of the human soul; joy is a formal effect of perfect knowl-

DIVISIONS OF FORM

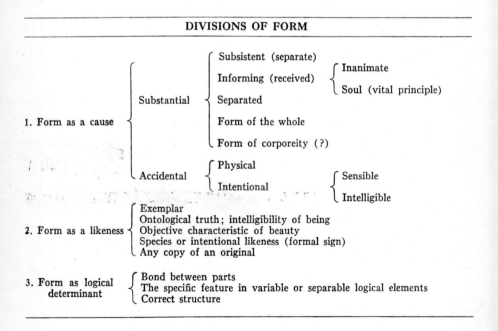

edge and love of God; some form of extension follows formally from quantity.

formal object, see OBJECT.

formally, *adv.* **1.** according to the definition of a thing; in its precise or proper meaning, descriptive of its specific nature alone and distinguished from all other associated meanings or attributes. **2.** as from or according to the form.

formula, *n.* **1.** the essence or especially the form of a thing. **2.** the definition of the essence or form. **3.** the exact statement or formulation of a principle. In sense 3, we have a *logical* formula which states a general truth or proposition in terms of thought or speech about objects; and an *ontological* formula which states a general truth in terms of being. ABBR. – *f.*

fortitude, *n.* courage; the habit of restraining fear and moderating rashness in the presence of dangers so that a man follows the rules of reason in doing good and enduring evil in spite of the dangers. REF. – *N. Eth.,* III, C. 9. *S.T.,* II–II, 123.

fortunate (the), *adj. as noun.* one to whom something good happens apart from his intention. REF. – *C.G.,* III, C. 92.

✓**foundation,** *n.* **1.** ground; basis. **2.** substratum. **3.** the objective reason for or the objective factor corresponding to some relation. *Foundation* is sometimes contrasted with *form;* and so, *fundamentally* is sometimes contrasted with *formally.*

foundation of an argument, opinion, *or* hypothesis, etc., the alleged reason or evidence offered in support.

foundation of a distinction, the parts or the diverse attributes upon which a distinction is based.

foundation of a relation, the reason why one term is or is thought or said to be related to another.

foundation of a right, the law and the title on which the subjective right is based; the reason why the right exists.

foundation of a universal concept, the nature of a finite thing inasmuch as its nature as known does not formally include individuation and is like other things.

✓**free,** *adj.* not bound or compelled to act by any person or anything contrary to its nature or by something external to the power that acts; that which is its own master; that which can actively determine its own act for its own end; that which is independent of external forces and authority so that it can decide for itself what it will do.

free act, choice; human act.

free choice, the act of the will causing itself to select one of two or more alternative means proposed to it by knowledge.

free knowledge, knowledge of contingent matters and means which leave the will free to choose, or not choose, to choose some one or other among them.

free will, the spiritual appetite for an intellectually known good insofar as it is of itself actively indifferent with regard to contingent goods or means and actively determines its own course of action and removes its indifference to such goods; the power of tending to an intellectually known good of a contingent means in such a way that even when all the conditions and causes for action are present and set, it can act or not act, can do this or that, or can choose this or that according to its own preference.

freedom, *n.* **1.** *in general.* immunity from determination or compulsion. **2.** absence of all antecedent necessity, both internal and external. ANT. – *necessity.*

civil freedoms, positive civil rights.

freedom of contradiction, the freedom to act or not to act, to perform or omit an act. It is sometimes called *freedom of exercise.*

freedom of specification, freedom to determine in which of two or more ways one shall act; freedom to do this or that or the other; the power or act of choosing any one among various contingent means to an end.

freedom of spontaneity, capacity of moving or being moved in any direction.

moral freedom, immunity from moral obligations or binding commands and prohibitions in some matter; permission of moral law to act as one chooses. ANT. – *obligation* or *moral necessity.*

physical freedom, absence of external physical compulsion or violence so that one must act or not act or act in only one way because of the restraint imposed; spontaneity of action.

political freedom, 1. power and right to choose one's own form of government or one's rulers; not under the control of civil authority without one's consent. **2.** protection of rights (freedoms) by law.

psychological *or* **rational freedom,** immunity from determination by one's knowledge or psychological forces (as feelings) so that the will can decide for itself and is not necessitated by the motives, emotions, habits, etc.

REF. – *Met.,* I, C. 2. *N. Eth.,* III. CC. 2, 3 at end, 5; VI, C. 2. Boethius, *Major Commentary on Aristotle's De Interpretatione,* III, Prologue. *S.T.,* I, 83, aa. 1, 2; I–II, 13, aa. 1–5. *Truth,* q. 24; 22, aa. 1, 4, 15. *C.G.,* II, C. 48.

friend, *n.* a person whom one knows and loves well and by whom one is known and loved for virtuous reasons.

REF. – *N. Eth.,* VIII, CC. 2, 3; IX, C. 4. *Rhetoric,* II, C. 4. *S.T.,* II–II, 23.

fruition, *n.* enjoyment; the act of the will in the possession or achievement of the good.

✓ **function,** *n.* a natural specific activity of any power or organ.

functional group, *phrase.* a natural group with a natural common interest and common special activities; a corporative body. See SOCIETY.

fundamentally, *adv.* **1.** basically. **2.** essentially; necessarily. **3.** in source; in principle; in objective reason. It is contrasted with *accidentally, formally, in detail, unessentially, verbally.*

future, *adj. or n.* that which will happen; that which will exist (from the point of time at which the event is viewed as not having occurred). ABBR. – *fut.*

conditioned future, an event or act that would come to pass if some free being should choose it or start the chain of events which would include this event.

free future, an event that will come about because of the choice of some free agent upon which that act or result depends.

futurible, *adj. and n.* a conditioned future. Usually it refers to a *pure futurible* which is something that would be if a free agent would have chosen or done it but which never will exist because the free agent will not choose it.

G

gen., abbreviation for *genera, general, generally, generic, genus.*

general, *adj.* universal; common.

generalization, *n.* **1.** the mental act of forming the concept of a class. **2.** the process of inductive discovery of the definition of a thing. **3.** the process of inferring a general law from particular instances.

generation, *n.* **1.** *proper sense.* the origin of a living being from a living being of its own species. **2.** *specifically.* the conception of a human being. **3.** *transferred meaning.* the coming-into-being of a new substance or substantial form; and especially the change of the lifeless into the living.
Ref. – *S.T.,* I, 27, a. 2.

genus, *n., pl.* **genera.** the sum of the constituent notes that are common to two or more species, abstracting from the specific differences. ABBR. – *gen.*

lowest (proximate) genus, the immediate or proximate genus in a given series; that genus under which a certain species is immediately contained or classified.

supreme genus, the class which is contained under no higher genus; a category. REF. – *Topics,* I, C. 5. *Met.,* V, C. 28; X, C. 8. *On Being and Essence,* C. 2.

given (the), *part. as n. or adj.* the data; whatever is admitted as a fact or premise.

glory, *n.* knowledge of excellence, together with esteem and praise of it.

extrinsic glory, 1. (fundamental) glory because of something besides one's own being, such as one's works. **2.** (formal) glory given by some other person.

formal (subjective) glory, knowledge and deliberate praise of excellence; willing public recognition of goodness.

fundamental (objective) glory, the excellence that is worthy of admiration and praise; goodness considered as the objective reason for rendering formal glory to the good being or to its author.

intrinsic glory, glory, whether fundamental or formal, considered in the ex-

Kind of Glory → ↓	Fundamental Glory Object's excellence; reason for glory	Formal Glory Act of glorifying
A. *Divine* Glory Intrinsic	God's infinite goodness and excellence in all attributes	God's knowledge, honor, and love of Himself
Extrinsic	The excellence of God's works in all their grades, considered as signs of the excellence of their Author	Created knowledge, honor, praise, and love of God: (*a*) in His works, (*b*) in Himself
B. *Human* Glory Intrinsic	The dignity of human personality, and the added excellence of character, grace, and merits	Self-respect; well-ordered love of one's self
Extrinsic	Man's external accomplishments: in arts, sciences, business, family, profession, nation, etc.	Reputation, public regard, and honor for human intrinsic and extrinsic goodness

cellent being; therefore, the goodness of a thing or the act of acknowledging its own goodness in proper honor.

vainglory, vanity; glory that is undeserved, or sought in an improper measure or manner, or on an improper occasion; inordinate love of one's own excellence. REF. – Cicero, *De Inventione,* II, 55. *C.G.,* III, C. 29. *S.T.,* II–II, 131, 132.

‡**gnome,** *Latinized Greek, n.* discriminating good judgment in unusual and difficult cases where higher, not common, principles and equity must prevail. See the chart on VIRTUES under "prudence." REF. – *N. Eth.,* VI, C. 11. *S.T.,* I–II, 57, a. 6; II–II, 51, a. 4.

God, *n.* **1.** *common concept.* supreme Being or supreme Lord. **2.** *scientific or philosophical concept.* the first uncaused cause of the universe, necessary, all-perfect, and self-sufficient being, essentially existing, infinite, personal, Creator and last End of all things. **3.** *revealed concept.* the Blessed Trinity of persons in one divine nature.

good, *n.* **1.** *in its formal nature.* that which is suitable to or befitting a being. **2.** *in its formal effect.* that which all things desire; the desirable; the object of the natural needs or tendencies of a being. See the chart on page 53.

absolute good, 1. that which is suitable to the thing or nature of which the goodness is predicated or to which it belongs. **2.** divine perfection.

apparent good, that which merely seems to be good; that which suits some power or appetite of men sufficiently to become an object of choice, but not of morally right choice since it does not conform to the nature of man as a whole.

befitting good, perfective good.

common good, 1. that which is suitable to many; some benefit possessed or shared in by many; the welfare of some community. **2.** that which can be attained only by the united action of many persons. **3.** goods communicable and communicated to many.

external goods, property completely outside the owner's own being, as lands or cattle.

internal goods, goods existing in or constituting the being of something, as life, knowledge, virtue.

intrinsic goodness, the quality of those moral acts that are of their nature and necessarily conformed to the true norm of morals.

mixed goods, such goods as belong partly to the nature and attributes of a being, especially of a human being, and partly to other beings in relation to man; e.g., reputation.

moral good, what is suitable to human nature because conformed to the true moral standard; good in human acts or secondarily in the objects of moral choice.

moral goodness, see MORALITY.

perfect good, 1. the highest good or ultimate end of a nature. **2.** God.

perfective good, what is suitable to complete or improve the very nature of the being that desires it; a good desirable for its own sake as naturally fit for a nature; desirable for its own sake by a rightly ordered will.

pleasurable good, that which gives satisfaction or enjoyment to an appetite.

private good, a good belonging only or principally to a person or private group, or obtainable by private effort; the well-being of the individual. A *proper good* is incommunicable to many, as one's own soul.

relative good, that which is suitable to another being.

supreme good, the highest good for a nature. See END, SUPREME; END, ULTIMATE.

true good, moral good.

useful good, a means or instrument; something desirable not for its own sake, but as a help in the attainment of a perfective good or end. REF. – *N. Eth.,* I, CC. 1, 6–8. *Politics,* VII, C. 1. *Rhetoric,* I, C. 7. *S.T.,* I, 5, aa. 1, 7; I–II, 19, a. 5; II–II, 145, a. 3. *C.G.,* III, C. 37.

government, *n.* the authoritative management of things pertaining to the common good according to an official plan and law and compelling subjects to use the means for realizing the end of the plan; the

DIVISIONS OF GOOD

1. Absolute (intrinsic; good to and for itself)
   Relative (extrinsic; good to others)

2.
   Universal
   - All-perfect (divine) goodness
   - Of the universe

   Common (social)
   - Of private societies
   - Of the state; public good

   Private
   - a) Material; spiritual
   - b) Internal goods; external; mixed
   - c) Necessary; necessary for status; superfluous
   - d) Of individual person; of private societies

3. Supreme (unparticipated)
   Dependent (participated)

4.
   Perfective (befitting)
   - Moral (always a true or genuine good)
   - Physical
     - According to a being's constitution
     - According to a being's proper accidents and operations
     - According to its end
   - Apparent (a physical good contrary to moral good; but properly not a perfective good)

   Useful (means)

   Pleasurable
   - To sense appetites
   - To the spiritual appetite
   - To both (as corporeal beauty)

5.
   Good as end
   - Perfective
   - Pleasurable

   Good as a means   Useful

   Good as a means-end: in different relations perfective and useful

6.
   True (genuine)
   - Supreme
   - Moral

   Apparent

7. Natural
   Supernatural

establishment and maintenance of public order.

immediate government, exercise of executive authority directly by the holder of this authority.

mediate government, exercise of authority through delegates or subordinates acting as authorized by the higher ruler or executive.

REF. – *S.T.*, I, 103, aa. 1, 3.

grace, *n. theological term often used in philosophy in comparing nature with grace.* **1.** the will of God gratuitously bestowing something. **2.** a free gift of God. The principal distinction is between habitual or sanctifying grace and actual grace.

REF. – *C.G.*, III, C. 150. *S.T.*, I–II, 110, 111.

grade, *n.* degree or rank in any order or series of related things.

greater, *adj.* **1.** *quantitative sense.* bigger; wider, etc. **2.** *qualitative sense.* better; more intensive, etc.

guilt, *n.* the state of one who is liable to punishment for violation of law before he has made atonement and received pardon.

REF. – *S.T.*, I–II, 21, a. 2.

H

habit, *n*. 1. a permanent quality according to which a subject is well or badly disposed in regard to either its being or its operations; a relatively stable disposition of a living nature or power, inclining it rightly or wrongly to some perfection or end of its own being or of another being.

acquired habit, a habit obtained by one's own activity or by divine gift in the course of life, and modifying nature or natural powers.

bad habit, any vice, intellectual or moral.

entitative habit, a permanent quality added to nature and natural potencies and directly modifying its being rather than its operations.

good habit, any virtue, but especially any moral or theological virtue needed in leading a morally good life. See VIRTUE.

infused habit, one supernaturally given, not acquired by our own efforts; e.g., the virtues of faith, hope, charity, and the gifts of the Holy Spirit.

innate habit, 1. a habit with which one is born or supposedly is born. **2.** a habit that is all but innate since it is acquired very early in life, very easily, and by very few acts; e.g., the habitual knowledge of the principle of contradiction.

natural habit, a habit that comes from human nature in its origin, in its action, or in its direction to a natural object or end.

operative habit, an acquired quality added to a power of a rational being that is relatively permanent and inclines the agent to perform definite types of acts with ease, accuracy, and consistency. Operative habits imply the direction and control of reason. Their subject may be another power of man, as organized and controlled by reason; and so, there are motor habits, habits of the higher senses as of the imagination and memory, habits of the sensory appetites, habits of the intellect, and habits of the will. There also are related habit-groups, in which two or more habits form one composite principle of action in a certain way. In most scholastic writers, automatisms in the senses are not regarded as habits. To prevent confusion of a true human habit with an automatism some scholastic philosophers refer to *habitus* and avoid the term *habit*.

supernatural habit, one that is better than natural in origin and in purpose, and usually also in mode of action. See SUPERNATURAL.

REF. – *N. Eth.,* II, CC. 1, 2. *S.T.,* I–II, 49, a. 4 summing up the definition; 51, aa. 1, 4; 94, a. 1.

habit, *n*. 2. the relation of possession; having something internal or external as one's own. **3.** Sometimes it is used for the tenth category, "having on" or "state," namely, a determination of a being arising from its natural or normal physical adjuncts or its natural environment; as hairy, clothed, wearing jewelry, etc. It is also spelled *habitus.*

REF. – *Cat.,* C. 15. *Met.,* V, 20.

habitus, *n*. see HABIT, OPERATIVE; HABIT, sense 3.

haecceity, *n*. *Latin "haecceitas," thisness – used by Scotus.* that incommunicable feature of a being which constitutes a thing as an individual being in its class; individuality; singularity.

happiness, beatitude; contentment in the possession of a good. See BEATITUDE.

temporal happiness, happiness in the present lifetime of man.

REF. – *Rhetoric,* I, C. 5.

henological, *adj*. that which is one in source or in explanation of plurality.

hierarchy, *n*. an ordered arrangement of

beings or perfections of different degrees; the arrangement of powers, of operations, of arts and virtues, of authority, and other things that are related but unequal. REF. – *S.T.*, I, 108, a. 1. *C.G.*, IV, CC. 11, 75.

honor, *n.* reverence given to some being because of its excellence or its connection with an excellent person. REF. – *S.T.*, I–II, 2, a. 2; III, 25.

hope, *n.* 1. *as a passion.* the emotion of the irascible appetite which expects to obtain a future good even though it is difficult to attain. 2. *as a virtue.* the expectation of attaining a future good with divine help; the confidence of obtaining from God both Himself as man's beatitude and the means to Him. REF. – *S.T.*, I–II, 40, a. 1; II–II, qq. 17, 18.

human, *adj.* of or characteristic of persons, and particularly of persons in their entire humanity or in their special traits distinguishing them from irrational animals.

human act, *phrase.* an act proceeding from deliberate reason and free will; an act performed by the free will with knowledge of the end to which the act is directed. See ACT OF MAN.

commanded act, the act of some power dependent on the will and directed by the act of command. See COMMAND.

elicited human act, the act in the will itself; the deliberate intention or choice.

imperfect human act, one performed with some element of obscurity, haste, antecedent passion, or any factor that weakens freedom.

perfect human act, an act performed with full deliberation and choice.

REF. – *S.T.*, I–II, 1, a. 1; III, 19, a. 2.

human nature, *phrase.* man's being considered as a principle of human operations.

human nature adequately considered, man's constitution considered in itself in all the completeness of its parts and powers, their internal order, and in all essential human relationships to other beings.

human nature specifically considered, the rationality of man by which he is distinguished from animals.

human nature in state of integrity, human nature before being wounded by original sin.

hylemorphism, *n.* the theory of the natural constitution of matter and a definite form in all bodies; the theory that every natural body is composed of two substantial principles related to each other as potency and act and called prime matter and substantial form. It is also spelled *hylomorphism.*

hylozoism, *n.* the opinion that all things are in some degree alive.

hypostasis, *n.* a suppositum; subsistent being; sometimes restricted to mean a person.

hypostatic union, *phrase.* a composite unity of two natures combined in one hypostasis or person; and specifically, the union of the divine nature and the human nature of Christ in the one person of the Son of God.

hypothesis, *n.* a conditional or provisional explanation of observed facts or of their connection with each other; a tentative explanation suggestive of further experiment and verification. ABBR. – *hyp., hypoth.*

REF. – *Post. Anal.,* I, CC. 2, 10.

I

I, symbol for a particular affirmative proposition.

idea, *n.* **1.** *strict original sense.* the form or likeness of a thing existing apart from the thing itself. **2.** the exemplary form or mental type which the agent deliberately imitates in production; model. **3.** the principle of knowledge of a thing in the knower of that thing; species; similitude; concept. See divisions under CONCEPT. **4.** *loose and modern sense.* any image or any act of perception or cognition.

divine ideas, the things represented in the mind of God, but not distinct acts of God's intelligence; especially, the exemplary forms according to which God creates. REF. – *S.T.,* I, 15, aa. 1, 3. *Truth,* q. 3, a. 2.

ideal, *n.* standard; archetype; criterion or model of excellence.

ideal being, being as known. See BEING.

identity, *n.* sameness in some respect. See the chart under UNITY. ANT. – *difference, distinction, opposition.*

absolute identity, total sameness of a thing, without any change or difference.

formal identity, 1. intrinsic identity. **2.** specific identity.

intentional identity, sameness of the objective concept or form as known with the form in the thing.

intrinsic identity, sameness even in concept; implication of one concept in another concept. This is said especially of the terms in an analytic judgment.

materially identical, formally different, same in fact or in the being, but different at least in degree of distinctness of the concepts compared. See DISTINCTION, VIRTUAL.

moral identity, sameness of a society in continuity of purpose over a period of time even though there are many changes of members by birth, death, etc.

objective identity, present in the same object, as substance and attributes or subject and predicate in a synthetic proposition.

personal identity, the persistent substantial sameness of the person or especially of his soul with itself throughout life.

physical identity, 1. sameness of constitution or of membership. **2.** sameness of substance or of appearance in spite of some accidental and external changes.

specific identity, sameness in specific nature or essence; sameness of type. REF. – *Topics,* I, C. 7. *Politics,* III, C. 3.

ideogenesis, *n.* the process of acquiring or of forming ideas, especially of our primitive ideas.

ignorance, *n.* **1.** nescience; a lack of knowledge or of information in one who is capable of knowing. **2.** a lack of knowledge in one who is able and ought to know the particular matter. **3.** error produced by inference. Sense 2 seems to be the more proper sense. See ERROR; NESCIENCE.

affected ignorance, voluntary ignorance; deliberate ignorance particularly with the motive of not being impeded in one's desires to indulge self and violate law.

antecedent ignorance, ignorance preceding the act of the will and causing the act of the will inasmuch as the act would not have been performed had there been knowledge of law or of fact.

concomitant ignorance, ignorance associated with an act of the will that neither knowledge nor ignorance would have caused or stopped.

consequent ignorance, ignorance due to an act of the will; voluntary ignorance.

culpable ignorance, ignorance of something which we can know and have the obligation to know. It is *crass* or *supine* or *direct ignorance* when it is present in important matters where evidence is abundant and need of the knowledge is urgent. It is *indirect ignorance* when the lack of knowledge is due to negligence, sloth, etc.

ignorance of fact, lack of knowledge of a contingent event, person, or circumstance.

ignorance of law, lack of knowledge of a precept of law, of its meaning, or of its application to a given case.

invincible ignorance, ignorance that is unavoidable in the given circumstances because of the difficulty of the object to be known, scarcity of evidence, insufficient talent or opportunity of the knower, etc.

vincible ignorance, that which can be removed by ordinary care, inquiry, reflection, and similar means available to the ordinary prudent person. REF. – *Post. Anal.,* I, C. 16. *S.T.,* I, 101, a. 1; I–II, 6, a. 8; 76, esp. aa. 2, 3.

ignoring the issue, *phrase.* a fallacy in which one establishes some conclusion other than the precise point to be proved. Forms of this fallacy are: failure to define terms and issues; proving too much; ignoring the correctives required in analogical predication; in refutation, attributing to an opponent what he has not meant or claimed.

illicit, *adj.* unlawful, contrary to laws or rules; not permitted. Note that not everything illicit is invalid.

illicit process (of *major* or *minor term*), a violation of the rule of the syllogism which forbids that a term have a wider extension in the conclusion than it had in the premise.

illumination, *n.* 1. *in general.* manifestation of truth. 2. strengthening the intellect to know something. 3. *Thomistic sense.* the activity of the agent intellect which "lights up" the essence of a sensible thing so that it becomes intelligible by the possible intellect. 4. *Augustinian sense.* the function of the divine light within our intellect making new knowledge, especially of immaterial things and divine

truths, possible to a rational creature. 5. *theological use.* a grace to the intelligence, aiding knowledge, belief, understanding, judgment, or even vision in supernatural matters. REF. – *S.T.,* I, 85, a. 1 ad 4. *Truth,* q. 9, a. 5; a. 7 ad 4.

image, *n.* 1. *in general.* a representation or likeness of another. 2. *metaphysics.* a specific likeness to another in its characteristic being or operations. In this sense, image is opposed to trace and is the correlative of exemplar. 3. the sensitive impression in one of the internal senses; or more narrowly, the fantasm. 4. *more widely.* any sensation or expressed sensible species, present or past or recalled. REF. – especially for sense 2, *S.T.,* I, 35, a. 1; 93.

imagination, *n.* the internal sense which knows absent sensible things, but not as absent from the sense.

creative imagination, rearranges sense impressions previously acquired, divides and combines them in new groups of images, etc.

reproductive imagination, recalls previous sense impressions and repeats them; a function of (sensitive) memory. REF. – *On the Soul,* III, C. 3.

imitation, *n.* 1. the act or process of reproducing the form of one thing in another kind of potency, matter, or medium. 2. the object copied from another.

immanent, *adj.* 1. present in; operative in. 2. beginning within and remaining within the agent as a perfection of the agent; living. Note that an immanent act may also have some external or transeunt results. ANT. – *transeunt, transitive.* 3. *pantheistic sense.* describing God as present in and operating in the universe, but identifying him with the universe itself. ANT. – *really distinct, transcendent.* 4. *idealism.* describing the immediate object of knowledge as in the knower, not as external to the knower.

immaterial, *adj.* not having matter or the properties of matter; in some way free of matter.

negatively immaterial, that which, as considered by the mind or in abstraction

SENSES OF IMMATERIAL AND IMMATERIALITY

1. The non-corporeal; e.g., substantial form, the act of a body

2. The negatively immaterial, i.e., natures as abstracted from matter by the mind and represented without matter or material conditions; e.g., being, substance, goodness

3. Not limited as bodies and matter are, not restricted to the possession merely of its own form: hence, the acts of knowledge, both sensation and intellectual acts

4. Beings naturally (not merely by abstraction) without matter
   - Partially without matter, but intrinsically dependent on matter for its operation; e.g., the power of sensing (immaterial element) intrinsically needs a bodily sense organ (material element)
   - Wholly or positively immaterial
     - Intrinsically independent of matter; e.g., the human soul, the intellect, will, their acts
     - Intrinsically and extrinsically independent of matter; e.g., angels, their acts, God

from its concrete state, is without matter, e.g., the concepts of goodness, substance, unity.

partially immaterial, that which is free from the limitations of matter in some characteristic of its being or in some principle of its compound being; e.g., sensory knowledge.

positively and wholly immaterial, that which is intrinsically independent of matter in its being or activities; the spiritual.

immediate, *adj.* 1. next; intimate; present; elicited. 2. acting without any medium or aid or step between it and something else. 3. direct. 4. intuitive.

immensity, *n.* the quality of being immeasurable; a mode of presence which is not measured or limited by real (or possible) place and space in which the being is or can be present.

immortal, *adj.* free from death or the capacity to decay and disintegrate; subsistent apart from the corruptible; able to live forever in the future.

absolute immortality, eternity of life.

gratuitous immortality, the gift of living forever, but not naturally proportionate to a nature.

natural immortality, the capacity to live forever that is proportionate to a spiritual being or form by its very essence.

personal immortality, capacity of the individual person's soul to live forever.

racial immortality, capacity of the race to live indefinitely or forever in its descendants, but not in the life of the same individuals.

immovable, *adj.* 1. incapable of being moved. 2. moved with difficulty. 3. *extended sense.* the unmoved; what is at rest.

REF. – *Physics,* V, C. 2, near end.

immunity, *n.* 1. freedom from something. 2. *in particular.* (*a*) the freedom of the will from antecedent necessity; and (*b*) the person's right to be free from interference in exercising his right.

immutable, *adj.* unchanging and unchangeable; independent of all intrinsic change.

impediment, *n.* an obstacle to the validity or legality of some act or of its effects, as legal impediments to contracts or weddings.

diriment impediment, a condition, previous act, external circumstance, etc., which makes an attempted act null and void of effect.

impedient (prohibitive) impediment, a condition, previous act, external circumstance, etc., which makes an attempted act illegal or immoral but does not automatically nullify it.

natural impediment, an obstacle arising from the nature of things, of man, or from the natural law.

positive impediment, a diriment or impedient impediment set up by just positive law.

imperate (imperated), *adj.* commanded, as in *commanded* act.

imperfect, *adj.* 1. incomplete in some way. 2. not fully actual. See INCOMPLETE.

imperium, *n.* 1. the act of command, q.v. 2. specifically, the act of the reason of the superior making the law binding on subjects. 3. the right to command and to use public force to compel obedience to laws.

implication, *n.* any inference or deduction; something shown to be involved or concerned in another thing or statement.

impose, *v.* 1. to name. 2. to give an arbitrary meaning or definition to something by way of explaining or testing one's position.

impossible, *adj.* that which cannot be.

absolutely (metaphysically) impossible, that which can never be because it is intrinsically contradictory in being.

morally impossible, 1. *usual sense.* that which is so difficult that it cannot be done or be done most rarely by a free agent, though physically within his capacity. The difficulty may be due to lack of insight into the importance of the matter, insufficient motivation, opposition to natural inclinations, greatness of effort, much pain, or to the perseverance required. 2. relatively impossible because of its lack of interest, etc., to a free agent.

relatively impossible, that which cannot be under given circumstances in reference to which the opposite must be so. An impossibility due to lack of a physical cause able to make the possible become actual is a *physical impossibility*. If due to lack of a free cause adequately motivated to perform the act, it is a *moral impossibility*. If due to the impossibility of the simultaneous verification of two opposites, each of them individually possible, it is given no special name. REF. – *Power*, q. 5, a. 3. *S.T.*, I, 25, a. 3, a. 4 ad 1.

imprudence, *n.* the act or the vice of a lack of that prudence which one can and ought to have.

impute, *v.* to attribute praise or blame to someone because of a good or bad human act; to charge something to his merit or demerit.

in, to be in another, *phrase.* 1. as part or member is in a whole. 2. as a whole is in its parts. 3. as species is in genus. 4. as genus or specific difference is in the species. 5. as form is in matter. 6. as accident is in substance. 7. as events are in their efficient cause. 8. as power is in the ruler. 9. as existence and nature and their value and meaning are in their end. 10. as contained is in container. 11. as a body is in place or in space. 12. as the known is in the knower. REF. – *Physics*, IV, C. 3. *S.T.*, I, 39, a. 8 near end of corpus.

incapacity, *n.* privation of a capacity to act or be acted upon; impassivity; powerlessness. REF. – *Met.*, V, C. 12; XI, C. 1.

inclination, *n.* a tendency toward something; a movement of an appetite to its object.

incomplete, *adj.* 1. not perfect. 2. being a part, not a whole. 3. not fully actual. 4. not fully possessing its end. See PERFECT.

incomprehensible, *adj.* that which cannot be thoroughly known or understood by some types of intelligence: as God is incomprehensible to man.

inconceivable, *adj.* incapable of being thought of; beyond thought. The inconceivable is to be distinguished from the unimaginable.

incorporeal, *adj.* 1. lacking a body or the properties of a body. 2. different from the material body. The incorporeal may then be material (as substantial forms of mere bodies), immaterial as an animal soul, or positively spiritual as a human soul. See IMMATERIAL.

incorruptible, *adj.* 1. *in general.* what is incapable of decay or destruction. 2. what is fully actualized and unchangeable in substance or in proper accidents. 3. the immortal.

independent, *adj.* 1. free. 2. separate or disconnected from another. 3. not needing another and not supported in being by another. **4.** not subordinate to another person, government, or thing. ABBR. – *ind.* See DEPENDENT; FREE; NECESSARY.

extrinsic independence of matter, the state of not needing matter even as a condition for or aid to action; total independence of the material.

intrinsic independence of matter, the state of not needing matter as a co-cause of its natural being or of its action. With intrinsic independence there may be extrinsic dependence; thus, the human intellect in learning in this life extrinsically depends on material things and on sense images.

sovereign independence, political freedom belonging to a sovereign authority.

indeterminism, *n.* the doctrine that the will in some acts is free, i.e., it is not absolutely determined by environment, feelings, ideas, needs, or motives in all situations.

indifference, *n.* lack of determination or compulsion to one act or one course in a being or power capable of determination.

active indifference, the state of indetermination or variability in a power which can by its own action determine itself to one of two or more possible acts or courses of action; freedom.

indifferent act, a morally neutral act; an act which considered only according to its moral object is neither good nor bad, i.e., is not yet morally determined to be good or bad.

objectively indifferent judgment, a judgment concerning objects whose goodness is that of contingent means so that the judgment is not compelling to the will. It is contrasted with judgments about what is objectively and subjectively necessary.

passive indifference, the state of a passive potency in a being or power whose indetermination to some act or form is removed by its complete submission to an agent external to itself.

religious indifference, the attitude that all religions despite differences of doctrines and essential practices are equally good and equally acceptable to God; the opinion that there is no moral obligation

by natural or positive divine law to assent to or worship in one particular religious confession.

indirect, *adj.* **1.** deviating from a direct line or course in space, intention, relation, descent, contact, etc. **2.** mediate. **3.** secondarily connected with or proceeding from. **4.** negative, preventive, or removing obstacles to a being or cause; as, indirect conservation, indirect influence. **5.** not wanted, but permitted even though foreseen; as indirect effect, indirect scandal.

indissoluble, *adj.* that which cannot be broken apart and so terminated; hence, lifelong, perpetual.

individual, *adj. and n.* **1.** any singular thing which cannot be divided without losing its identity. **2.** pertaining to some one thing and no other and incapable of being found in its entirety in more than one. ABBR. – *individ.*

individuation, *n.* **1.** *metaphysics.* the basic or constitutive reason which differentiates the individual both from the universal or class and from every other individual in that class. **2.** *logic.* the recognizable individual features of a being whose sum identifies him as different from every other.

individuum, *n.* the individual regarded as one or as a unit; a singular, complete substance.

induction, *n.* **1.** the legitimate derivation of universal laws from individual cases. **2.** the derivation of the definition of an essence from knowledge of features common to the instances. **3.** an argument that moves from a more particular premise to a more general conclusion; an argument in which from our experience of particular instances we draw inferences concerning the universal subject or type to which these instances belong. ABBR. – *induc.*

complete induction, a conclusion drawn from the complete numbering of the members of a class; a summary of the attributes of all individuals of a class and of the class as a whole.

incomplete induction, a universal affirmation based on abstraction of a tested common feature of some members of a class.

REF. – *Post. Anal.*, I, C. 18. *Topics*, I, C. 12.

industrial council, *phrase.* the directive group in a corporative economic society.

ineffable, *adj.* exalted beyond human naming and description.

‡**in esse,** *Latin infinitive phrase,* in respect to existence. See CAUSE "IN ESSE."

inessential, *adj.* not pertaining to the essence either as part of its constitution or as a necessary property flowing from the essence; contingently accidental.

‡**in facto esse,** *Latin phrase.* in a complete state; in act, not merely undergoing change.

infallible, *adj.* certain and incapable of error.

inference, *n.* **1.** an act of the mind moving from the content of one or more judgments to a new judgment connected with the prior one(s). **2.** the judgment or proposition so derived.

immediate inference, an act of the mind deriving from one judgment another connected judgment without the aid of any additional term or judgment.

mediate inference, reasoning.

inferior, *adj. and n., usually pl.* **1.** objects of reference contained within the extension of a general concept. **2.** subaltern.

‡**in fieri,** *Latin phrase.* **1.** in respect to change. See CAUSE "IN FIERI." **2.** in the state of changing or becoming.

infinite, *adj.* unlimited; unbounded; immeasurable; inexhaustible.

actually infinite, a positive reality without limit.

infinitely perfect, unlimited in perfection of being or of operation; possessing every pure perfection in every perfect way and in perfect degree.

potentially infinite, a finite reality, capable of actual or conceptual increase without any limit or term.

REF. – *Physics,* III, CC. 4, 6, 7. *Met.,* XI, C. 10. James A. McWilliams, S.J., *Physics and Philosophy: A Study of Saint Thomas' Commentary on the Eight Books of Aristotle's Physics,* pp. 8, 135 on all

the meanings and uses of the term "infinite." *S.T.,* I, 7; III, 10, a. 3 replies. *C.G.,* I, C. 43. *Truth,* q. 2, a. 10; 20, a. 4 ad 1.

influence, *n.* causality.

information, *n.* **1.** the presence and communication of the substantial form in the potency. **2.** existence in another as in a substantial substrate.

informed, the state of the potency when it has received and been united with and been specified by the formal element. Thus, the body is informed by the soul; the intellect is informed by a species; virtues are informed by charity.

informing, exercising formal influence in the composite being.

infused, *part. as adj.* **1.** received from without, not educed from within; as, the human soul is infused. **2.** received from without by gift of God working in the soul, and not by natural development from the subject or power affected; as, infused knowledge, infused supernatural virtues.

infusion, *n.* the act of uniting the human soul to the body. Compare with eduction which is the development of the form out of the matter.

inherence, *n.* existence in another being as in a subject of being or as a modification of another being. Accidents are said to inhere in substance. ANT. – *perseity.* Compare SUBSISTENCE.

injustice, *n.* the act or the vice of not giving to another what is his due. See JUSTICE for types.

REF. – *N. Eth.,* V, C. 2. *S.T.,* II–II, 61, a. 3.

innate, *adj.* inborn; congenital; given with the nature, not learned, acquired, infused, nor otherwise obtained after birth.

‡**in re,** *Latin phrase.* in the thing; really, objectively, and actually. It occurs as (1) a contrast to *in intellectu,* i.e., in the intellect, in the mind; (2) a contrast to *in spe,* in hope, desire, or claim. See JUS IN RE.

In Sent., In I Sent., etc. abbreviated reference to Commentary on Peter Lombard's *Books of Sentences,* Bk. I (or II, III, IV). A number of scholastics have such commentaries.

instinct, *n.* a natural power or internal sense which guides brute animals in performing complex acts useful for the preservation of the individual or of the species; the estimative power. Some authors prefer to call the *power* here the estimative power, and to call the *acts* performed dependently on this power, with their uniformity throughout the species, instinctive activities.

instrument, *n.* **1.** a tool. **2.** a means. See under sense 2 of CAUSE. ABBR. – *inst., instr.*

integral, *adj.* internally belonging to some whole. See PART; UNIT; VIRTUE.

intellect, *n.* **1.** the spiritual cognitive power or possible intellect; the power of knowing in an immaterial way; the thinking power higher than senses and imagination. **2.** the intellectual act known as intuition. **3.** knowledge of essences and of meaning. **4.** the habit of knowing the first principles of demonstration. **5.** the intellectual soul. **6.** an angel; an intelligence.

agent intellect, active intellect (*intellectus agens*), the immediate principle which makes sensible things to be actually intelligible; the power with the functions of abstracting from the material and singular, of illuminating the sense image so that the potentially intelligible sense datum becomes actually intelligible, and of producing the intelligible species in the possible intellect.

passible intellect, possible intellect, the spiritual power of knowing or understanding.

passive intellect, a now rare term for cogitative power.

practical intellect, the possible intellect in its function of seeking knowledge for

---

SENSES OF INTELLECT

1. An immaterial power of knowledge (said to be the fundamental sense)

2. Intellectual beings
   - Angels, separated substances, intelligences
   - Human souls

3. Any immaterial power
   - *a.* Comprising intellect and intellectual appetite
     - Restricted to knowledge
       - Preparing it: agent intellect
       - Identified with reason: possible intellect
       - Distinguished from reason: pure intellect
   - *b.* Cognitive power
     - Directed to truth for its own sake: speculative intellect
     - Directed principally to action: practical intellect

4. A habit in the intellect
   - Habit of the first principles (speculative)
   - Synteresis
   - Immediate knowledge of singulars
   - The gift of the Holy Spirit

5. An act of the intellect
   - The activity of the power
   - The concept formed by the activity

6. **The object known by the intellect:** the objective concept or the intelligible in act (Latin usage cognate to English use of information or intelligence received)

the sake of action or about matters directly connected with action.

speculative intellect, the possible intellect in its function of seeking and considering truth just for its own sake. REF. – *On the Soul,* III, CC. 4, 5. *N. Eth.,* VI, C. 2. *In Boeth. de Trin.,* q. 5, a. 1. *S.T.,* I, 54, a. 4 ad 2; 79, a. 11; III, 12, a. 1 ad 1. J. Peghaire, *Intellectus et Ratio selon S. Thomas d'Aquin,* p. 25.

intellectual light, *phrase.* 1. the mind considered as revealing truth to the person. 2. illumination, q.v. 3. the abstractive activity of the agent intellect making the form in material things actually intelligible by freeing it from sensory conditions and limitations. See LIGHT.

intelligence, *n.* 1. intellectual activity or its result in the way of habitual knowledge or intellectual virtues. 2. the possible intellect. 3. an intelligent being, especially a pure spirit.

simple intelligence, God's knowledge of His ideas and of all the possibles by knowing all the ways in which His own essence is imitable.

intelligible, *adj. or n.* knowable by the intellect; capable of being received by the possible intellect.

accidental intelligible (*intelligibile per accidens*), some form or note immediately known by the intellect only in association with intellectually perceived accidents; as, our soul is knowable directly only together with knowledge of its acts. Compare SENSIBLE, ACCIDENTAL.

essentially *or* **directly intelligible** (*intelligibile per suam essentiam or per se*), something whose essence is immediately perceived by the intellect without needing the media of accidents or association with perceived accidents.

intelligible matter, see MATTER.

intension, *n.* comprehension of a term.

intention, *n.* 1. *ethics, philosophy of man.* **a.** the act of the will toward an end that is or is thought to be obtainable. **b.** the purpose of an act. See the chart on END.

actual intention, 1. the intention made in and for the present act of the will. 2. the good sought in this present act.

habitual intention, a permanent purpose

of the will that has not been retracted explicitly or implicitly by doing the contrary of the purpose.

intentionally, deliberately; with design.

intention of nature, intrinsic end; natural finality.

virtual intention, an intention whose efficacy persists in the present moment, controlling one's activities here and now, without renewal of the former actual intention. REF. – *S.T.,* I–II, 12, aa. 1, 2, and 4 ad 3. *Truth,* q. 22, aa. 13, 14.

intention, *n.* 2. *logic, epistemology, philosophy of man.* **a.** mental representation or cognitive likeness of something. **b.** the object or being that is represented in knowledge; the objective concept, and especially the universal.

first (direct) intention, a. mental attention to the thing itself as the object of its knowing. **b.** the formal object or being that is directly known. See CONCEPT, DIRECT UNIVERSAL.

intentional being, the being or form as mentally represented; the being that belongs to something as it is in the mind or as affected by the mind's activity, such as its immaterial or universal status; representative being as opposed to physical (natural) being.

intentionally, in a cognitive way; by way of similarity to the thing known; as a sign of the form of the thing known.

second (logical, reflex) intention, a. directing mental attention to and representing an object as it exists in the mind. **b.** the object as it exists in the knower; e.g., the predicables, grammatical relationships, etc. See REFLECTION.

intention, *n.* 3. *metaphysics.* the direction or application or causal power to an effect; the influence of the principal cause on the instrument. This may be the primary meaning of intention as it best shows the notion of directing or tending on the part of a being or power.

intermediate, *adj.* being in some way between first and last or between contraries.

internal, *adj.* within a being or within a power.

SOME SENSES OF INTENTION

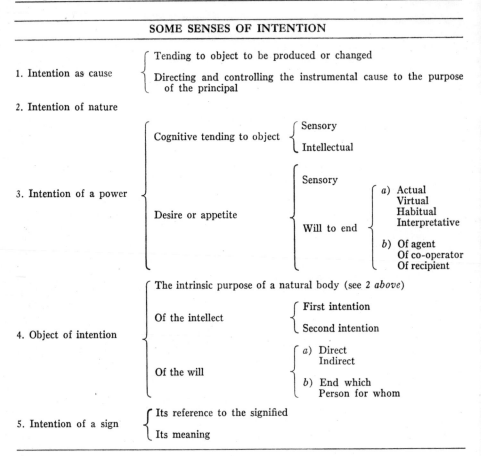

1. Intention as cause
   - Tending to object to be produced or changed
   - Directing and controlling the instrumental cause to the purpose of the principal

2. Intention of nature

3. Intention of a power
   - Cognitive tending to object
     - Sensory
     - Intellectual
   - Desire or appetite
     - Sensory
     - Will to end
       - *a)* Actual / Virtual / Habitual / Interpretative
       - *b)* Of agent / Of co-operator / Of recipient

4. Object of intention
   - The intrinsic purpose of a natural body (see *2 above*)
   - Of the intellect
     - First intention
     - Second intention
   - Of the will
     - *a)* Direct / Indirect
     - *b)* End which / Person for whom

5. Intention of a sign
   - Its reference to the signified
   - Its meaning

---

interpretation, *n.* explanation of the meaning or force of something, as of a law, proposition, or purpose. Interpretation may be authentic or doctrinal, broad or narrow, restrictive or extensive.

intrinsic, *adj.* 1. pertaining to the nature of a thing or person; constitutive. 2. contained or being within; internal. 3. inherent.

introspection, *n.* 1. the act of looking within one's self; self-reflection; psychological reflection. 2. self-examination. 3. consequent conscience judging the morality of an act performed.

intuition, *n.* 1. immediate knowledge of a present object, especially the act of vision by angelic or divine intelligence. 2. the intellectual virtue of insight, without reasoning, into the truth of the primary premises. REF. – *Post. Anal.,* II, C. 19. *N. Eth.,* VI, C. 6.

invalid, *adj.* having no force; having no obligation; void; null. Compare ILLICIT.

involuntary, *adj.* 1. not under the control of the will; spontaneous; automatic. 2. contrary to one's will or choice; violent. REF. – *N. Eth.,* III, C. 1; V, C. 8. *S.T.,* I–II, 6, a. 5.

irascible appetite, *phrase.* the sensitive passion that is aroused to fight a danger that is sensibly recognized. See APPETITE.

irrelevant, *adj.* not related or pertinent to the topic, question, or argument.

irritability, *n.* the property of living matter which reacts purposefully to a stimulus. In philosophical usage irritability is not to be confused with irascibility.

J

join, *v.* **1.** to unite. **2.** to affirm a predicate of a subject in a judgment.

joy, *n.* the act of the will delighting in the possession of a loved good. See ENJOYMENT.
REF. – *S.T.,* I–II, 31, a. 3. *C.G.,* III, CC. 26, 90.

judgment, *n.* **1.** *epistemology.* **a.** an act of the mind combining two objective concepts in an affirmation or separating them in a negation; an act of the mind assenting to the known objective identity or difference of concepts. **b.** an act of the mind asserting or denying existence of some subject. This is sometimes called an *existential* judgment. **c.** affirmation or denial of some conclusion. **2.** *ethics.* **a.** a right decision about what is just. **b.** a judgment of a superior, prescribing and administering justice. **c.** a right decision in any speculative or practical matter.

analytic judgment, a judgment in which the identity or difference of the objects, concepts, or terms is known by mere inspection or comparison of the concepts of subject and predicate. The comparison may be made immediately between the two objects or concepts or mediately through others. ANT. – *synthetic judgment.*

a posteriori judgment, 1. a judgment in contingent, variable, or historical matter. **2.** a judgment that can be known as true only after experience of the connection or separation of the objects or objective concepts of the subject and predicate.

a priori judgment, 1. a judgment in necessary matter. **2.** a judgment that is formed, or at least can be formed, from inspection of the terms without prior experience of the combination or separation of the objective concepts.

attributive judgment, a judgment that asserts or denies a predicate other than existence.

immediate judgment, a judgment formed without a middle term, i.e., without reasoning.

mediate judgment, an assent reached after reasoning on the matter.

natural judgment, an act of the estimative power in a concrete situation of good or evil for the animal. It is only analogous to a genuine act of judgment.

practical judgment, a judgment whose subject matter is action or operable objects.

ultimate practical judgment, 1. the judgment immediately preceding choice or decision. **2.** the judgment of antecedent conscience, immediately preceding good or evil choice.

rash judgment, a judgment ascribing evil to another person without sufficient evidence; unfounded suspicion of evil in another's acts or intentions.

speculative judgment, one concerned with the truth of its objects for truth's sake.

synthetic judgment, a judgment based on experience of the connection or separation of its subject and predicate.
REF. – *S.T.,* I, 79, aa. 4, 9; 85, a. 5. *S.T.,* II–II, 60, a. 1. *Truth,* q. 1, a. 3; 14, a. 1.

juridical, *adj.* relating to law; juridic.

juridical action, the activity or the legitimate action of a juridical cause.

juridical cause, a moral agent who validly (with lawful right) produces some juridical effect. Such a cause is distinguished from an historical or merely *de facto* cause.

juridical duty, an obligation arising from law and binding in justice. It is distinguished from ethical duty.

juridical effect, one binding in law and in justice.

juridical order, the total system of rights and justice, including laws, duties, rights, and the persons concerned in these in all three types of justice.

juridical succession, legitimate transfer of power from one to another.

juridical unit, a moral person or a society established by law acting officially.

‡**juris,** *n., Latin, genitive sing. of "jus."* pertaining to law or right; a subject of law and of rights. See PERSON, "SUI JURIS."

jurisdiction, *n.* **1.** the right to exercise official and public authority in some capacity; rightful public power in a perfect society. **2.** the territory within which or the matter over which such public authority may be lawfully exercised.

jurisprudence, *n.* the philosophy of law and of rights.

‡**jus ad rem,** *Latin phrase.* a right to a thing over which one has a claim, but which one does not actually hold in one's possession; as a right to payment of a debt.

‡**jus gentium,** *Latin phrase.* law of the nations; law agreed upon among all men.

‡**jus in re,** *Latin phrase.* a right to keep or dispose of a thing which one holds.

just, *adj.* **1.** what is due to a fellow man. **2.** the equal thing that belongs to another. **3.** the lawful. **4.** the fair; what should be proportionally shared according to the varying measures of each one's capacities, needs, and merits in a community.

justice, *n.* **1.** *general sense.* the virtues that make a man's actions habitually conformed to the law; human goodness. **2.** *as a particular form of human goodness.* the perpetual and constant will to render to another his right. See the chart on VIRTUES for the parts of justice.

civic justice, justice in civic or state matters; and therefore, both distributive and legal justice.

commutative justice, the justice of exchange of rights between individuals or equals and measured by strict equality of the goods rightfully transferred.

distributive justice, justice of the community in dealing with its members proportionately to their capacities, merits, services, and needs, without discrimination or respect of persons.

legal justice, **1.** justice to the community to be paid by its members, both rulers and ruled, in obeying the laws for the sake of the common good. **2.** justice as prescribed by positive law. In this second sense, justice is subject to correction by equity, q.v.

natural justice, justice as prescribed by the natural law, and especially commutative justice and equity.

social justice, 1. any act of justice which has important social or general effects; in this sense, commutative, distributive, and legal justice are included. **2.** the justice practiced in organizing and supporting social institutions for the common good, whether these are of a semipublic, public, or international character. It is disputed whether social justice is the same as sense 1 of JUSTICE, LEGAL.

REF. – *N. Eth.,* V, CC. 1–7; VIII, C. 1. *S.T.,* I–II, 113, a. 1; II–II, 57, 58, 61. William Ferrée, S.M., *The Act of Social Justice.*

K

kind, *n.* class, whether genus or species.

knowledge, *n.* any act, process, state, or fruit of mental representation; cognition; the immanent activity which possesses the form of another by its intentional likeness; any act whether of sensation, imagination, apprehension, reasoning, etc., in which there is an intentional union of knower with the known. Knowledge is usually regarded as indefinable.

analogous (analogical) knowledge, conception or understanding of something either through analogous concepts or by imperfect comparison with other things properly known.

discursive knowledge, knowledge in successive acts or by coming to know one thing through another; reasoning.

divine knowledge, 1. God's act of knowing. 2. what God knows.

immediate knowledge, knowledge through the direct presence of the object to the knower; perception; experience; intuition; vision; immediate consciousness.

infused knowledge, knowledge through species implanted by God in the possible intellect of a man or in the intellect of an angel.

intellectual knowledge, the act or fruit of knowing by the intelligence, in a supra-sensitive way.

middle knowledge (intermediate knowledge, *scientia media*), the knowledge of the futuribles which is a stage or "sign" intermediate between God's necessary and free knowledge as well as between His knowledge of the possibles by simple intelligence and His knowledge of the existents by vision.

natural knowledge, 1. that which results from something implanted in us by nature; as knowledge of first principles by the power of the agent intellect. 2. that kind and degree of knowledge of objects which natural cognitive powers can reach by their own activities without special divine help or revelation.

philosophical knowledge, knowledge of being, its causes, and structure, gained by properly philosophical methods.

practical knowledge, knowledge concerning action and especially concerning doing or making singulars.

proper knowledge, understanding of something through a proper concept or through representation of it as it is, not by way of an imperfect likeness with something else.

sensitive knowledge, knowledge possessed by men or animals through the activities of the external or internal senses.

speculative knowledge, 1. merely speculative knowledge; knowledge of things which the knower cannot affect by action. 2. knowledge of matters of action and of practice for the sake of knowing the truth about them, not for the sake of applying the knowledge. 3. the consideration of the truth of the end of any thing, for the mere sake of knowing the end.

REF. – *Met.,* II, C. 1. *Physics,* I, C. 1. *S.T.,* I, 14, esp. aa. 9, 12, 16; 16, a. 1; 85, a. 3; I–II, 5, a. 5; II–II, 9. *C.G.,* I, C. 47. *Truth,* q. 2, a. 2; a. 9 ad 2, 3; q. 8, a. 15; q. 18, a. 4 c. and ad 10. J. Maritain, *Degrees of Knowledge,* C. VII, on practical and speculative knowledge.

L

l., abbreviation for *law*.

language, *n.* any arbitrary sign or system of signs, invented by man to express or communicate to men one's knowledge and other mental states such as one's feelings and decisions. ABBR. – *lang.* See SPEECH.

latria, *n.* the internal and external adoration or worship due and rendered to God alone. See ADORATION.

REF. – *S.T.,* II–II, 81, a. 1, esp. ad 2, 3; 84, a. 1; 85, a. 2. *C.G.,* III, C. 120.

law, *n.* **1.** *in general.* a rule of action. **2.** *specifically of authoritative orders.* an effective and promulgated command of reason made for the common good by one in charge of a perfect community; "an ordination of reason for the common good, made by one having charge of the community, and promulgated" (St. Thomas). ABBR. – *l.*

canon law, ecclesiastical law, especially of the Roman Catholic Church.

change of law, 1. *objective change.* modification of the precepts, rules, or content of the law. **2.** *subjective change.* modification of one's understanding or observance of the law without change in the law itself.

> **formal change,** *applied to sense 1.* an addition to or subtraction from the precepts or permissions of the law; new law. *Extrinsic* change is caused by the lawgiver dispensing, derogating from, or abrogating the law in whole or in part. *Intrinsic* change is in the law itself when it becomes injurious or harmful to the common good, and thereby ceases to bind.

> **material change,** change in the relevant circumstances under which a legal act, right, or omission concretely occurs without change in the law itself. Thus, the law commands modesty; but modesty is variable under many types of circumstances.

civil law, 1. positive law of states. **2.** Roman law, especially the part of it applied to Roman citizens.

declarative law, positive law which restates some precept of natural law.

determinative law, positive law which adds to natural law or definitely settles some matter not adequately contained in or determined by natural law. This is positive law in its fullest sense.

divine law, any law directly from God; therefore, either eternal law, natural law, or divine positive law.

eternal law, "the plan of divine wisdom in as much as it is directive of all acts and motions" (St. Thomas); the immutable, effective decree of God binding the whole universe to its end and to the use of the means for attaining this end as these are adapted to each nature.

law in the active sense, law as in the lawgiver's mind and will.

law of nations, 1. *jus gentium,* q.v. **2.** positive international law.

law of nature, 1. *usually.* physical law. **2.** *sometimes.* natural moral law.

law in the passive sense, law as in the subject.

law in sign, law as given in the code; the formulation of the rules of the law in words, customs, legislative enactments, judicial decisions, etc.

law of thought, any one of the basic principles of reasoning, especially the principles of contradiction, excluded middle, sufficient reason, and the *dictum de omni et nullo.*

moral law, a rule of action binding the actions of free beings and whose deliberate violation is a sin.

natural law, 1. *moral natural law.* the universal, practical obligatory judgments of reason, knowable by all men as binding them to do good and avoid evil, and discovered by right reason from the

68

TYPES OF LAWS AND SOME OF THEIR RELATIONSHIPS

1. The Eternal Law

In God — directs

all creatures

in all their activities,
namely.

Angels and their acts by	Men's human acts by	Acts of men, things, and their activities by
2. *Angelic natural law*	3. *Natural (moral) law*	4. *Many physical laws* (laws of nature) rarely supplemented by
supplemented by	supplemented by	
5. *Divine positive law* for angels		miracles

(in the church)	(in the family)	(in the state)
6. *Divine positive law* for men	9. *Precepts* of parents, guardians, and their delegates	10. *Civil positive law* of

a) Primitive
b) Mosaic (Old Law)
c) Christian (New Law)

10a. *Sovereign states*   11. *Associated sovereign states* (treaties: international law)

supplemented
by

supplemented
by

7. *Canon law*

12. *Local ordinances*   13. *Orders* of military officers, etc.

supplemented
by

8. *Precepts*
of
a) The Pope
b) Local bishops
c) Religious superiors

14. *Concordats* between Church and sovereign states

---

nature of man adequately considered; the sharing in the eternal law by the rational creature; the dictates of right reason concerning the necessary order of human nature.

Christian natural law, the natural law as clarified, interpreted, and confirmed by the truths of Christian faith and Christian tradition guiding reason's knowledge of the law.

natural law formally considered, the body of precepts and rights which constitute the law; the judgments or dictates of the law.

natural law fundamentally considered, the objective natural norm of morality; the evidence for the law.

natural law virtually considered, right reason; reason's capacity and tendency to know the law.

natural law, 2. physical law; law of nature.

new law, the divine positive law promulgated by Christ.

old law, the divine positive law promulgated especially by Moses.

penal (purely penal) law, a human law having only a disjunctive obligation; a human law binding subjects either to obey the law or to accept justly imposed sanctions for disobedience so that violation of the direct precept of the law is not of itself morally wrong. See OBLIGATION, DISJUNCTIVE.

physical law, 1. an intrinsic tendency in a natural body or other nature to produce definite effects proper to its nature in a definite uniform way and measure or by determinate means; the sharing in the eternal law by the irrational creature. **2.** the scientific or mathematical expression of this constant way in which a natural body or other nature acts; the statistical constant expressing the average way in which natural bodies act.

positive law, a reasonable ordinance of a legitimate superior which constitutes a general and just rule for the common benefit of the subjects and is properly promulgated by some external sign.

  divine positive law, positive law decreed and promulgated by God.

  human positive law, positive law decreed and promulgated by legitimate human authority, and especially by supreme civil authority.

principle of law, a general rule or precept of conduct.

  primary principle of natural law, a simple, all but self-evident, very broad rule of action; as, "Do good, avoid evil."

  secondary principle of natural law, a rule connected closely and necessarily with the primary principle, concerning an important interest in human life, of frequent occurrence, and abundantly evident so that normally developed minds readily reason to it; as, "Honor parents."

  tertiary principle of natural law, a precept of the law which is discoverable only by complex and subtle reasoning and considerable attention to circumstances and detachment from emotional impediments to clear thinking; e.g., "One must banish evil desires."

REF. – *N. Eth.,* V, C. 1. *Rhetoric,* I, CC. 13, 15. St. Augustine, *On Free Choice,* I, C. 6. *S.T.,* I–II, esp. 90, 91, 93, a. 1; 95, aa. 2 and 4; 99, aa. 3, 4; 104, a. 1. *C.G.,* III, C. 114.

learning, *n.* **1.** any acquisition of knowledge or skill, even if not understood. **2.** the knowledge, habit, or skill acquired.

lemma, *n.* a proposition assumed to be true. See AXIOM.

liberty, *n.* **1.** freedom, independence. **2.** a right. See FREEDOM.

liceity, *n.* lawfulness; permissibility.

licit, *adj.* lawful; allowed or permitted by law. Sometimes it may mean the same as valid, especially in reference to right applications of laws of reasoning.

lie, *n.* formal speech contrary to one's mind. The definition is disputed, so that some authors define a lie as a denial of the truth due to another, or as a statement of something false with the intention to deceive.

REF. – *N. Eth.,* IV, C. 7. *S.T.,* II–II, 109, aa. 3, 4; 110; 113.

life, *n.* **1.** the natural capacity for immanent or self-perfective activity; the power of a substance to move itself toward its own good or perfection. **2.** living activity or immanent activity. **3.** the essence of a being which has vital activity, particularly on the vegetative level since life at higher levels is referred to as sentience, intelligence, and by other proper names. **4.** the form of being of some level of living things. **5.** the abstract term for vital or immanent activity.

active life, human life which is mainly occupied with, intent upon, and pleased with external activities.

common life, life spent together by two or more sharing home, goods, companionship, etc.

contemplative life, human life which is mainly occupied with, intent upon, and pleased with consideration of truth. REF. – *Truth,* q. 4, a. 8. *S.T.,* I, 18, aa. 1–3. *C.G.,* I, CC. 97, 98.

light, *n.* **1.** *in general.* a source of understanding or of insight. **2.** the intellect's power of knowing. **3.** a medium of knowledge. **4.** a pure act of knowledge. **5.** a manifestation of knowledge or of truth. See AGENT INTELLECT; ILLUMINATION.

light of glory, the disposition whereby the created intellect is raised to the capacity of the vision of the divine essence.

natural light, 1. reason or reason unaided in its activity by supernatural means of faith, infused knowledge, etc. **2.** the principles known by natural reason. REF. – *S.T.,* II–II, 15, a. 1. *C.G.,* IV, C. 12; III, C. 53 near end.

likeness, *n.* agreement of two or more things in a form. See ANALOGY; IMAGE; KNOWLEDGE; NORM; SPECIES. REF. – *S.T.,* I, 4, a. 3; 93.

intentional likeness, the cognitive representation of an object in the image or concept. It is contrasted with physical or entitative likeness between beings. See INTENTION; REPRESENTATION.

limitation, *n.* **1.** *metaphysics and philosophy of nature.* an intrinsic factor, as a passive potency, holding the being or its operations or perfections within a finite measure. **2.** *ethics.* some restriction or boundary within which some act is lawfully performed or some right justly exercised. REF. – *Met.,* V, C. 17.

limited, *part. as adj.* finite; restricted.

locomotion, *n.* motion in place or through space. This is the most proper sense of motion. REF. – *Physics,* V, C. 2.

logic, *n.* the art or science of reasoning. ABBR. – *log.*

art of logic, intellectual skill in reasoning with order, with ease, and without error.

major (material) logic, epistemology or theory of knowledge. (This usage, found chiefly in Latin texts, is probably a misnomer.)

minor (formal) logic, the study of the rules and procedures of correct thinking. Note that many authors speak of these two (major-minor, material-formal) in other meanings. Thus, induction and more modern scientific methods are called material logic.

science of logic, the science of the first principles of conceptual beings; the science of second intentions; the discovery, analysis, proof, and organization of the principles and rules of clear, consecutive, consistent thinking.

logical, *adj.* **1.** pertaining to logic. **2.** conformed to the rules of logic; orderly; consistent. **3.** *in contrast to the ontological or real.* mental; pertaining to thought or knowledge but not directly pertaining to beings. USES – *logical* being, distinction, order, relation, unity, etc.

love, *v.* to will a good to someone; to desire, seek, appreciate, or rejoice in the good for someone.

intellectual love, an act of love in the will, following upon intellectual knowledge.

love of concupiscence, love of another thing or person for one's own sake, as something useful or pleasant to the one who loves it or him.

love of friendship, love of another for his own sake, for his good; love of benevolence.

natural love, love of a natural good for a natural motive.

sensible love, a desire for union with an object agreeable to a sensitive appetite. REF. – *S.T.,* I, 20, aa. 1, 3; 60, aa. 1, 2, 3, 5; I–II, 25, a. 2; 26, aa. 1, 4; 27, aa. 1, 2. *C.G.,* I, C. 91.

M

m., abbreviation for *middle*.

machine, *n.* an artificial body of a specific type, made by man for a special purpose or as a special tool, and operating by local movement of its parts.

macrocosm, *n.* the universe regarded as the great order of all nature.

maieutic, *n.* the art of aiding someone to bring forth knowledge from the mind by a series of pertinent questions. This intellectual "midwifery" is part of the Socratic method preparatory to formulating a definition or recalling past knowledge.

make, *v.* **1.** to alter; to produce change in another being external to the agent. **2.** to create (make from nothing). **3.** *loosely.* to cause in any way. See "AGIBILIA"; ART; DO.
REF. – *Met.*, VI, C. 1. *N. Eth.*, VI, C. 4.

malice, *n.* **1.** deliberate choice of evil, i.e., of temporal good instead of a necessary spiritual good. **2.** a bad habit of evil choice. **3.** bad will. Malice connotes defiance, hardness, contempt of good as contrasted with the weakness of passion. See SCANDAL; SIN.

man, *n.* **1.** *physical definition.* a living substance composed of a material body and a spiritual soul as its form. **2.** a creature composed of a body and spiritual soul, made to the image of God and for the glory of God and His own beatitude. **3.** *metaphysical definition.* a rational animal. **4.** the human species, the human race.

marriage, *n.* **1.** the contract by which a man and woman with juridical capacity mutually associate themselves and are conjoined into one principle for acts suited to the proper procreation of children; the wedding or act of beginning the married state. **2.** wedlock or the married state; the permanent moral union, legitimately formed, of a man and a woman for the proper procreation and proper education of children.

Christian marriage, 1. the sacrament of marriage. **2.** the married state as reformed and elevated by Christ, with specific reference to its unity, perpetuity, and religious character.

consummated marriage, marriage made complete by the first use of marriage rights after the wedding.

mastership, *n.* ownership, q.v.

material, *adj.* **1.** that which is composed of matter or has matter as part of itself. **2.** that which intrinsically depends on matter for its being or has or can have its being only as present in matter. **3.** of or pertaining to matter or potency as opposed to form or to act.

material cause, that from which something is produced or a form educed; the constituent potential principle of a composite thing; the passive subjective potency in which change occurs; the passive subjective potency which is united to the (new) form, with which it shares its being and intrinsically constitutes one being; the subject determined or modified by causal action; the substratum or determinable subject of change.

material object, see OBJECT.
REF. – *Generation*, I, CC. 3, 4. *In Boeth. de Trin.*, q. 5, a. 3 ad 2.

materialism, *n.* **1.** *metaphysics, philosophy of nature.* the view that only matter or bodies exist. **2.** *philosophy of man.* the view that man is entirely material, having no spiritual soul or spiritual powers. **3.** *ethics.* the view that material goods and interests are the only or at least the chief goods for human living.

materially, *adv.* **1.** pertaining to, belonging to, or found in the same material or whole object; as, "Being and goodness are materially identical." **2.** like that from

SOME USES OF MATERIAL CAUSE AND OF MATTER

1. As passive potency (substratum; determinable constituent)	As subject of form	{ Prime matter Disposed matter Second matter	
	As subject of change or privation	Second matter as subject	{ Of substantial change Of accidental changes
		Powers as subject of new acts and habits Finite good as subject of evil or defect	
2. As source from whose substance	Real	{ Elements Raw materials, resources (such as mines, etc.) Integral parts of some whole, especially of artefacts Members of a society	
	Logical	{ Terms for propositions Premises for conclusions Individuals for universals	
3. As object about which	{ Terms of a relation Objects of rights, of contracts, etc. Objects of living powers Objects of habits and virtues Objects of mental operations Objects of order, union, organization Subjects of law		
4. As object of perception and abstraction	{ Signate matter Sensible matter Intelligible matter Material object Formal object		

which something can be formed; as, "The nature of a singular thing is materially universal."

mathematics, *n.* the sciences that deal with abstract quantity, numbers, measurement, and their many relationships. See ABSTRACTION.

matrimony, *n.* marriage.

matter, *n.* **1.** being or substance in bodies, and usually possessing such characteristic accidents as quantity, extension, inertia, mass, weight, volume, etc. **2.** bodily substance as distinct from spirit and from its own accidents. **3.** the material cause or passive subjective potency, as distinct from form; an intrinsic capacity for perfection. **4.** the objects about which some mental operation or power or habit is concerned.

common matter, prime matter considered as not divided into many material beings.

designated (signate, individual) matter, matter considered together with its dimensions, but abstracting from substantial form; the individual piece or amount of matter in an individual body.

disposed matter, a material subject in proximate potency to receive some definite form that is proportionate to the dispositions.

intelligible matter, that which is present in sensible things, but is not perceptible as sensible and changeable; e.g., the object of mathematics (at least of arithmetic and Euclidean geometry).

necessary *and* **contingent matter,** the subject matter or enunciable of a judgment insofar as it is a necessary truth or a contingent truth.

prime matter, pure passive potency of substance, without any form, species, or privation, and receptive of any forms or subsequent privations; completely undifferentiated or indeterminate basic material of the physical universe, subject to all changes, informations, and privations; the first intrinsic and potential principle of a corporeal essence.

second matter, informed matter; a natural body; a sensible body completely constituted as a particular substance by union of prime matter with some substantial form; matter already actuated by form.

sensible matter, physical matter with its physical characteristics in nature, and therefore knowable by the senses.

REF. – *Met.,* VII, C. 3 (Aristotle's famous description of prime matter); C. 10; IX, CC. 1, 7. *S.T.,* I, 85, a. 1 ad 1. *Power,* q. 1, a. 4, end of c. *Truth,* q. 2, a. 6 ad 1.

matter, in phrases. 1. *matter* of a contract: the object about which there is mutual agreement. 2. *matter* of a proposition: the subject and predicate considered independently of the copula or form. 3. *matter* of a right: the object or term of the right. 4. *matter* of a syllogism: the three terms of the premises.

mean, *adj. and n.* 1. something in between others. 2. middle, as "mean term" of comparison. 3. intermediate between contrary extremes and partaking of some characteristics of both extremes. 4. the moderate and reasonable way between opposed vices; the mean of moral virtue which does the right thing in the right way in the right measure at the right time and place and to the proper person. 5. the mean condition of states, i.e., control by the middle class.

REF. – *Met.,* X, C. 7. *N. Eth.,* II, CC. 6, 9. *Politics,* IV, C. 11. *S.T.,* I–II, 64.

meaning, *n.* 1. what is meant; that for which something else is a sign; what is intended to be or actually is indicated, referred to, signified, or understood; the object intended. 2. the intelligibility of relations; especially representation of a thing by a conventional sign.

means, *n.* 1. a useful good. 2. instruments of an agent. See CAUSE, INSTRUMENTAL. 3. environment, property, or conditions as aids to life.

means-end, *n.* some good which in one respect is sought for its own sake and is an end, and in another respect is sought for the sake of something else and is a means. See END.

measure, *n.* 1. a standard or unit of measurement of quantity and its properties and relations. 2. a criterion of judgment, valuation, or comparison. 3. a proportion, degree, or limit; as, "Equality is the *measure* of justice." 4. a law. 5. a means or (*pl.*) a set of means in a course of action.

mechanism, *n.* 1. the view that all the activity of bodies is in the last analysis only like the movement of machines, i.e., a movement in time and a rearrangement in place of internally unchanging parts. 2. the view that even living things, other than the human soul, are only highly complex machines, so that all organic life is only a variation of the physico-chemical activity of matter. ANT. – *vitalism.*

mediate, *adj.* 1. being in between two others; intermediate. 2. prior to the immediate in a series of related steps. 3. acting through an intervening agent. 4. indirect; indirectly connected. 5. resulting from indirect or intermediate agency.

medium, *n.* 1. a mean; something intermediate between two others. 2. something that in some way unites the extremes. 3. a means; an intervening agent or instrument; an intervening thing through which agency or force or action is transmitted or produced. 4. surrounding or pervading substance in which bodies exist or move; the environment. 5. the material or potency in which the artist works.

medium of knowledge, *phrase.* that which is between the knower and known and somehow assists or effects the union of known with knower. The medium is *subjective* in the knower, and *objective* if external to the knower. Terminology on the divisions varies among the scholastics. Also see SIGN.

medium *in quo* (in which), 1. in the knower: the expressed species. 2. in the object: that reality or note of a reality which is the reason why something else is and in which it is simultaneously known; e.g., God's essence as imitable is the medium in which God knows the possibles simultaneously with knowing Himself perfectly.

medium *quo* (by which), that which leads to knowledge of another but need not be itself known before that other object is known; e.g., the intentional likeness or impressed species whereby the knower immediately knows the object.

medium *quod* (which), an object or form which must be known before it can lead to knowledge of another. This medium may also be referred to as the *medium "ex quo" (from which)*.

medium *sub quo* (under which), 1. the light or source of knowledge, as reason or revelation, enabling one to know. 2. the formal motive of assent.
Example: St. Thomas, in *Quodlibetum VII*, a. 1, calls the agent intellect the *medium sub quo*, the intelligible species the *medium quo*, and effects as leading to knowledge of causes, or a contrary leading to knowledge of its opposite, as *medium in quo*.
REF. – *S.T.*, I, 94, a. 1 ad 3. *Truth*, q. 2, a. 6 ad 10; 10, a. 8; 18, a. 1 ad 1.

meekness, *n.* the virtue that mitigates the passion of anger.
REF. – *S.T.*, II–II, 157.

memorative power, *phrase.* the internal sense which retains past judgments of the estimative sense for future recall. It is a different sense than the imagination in its function of memory.
REF. – *S.T.*, I, 78, a. 4.

memory, *n.* the general power of retaining, recalling, and recognizing past experiences or states or their objects.

intellectual memory, 1. the retention, recall, and recognition of past intellectual or voluntary experiences or their objects. Often this may be knowledge in the state of habit. 2. reminiscence; the sense memory guided by reason and recognizing the past as past.

sense memory, 1. the function of the imagination in retaining and recalling past sensible experiences or their images. 2. the combined action of imagination and estimative power in recognizing past experiences concretely as past.
REF. – *On Memory and Reminiscence. Post. Anal.*, II, C. 19. *S.T.*, I, 79, aa. 6, 7. *Truth*, q. 10, a. 2. George Klubertanz, S.J., *Philosophy of Human Nature*, C. 7.

mental, *adj.* 1. existing in the mind; existing as a quality of the mind knowing them. 2. having a purely logical, but not a real status of being. See BEING; DISTINCTION; ORDER; RELATION; etc.

mental restriction, *phrase.* mental reservation. See RESERVATION.

mercy, *n.* goodness and charity to one who is in need.
REF. – *S.T.*, I, 21, aa. 3, 4; II–II, 30.

merit, *n.* 1. *in general.* a good deed, freely done as a service to another and of itself deserving something in the form of a reward. 2. *abstractly or in the abstract sense.* the value of the deed as worthy of reward; the title or exigency for reward. 3. *concretely.* the deed performed for another. 4. *in active sense.* the good deed done. 5. *in passive sense.* the reward due for the deed or the reward given for the deed.

condign (true) merit, a good deed which earns a reward on the title of justice or at least on the title of fidelity to a promise that binds in commutative or distributive justice.

congruent (appropriate) merit, a good deed which is rewardable on grounds less than justice, such as friendship, pity, public spirit, etc.

supernatural merit, a good deed done with the help of grace or in the state of grace and deserving some supernatural reward.
REF. – *S.T.*, I–II, 21, aa. 3, 4; 114, a. 1. *Truth*, q. 14, a. 3, near end of c.; q. 29, aa. 6, 7.

metaphysical, *adj.* 1. pertaining to metaphysics. 2. concerned with ultimates, with basic principles, or with being in a general way; ultimate or radical. 3. the necessary. 4. abstract or beyond the physical; the intelligible but not sensible characteristics of things. ABBR. – *met.*

metaphysics, *n.* the science of the absolutely first principles of being; the science of being as such. It is also called ontology, first philosophy, philosophy of being, wisdom. ABBR. – *met.*
REF. – *Met.,* IV, CC. 1, 2; VI, C. 1; XI, C. 7.

metempsychosis, *n.* the doctrine of transmigration of souls from body to body in successive lives.

method, *n.* **1.** a way or mode of doing something. **2.** a way of keeping order in a series of operations so that a definite end may be achieved. **3.** a systematic manner or set of rules for seeking truth.
logical method, an orderly way of advancing in mental operations in order to reach truth.
scientific method, the method of observation, experiment, and critical testing of hypotheses, inductions, etc.
Socratic method, the method adopted by Socrates of using questions and answers in a planned series in order to reach a conclusion or a refutation. See MAIEUTIC.
methodical doubt, *phrase.* see DOUBT.
methodology, *n.* the science of method; the department of logic dealing with methods of right thinking and right investigation of truth.
microcosm, *n.* **1.** a little world or universe. **2.** specifically, man as possessing all levels of finite being and life in human nature.
middle, *adj.* see TERM, MIDDLE. ABBR. – *m., mid.*
mind, *n.* **1.** any state or activity of consciousness, whether sensory or intellectual. **2.** collective term for all conscious powers, states, and activities. **3.** in scholasticism it commonly but not always means the possible intellect.
REF. – *Truth,* q. 10, a. 1.
minor, *adj.* see TERM, MINOR. ABBR. – *min.*
miracle, *n.* a sensible effect produced by God within the limits of sensible nature and surpassing the power and order of all created nature.
intellectual miracle, a genuine prophecy concerning free future events.

moral miracle, one that surpasses the capacities of human virtue left to man's unaided powers.
physical miracle, an act or event that surpasses the powers of physical nature. A miracle *supernatural in substance (supra naturam)* is one which no created agent can perform. A miracle *supernatural in manner* is an event which no created agent can do in this way *(praeter naturam)* or which is opposite to the normal course of nature *(contra naturam).*
REF. – *S.T.,* I, 105, aa. 7, 8; 110, a. 4; 113, a. 10; II–II, 178. *C.G.,* III, C. 101. *Power,* q. 6, a. 2. J. A. Hardon, S.J., "The Concept of Miracle from St. Augustine to Modern Apologetics," in *Theological Studies,* XV (1954), 229–257.

mode (of being). a way in which something has being; any modification or determination of being.
common modes, the transcendentals; attributes or aspects of reality common to all things.
modes (in Descartes), inseparable attributes of substance, identified in reality with the essence of the substance. Thus: thought for spirit, extension for bodies.
modes (in pantheistic thought), appearances of the divine or manifestations of the divine in the beings of this physical universe.
modes (in Suarez), determinations of being.
metaphysical modes, aspects of a being only metaphysically (logically with a real foundation) distinct from the subject; thus, shape is a mode of extension.
physical modes, determinations really distinct from the subject.
physical accidental modes, a positive immediate determination of the being of something (but not a new being) conferring upon it something over and above its whole individual real essence and giving it its last complete status in existence. See ACCIDENT.
modes of a proposition, see PROPOSITION, MODAL.
proper modes, the primary divisions of being or the supreme classes of things;

as substance, accident, God, creature, act, potency, etc. See chart on BEING.

REF. – *Truth*, q. 1, a. 1. For Scotistic use of "mode" see F. Garcia, *Lexikon Scholasticum Philosophico-Theologicum*.

mode and dictum, *phrase*. *logic*. the mode is the modification of the copula in a modal proposition ("can," "cannot," "must," "may," etc.); the dictum is the absolute statement considered without the mode attached to the copula.

model, *n*. exemplary cause; that form which the agent deliberately imitates in his action; the original form or idea in whose likeness something can be made; that which causes by guiding action according to a preconceived plan. An *internal* model is an idea or mental plan; an *external* model is an object or sketch imitated. REF. – *S.T.*, 44, a. 3. *Truth*, q. 3, a. 1.

moderation, *n*. 1. reasonable use of what is sensibly pleasurable. Hence, it describes frugality, abstinence, etc. 2. the general control of all excess in various virtues related to temperance, as in humility, studiousness, good manners, orderly recreation, etc. See chart on VIRTUES under "temperance."

modesty, *n*. decent reserve and propriety; the virtue that controls internal and external acts that are the safeguards of chastity, as one's bearing, behavior, curiosity, dress, speech, etc.

Molinism, *n*. the doctrine advocated by Luis Molina, S.J. (1535–1600), that God foresees futuribles in His *scientia media* and offers His simultaneously indifferent concurrence (and actual grace) to human free will.

monad, *n*. an indestructible unit; a simple and indivisible substance (used especially by dynamists and Leibniz).

monism, *n*. any one of many views that all things are a single ultimate reality, with merely accidental or apparent variations, modifications, and manifestations of it. See DUALISM; PANTHEISM.

monogamy, *n*. the state or institution of marriage in which husband and wife may have only one marital partner; the unity of marriage. ANT. – *polygamy*.

monopoly, *n*. exclusive control of anything, especially of goods, credit, services, or certain types of activities.

mood, *n*. *of a syllogism*. a correct arrangement of the quantity and quality of propositions of a syllogism; as *Barbara Celarent* in the first figure.

moral, *adj*. 1. pertaining to moral beings. 2. pertaining to the intellect and free will; voluntary. 3. the ethically good. 4. pertaining to human conduct or to the science of human conduct. USES – *moral* argument, certitude, conduct, good, law, man, necessity, order, person, philosophy, possibility, theology, universality, etc.

moral determinants, the factors that have a bearing on the morality of an act, namely, the object, the end, and the intrinsic circumstances.

moral judgment, 1. a judgment about human good and evil. 2. a judgment of conscience. 3. a prudential judgment without absolute certitude.

morals, 1. moral principles. 2. regular behavior consistent with principles.

moral sense, an alleged innate ability to make moral judgments and decisions, to know the natural law and right applications of it.

philosophy of morals, ethics.

morality, *n*. moral goodness or moral evil; the quality of conformity or non-conformity of a human act to the right standard of moral conduct.

objective morality, the conformity or nonconformity of the act done to the moral standard, but abstracting from the agent's knowledge of its conformity or non-conformity. Thus, theft is objectively evil even though this person did not consider this particular act a theft.

subjective (formal) morality, the known conformity or non-conformity of the act to the standard of moral judgment; the judgment of conscience about the good or evil of the act.

mores, *n*. *pl*. 1. customs. 2. fixed folkways having ethical significance. 3. manners or even mere conventions that have acquired the force of law in some community.

motion, *n*. 1. *strictest sense*. change of

place; local motion and rearrangement. **2.** *broadly.* any passage of something from potentiality to actuality; any change; any reception of a perfection. See CHANGE and chart on CHANGE.

natural motion, 1. one whose source of motion is in the thing itself. **2.** one which brings to act the natural potencies of a thing.

spontaneous motion, the living non-voluntary movement of an organism consequent upon sensation and sense appetite, directed toward satisfying the desires of that appetite.
REF. – *Physics*, VII, C. 7; III, C. 1; V, C. 5; VIII, C. 4. *S.T.*, I, 2, a. 3.

motive, *n.* some known good that incites to action or choice.

motive of assent, the evidence or other reason which moves an intellect to make a judgment.

motive power, the power of causing motion.
REF. – *S.T.*, I, 75, a. 3 ad 3.

moved, to be moved, *v.* to undergo change of any kind; esp. to be changed in place.

to be moved accidentally *or* **indirectly,** to be moved because of association with something that is being directly moved, as the soul is moved when the body walks to another place or a glass on a table is moved when the table is moved.

to be moved essentially *or* **directly,** to be in virtue of itself the subject of motion, such as a natural body.
REF. – *Physics*, VIII, CC. 4, 6.

movement, *n.* a change (the concrete noun for motion).

movement in the improper sense, 1. an act of the perfect; an immanent act, as an act of knowledge or volition; self-motion. **2.** *in creatures.* the passage of an agent from substantial act to operation within itself.
REF. – *On the Soul*, III, C. 7. *S.T.*, I, 18, a. 3 ad 1.

movent, *n.* a mover. It is also spelled *movant.*

mover, *n.* the being that initiates change. This may be the end or the agent; it is more commonly applied to the agent.

moved mover, a cause of motion in another which is itself also moved by another while imparting motion. See CAUSE, SUBORDINATE.

prime mover, a first cause originally starting motion or change.

unmoved mover, a cause of motion in another but which itself is not moved.
REF. – *Physics*, VIII, CC. 5, 6. *Met.*, XII, C. 7.

multitude, *n.* a large number of things; the many opposed to the one.
REF. – *S.T.*, I, 11, aa. 1, 2.

mutilation, *n.* **1.** the act by which some member of the body is temporarily or permanently injured, destroyed, or separated from the body, or made functionally useless. **2.** the resulting injury or privation of the body or of its functions.

mystery, *n.* **1.** a hidden truth. **2.** something of which the fact is known, but the reason of the fact or its harmony with other facts and truths is not understood.

strict mystery, a truth so far exceeding the capacities of human reason that its full meaning cannot be comprehended by us nor a natural proof of its truth be discovered even after God has revealed that truth to men.

myth, *n.* **1.** *Platonic sense.* a parable or allegory used to illustrate some truth or to attempt a proof. **2.** *Sorel, others.* a popular contemporary hope, ambition, or social ideal.

N

n., abbreviation for *number*.

name, *n.* **1.** a noun; a term indicating a substance or something represented after the manner of a substance. See TERM. **2. divine name,** a divine attribute or perfection (since all divine perfections are substantial, even though conceived by us as multiple). See PERFECTION.

nation, *n.* a community with a distinctive culture and a language in common, even if it is not politically independent. A state might include more than one nation or national minority.

natural, *adj.* **1.** as found in nature: belonging to nature. ANT. – *artificial, mechanical.* **2.** what a being has from birth; connatural. ANT. – *acquired.* **3.** what is only from the essential principles of a being; acting according to natural powers, moved by natural tendencies, and for natural and common needs of a nature. ANT. – *merely arbitrary* or *conventional, unnatural, violent.* **4.** conformable to natural laws, whether these be physical or moral; not surpassing natural laws and powers and ends, as the supernatural, preternatural, and miraculous do. **5.** the merely physical and non-intelligent, as natural bodies. ANT. – *rational, voluntary.* **6.** produced by nature. ANT. – *accidental, artificial.* ABBR. – *nat.* USES – *natural* action, appetite, beatitude, body, end, knowledge, law, love, necessity, order, philosophy, right, science, theology, title, unit, virtue, etc.

natural philosophy, philosophy of nature, q.v. ABBR. – *nat. phil.*

natural theology, see THEOLOGY. ABBR. – *nat. theol.*

REF. – *Physics,* II, C. 1. *S.T.,* I–II, 41, a. 3; 63, a. 1; 71, a. 2; 94, a. 3 ad 2. *C.G.,* III, C. 129.

naturalism, *n.* the view that all facts and events have only natural causes and natural significance, so that nature alone suffices to explain itself. It usually includes a denial of finality in nature, of creation, of all supernatural order and events. It is only loosely the same as materialism and positivism.

nature, *n.* **1.** the origin of growing things. **2.** the essence considered as the internal principle of growth. **3.** the essence or substance considered as the intrinsic principle of activity and passion or of motion and rest. **4.** the intrinsic first principle of the specific operations of a thing; therefore, substantial form. **5.** sometimes, the raw material of a product; as a bench is by nature wood. In senses 2–5, nature is almost like essence or substance, but considered actively. **6.** the totality of objects in the universe considered prior to free human modifications of them. ANT. – *artefacts, supernatural, voluntary.*

absolute nature, see CONCEPT, UNIVERSAL; ESSENCE, ABSOLUTE.

according to nature, 1. acting from natural powers and for the good of a nature. **2.** *in man.* according to right reason. See meanings 3, 4, 6 *above.*

contrary to nature, 1. unnatural; altogether opposite to the being, activities, mode of action, order, or end of a particular nature or of nature generally. **2.** using nature against the good of nature, or as destructive of the functioning or purpose of a nature or natural power. **3.** *in man.* acting contrary to the order of right reason especially in matters grossly violating natural appetites and purposes.

course of nature, the long and continuous series of ordered events in the universe. Compare MIRACLE.

individual (singular) nature, the real concrete one principle of action or passion, usually existing. See INDIVIDUAL ESSENCE.

order of nature, see ORDER, NATURAL.
REF. – *Physics,* II, C. 1. *Met.,* V, C. 4.
Boethius, *Liber de Persona et Duabus Naturis,* I; *On Being and Essence,* CC. 1, 3. *S.T.,* I–II, 85, a. 6; III, 2, a. 1. *C.G.,* IV, CC. 35, 41. *Truth,* q. 13, a. 1 ad 1, 2. St. Thomas Aquinas, *Quodlibetum VIII,* a. 1.

necessary, *adj.* **1.** that which cannot not-be. **2.** that which must be and be as it is. **3.** that which must act as it does and which cannot act otherwise; that which is not free in its action. **4.** that which must be related as it is and cannot be without this relation. **5.** required; needed; indispensable. **6.** resulting from what is necessary, either as a real effect or a logical consequence; inevitable; what is consequently necessary. See CONTINGENT; FREE; TRANSCENDENTAL.

necessity, *n.* **1.** the state or condition of being necessary or required; the condition, state, or characteristic of a thing according to which it must be as it is and cannot not-be or be otherwise; constraint; compulsion; restriction to only one state or act.

absolute necessity, metaphysical necessity, q.v.

antecedent necessity, necessity even before the fact or act occurs; that which prior to the actual fact or event must be or must act in only one way or must happen in only one definite way and cannot be, act, or happen otherwise; lack of freedom to be, to act, or to occur in any but one way.

conditional necessity, 1. relative necessity. **2.** that which must be or must act or must follow only on the supposition that a certain condition will be verified. Such an event is antecedently contingent.

consequent necessity, what must be so because of the reality and nature of some other event, fact, decision, truth, or premise upon which it depends and from which it necessarily follows; *de facto* necessity. Consequent necessity is compatible with antecedent contingency as well as with freedom.

essential necessity, a real necessity dependent on the reality of some essence;

as will must be in any intellectual being.

existential necessity, the necessity of existence.

extrinsic necessity, a necessity whose source is outside the thing itself which is said to be necessary; necessary dependence on another.

intrinsic necessity, a necessity internal to the nature or thing said to be necessary. This may be metaphysical or physical necessity.

logical necessity, the conclusions or implications that are unavoidable or alone valid in the given assumptions and premises.

metaphysical necessity, the impossibility of being otherwise under all conditions so that even God cannot cause an exception.

moral necessity, 1. something required by the common and constant dispositions and abilities of men, but which men can exceed or fail in under very unusual circumstances of heroism or weakness or malice; that whose opposite is practically impossible to human nature generally. **2.** moral obligation.

natural necessity, 1. what a nature requires. **2.** what results from natural (non-voluntary) operations of natural bodies. **3.** intrinsic necessity.

necessity of the end, the good for which a nature exists and which it requires for its own proper perfection and for which it has innate capacities and tendencies.

necessity by supposition, that which must be because it is so or because it follows from a conceded fact or assumed proposition; consequent necessity.

negative necessity, impossibility or necessary exclusion.

physical necessity, 1. the necessity of natural agents, but whose operations may be impeded or supplemented by miraculous works of God. **2.** bodily needs.

relative necessity, a necessity either moral or physical which bears exceptions.
REF. – *Met.,* V, C. 5. *S.T.,* I, 25, a. 5; 41, a. 2 ad 5; 82, a. 1; III, 14, a. 2; 46, a. 1; 65, a. 4. *C.G.,* II, CC. 28–30. *Power,* q. 5, a. 3.

necessity, *n.* **2.** moral obligation **3.** legal obligation.

necessity, *n.* **4.** need or want; a condition or situation of difficulty or poverty in which some goods are required or desired to give supply or relief to the need.

extreme necessity, a very pressing need involving great risk, great sacrifice, or very important human goods such as life and danger of life.

necessities of status, goods useful or required not for life and health of one's self or family, but for maintaining one's present status of prosperity or one's public position, etc.

ordinary necessity, a need that is usual and widespread among men and that can be relieved by normal care, effort, and supplies.

serious necessity, an urgent need of some importance, intermediate between ordinary and extreme necessity.

negation, *n.* a judgment that divides predicate from subject.

way of negation, the mode of knowing God by denying of Him the imperfections and limitations which a creature has.

negative attribute, *phrase.* a perfection of a spirit or of God which is known by way of denying material limitations or finite limitations; as immortality in a spirit, infinity in God. See PERFECTION.

nescience, *n.* mere lack of knowledge. See IGNORANCE.
REF. – *S.T.,* I, 101, a. 1.

no., abbreviation for *number.*

noble, *adj.* **1.** excellent, especially in moral qualities. **2.** deserving of high praise.
REF. – *Rhetoric,* I, C. 9.

nominal, *adj.* **1.** pertaining to or explaining a name. **2.** existing in name alone. See DEFINITION, NOMINAL; DISTINCTION, NOMINAL.

nominalism, *n.* the view that universals are only names, not concepts and not founded on reality. See CONCEPTUALISM; REALISM, MODERATE; UNIVERSAL.

‡**non sequitur,** *Latin phrase.* "It does not follow." This is said of an inference or conclusion which does not follow from the evidence or premises advanced in its favor.

norm, *n.* a standard or measure of comparison; a criterion; a measure; a rule.

normative, something which sets up rules for guiding some activity.

norm of morality, the standard for distinguishing and evaluating good and evil in human acts.

norm of truth, the standard for assent or dissent in judgment or for determining what is true and what is false.

note, *n.* a knowable attribute of an object.

analogous note, a characteristic or form in which two or more are simultaneously like and unlike each other.

formal note, the specific, exclusive, characteristic, or differentiating note.

nothing, *n.* **1.** the non-existent. **2.** what is incapable of existing; the impossibles and beings of reason.

notion, *n.* concept; mental apprehension.

logical notion, a second intention.

‡**notum quoad nos,** *Latin phrase.* known to us. See EVIDENT.

‡**notum quoad se,** *Latin phrase.* known in itself. See EVIDENT.

noun, *n.* a part of speech signifying a substance or something conceived after the manner of a substance; a name. For divisions see SUPPOSITION and TERM.

nous, *n.* **1.** mind (in general, as contrasted with nature and the non-cognitive). **2.** *specifically.* simple understanding or intuition.

now, *n.* the end of the past and the beginning of the future; the flowing point of time.
REF. – *Physics,* IV, CC. 10, 13.

number, *n.* a plurality measured by some suitable unit. ABBR. – *n. no., num.*

cardinal number, a plurality of units of the same kind, as four.

ordinal number, a measure indicating the position or rank of a member in a series or set, such as fourth, ninth, etc.

O

O, symbol for a particular negative proposition.

o., abbreviation for *order*.

oath, *n.* an act calling upon God or some revered object in support of the truth of one's statement or the interior sincerity of one's promise.
REF. – *S.T.*, II–II, 89.

obedience, *n.* 1. the general observance of the commands and prohibitions of law. 2. the special virtue related to justice by which one willingly fulfills the commands of a superior.
REF. – *S.T.*, II–II, 4, a. 7 ad 3; 104, a. 2.

obj., abbreviation for *object, objection, objective*.

object, *n.* 1. *metaphysics.* **a.** end or final cause; what is aimed at. **b.** the patient; the recipient of causal action. 2. *epistemology.* anything external to the knowing act and which is knowable by sense or by intellect; that which is known; the object of cognitive attention; the essence represented in knowledge. 3. *philosophy of man.* anything to which action, thought, feeling, or willing is directed. 4. *ethics.* **a.** the term of moral choice; the deed done or to be done that is external to the elicited act of the will. **b.** the just thing or that over which a person has a right. ABBR. – *obj.*

adequate object, all that can be reached by a power; the sum of all those objects in which the formal object can be found.

connatural object, that object to which a power is naturally and primarily related; the object which a power primarily, most readily, and best attains in its natural conditions of operation; proportionate object.

direct (immediate) object, that to which a power is first ordered in any series or chain of objects with which its activity is concerned.

formal object, that particular perfection in an object which a power, habit, or act primarily (directly) and naturally (essentially, *per se*) attains, to which the power, habit, or act is essentially adapted, and by means of which it reaches the material object; the definite, precise characteristic engaging a power in a complex whole; the special, primary, immediate characteristic or aspect considered or sought in a material or whole object.

indirect object, an object reached through the medium of another object, secondarily or dependently or by association with the direct object.

material object, 1. the indeterminate or general object. 2. the total object or the thing in all its reality, and not merely the particular feature falling under the action of a power or habit or act. 3. the general or common subject matter, rather than the specialized feature of study or the specialized viewpoint under which the subject is studied.

moral object, the matter about which a human act is concerned. See meaning 4a *above*.

primary object, 1. what is both the direct and formal object, as God's essence is the primary object of God's knowledge. 2. a primary quality. See QUALITY.

proper object, 1. an object suitable to the operations of a power in its natural state. 2. the same as formal object.

proportionate object, 1. connatural object. 2. an object which meets but does not exceed the capacity of a power under the given set of conditions. Thus, the free futures are a proportionate object of God's knowledge, but not of our knowledge.

sensible object, one that can affect the senses or sense appetites or be known and desired by sensory powers. See SENSIBLE.

MEANINGS OF OBJECT AND SUBJECT

	Object	Antonym
Grammar	The noun or substantive to which the action of the verb is directed or which is governed by a preposition	Subject
Metaphysics	End or purpose; objective Recipient of causal action Material thing (infrequent in scholasticism)	Means Cause, either efficient or formal Person
Epistemology	The known or knowable, as other than the act of knowing and related to it Divisions: formal and material; direct and indirect; *per se* and *per accidens*	Subject, percipient
Philosophy of Man	That to which the acts of a power are directed Divisions: formal and material; connatural (proper) and adequate; direct and indirect	Power, habit, or act
Ethics	End or purpose Object of choice The just thing or matter of a right	Means The act of choosing Holder of the right

	Subject	
Logic, grammar	Term about which predication is made The inferior of a universal concept or term The material object or subject matter of a science, a discourse, argument, etc.	Predicate Nature in the concept or term Formal object
Metaphysics	Substance First term of a relation; referent	Accident Referend
Epistemology	Conscious being; a knower	Object
Philosophy of Nature	Substrate or potency	Form, agent
Philosophy of Man	The self The recipient of a habit	The outside world The habit
Ethics	Holder of a right The person under authority	Matter of right (object) Ruler, superior

objection, *n.* a reason or difficulty proposed against an explanation, proof, or conclusion. ABBR. – *obj.*

objective, *adj.* 1. *epistemology, the usual usage.* what belongs to things themselves or is grounded in things, prior to and independently of the mind's consideration of them. 2. ontological, as contrasted with the merely mental or logical. ABBR. – *obj.* USES – *objective* concept, evidence, identity or difference, morality, validity, etc.

objective reference, see OBJECTIVITY, sense 1.

objectivity, *n.* 1. the conformity of mental representation to the object known; the characteristic of knowledge as measured by the object. 2. the state of critical and impartial reflection in which the mind considers things as they are in their own reality and under their own real conditions, detaching itself from personal tastes, interests, preferences, etc.; as the objectivity of sciences. **3.** a general philosophical viewpoint that regards external or extra-mental being as real, independently of the knower, and measures true knowledge by the real.

obligation, *n.* **1.** the moral necessity of freely obeying a law or other command of a superior. **2.** a duty, especially a juridic duty.

absolute obligation, a duty binding all men always in every condition of human nature.

directly moral obligation, a duty binding one in conscience to do or omit the act named in the law.

disjunctive obligation, a duty binding one in conscience either to do (or omit) the legally specified act or at least to obey by accepting the justly imposed penalty for violating the law. Sometimes such an obligation is referred to as a merely penal law.

hypothetical obligation, a duty that arises only from a special free act of a superior or of a subject. Examples are the obligations from divine positive law, vows, contracts, and human positive laws and precepts.

observance, *n.* honor, tribute, and obedience to persons in positions of dignity. REF. – *S.T.,* II–II, 102, a. 2.

obversion, *n.* an immediate inference with the same subject and predicate as the original (obvertend) proposition with negatives appropriately added to retain a proposition equivalent to the original.

occasion, *n.* a principle or circumstance that favors or makes opportune the present action of a free cause. It is sometimes referred to as an accidental cause.

occupation, *n.* the act of taking hold of and making unowned or abandoned property one's own.

occupational group, *n.* a functional group.

omission, *n.* non-fulfillment of a good that is due and to which one is bound. REF. – *S.T.,* II–II, 79, a. 3.

omnipotent, *adj.* all-powerful; possessing causal ability to do or to make all that is intrinsically possible. REF. – *S.T.,* I, 25, a. 3.

omnipresent, *adj.* present everywhere; being simultaneously wherever there is being.

one, *adj. and n.* **1.** that which is undivided in itself and distinct from every other. See UNIT. ANT. – *many.* **2.** the standard for measurement of number.

ontogenesis, *n.* development of the individual living being.

ontological, *n.* **1.** pertaining to being; implied in being. **2.** real as contrasted with the mental, logical, verbal. USES – *ontological* argument, order, reflection.

ontology, *n.* metaphysics; the science of being; especially, the study of general topics in metaphysics and so excluding natural theology and epistemology. Some scholastics do not wish to accept the name as a proper equivalent of metaphysics because of its association with and misuse by semi-scholastic and non-scholastic writers.

operation, *n.* **1.** activity; the second act of a power. There seems to be a preference for using operation for living and immaterial activity, and action for transeunt activity. **2.** *ethics.* surgery performed especially on a human being.

opinion, *n.* **1.** assent to a probable proposition that does not certainly exclude its contradictory as untrue. **2.** a conclusion resting on a probable or dialectical proof. **3.** *among the Greek philosophers.* knowledge of contingent facts or relationships or of individuals and accidents, as distinguished from science or understanding of universal and necessary substances and their relationships. REF. – *Post. Anal.,* I, C. 33. *Met.,* VII, C. 15. *S.T.,* I, 79, a. 9 ad 4. *Truth,* q. 14, a. 1.

opportunity, *n.* **1.** *metaphysics.* a favorable occasion. **2.** *ethics.* the positive aspect of right, namely, freedom for something as contrasted with immunity or freedom from something.

opposition, *n.* the state of being other or against; difference.

logical opposition, a difference between propositions in quantity or quality or both, though treating of the same subject and predicate. See CONTRADICTORY; CONTRARY; SUBALTERN; SUBCONTRARY.

privative opposition, the difference between lacking and possessing the same
natural characteristic.

square of opposition, the schematic
arrangement of the contrasts and relationships of logically opposed propositions.
REF. – *Cat.*, CC. 10, 11. *Met.*, V, C. 10.

order, *n.* 1. the arrangement of many
things into some unity according to some
principle. The chief kinds are the order
of parts to a whole and of means to one
end.

actual order, an order really existing
among things or in minds.

artificial order, an order imposed on
things by free human action; a rearrangement of natural objects in human
production; mechanical order.

dynamic order, an order of activity,
maintaining the unity of order during
change and development.

extrinsic order, artificial order; an arrangement imposed on the many by an
agent who uses and arranges already
existing but unrelated natures.

intrinsic order, a unity that develops
from the very nature of the ordered
multiplicity. The unity may be within the
being itself or between it and the beings
to which it is naturally related in its
environment.

juridic (juridical) order, the order of
justice or of rights among men; the body
of those rights and duties which justice
grants, protects, and imposes.

logical order, correct arrangement of
concepts, language, propositions, arguments, numbers, and other mental
entities.

mental order, logical order.

metaphysical order, the necessary order
among things, as of necessary dependence,
similarities, and other relationships.

moral order, 1. the proper direction of
human acts to man's end; the conformity
of acts to the norm of human conduct.
2. the relations of moral causes and
effects, of moral purposes and means, of
moral parts or members to the whole, and
of comparative moral excellence. 3. the
legally established body of rights and
duties among human beings.

natural order, 1. an arrangement intrinsic to things, belonging to them inherently,
and developing from the very natures of
the things in which or among which the
order is found. ANT. – *artificial order.*
2. the arrangement and adaptation of
natural objects to the good of the whole
of nature and the general benefit of
each. 3. the sum of all natures, natural
powers, and natural activities related to
the end of nature and the particular
ends of each nature; the order in the
whole of nature. ANT. – *supernatural order.*

ontological order, 1. order among beings
or their principles and parts. 2. the
hierarchy of being arranged according to
intrinsic excellence of natures and operations. 3. real (as distinguished from
logical) order.

physical order, natural or artificial order
among mere things, as distinguished from
moral and juridic order.

real order, an objective arrangement of
many things into some real unity; ontological order.

social order, 1. the arrangement of rights,
duties, and advantages of members of
society so that all members justly and
fairly share in the common good, in
common obligations, and in common protection of their rights. 2. *loosely.* any
order that affects a number of people.

subordination, the relation of lower to
higher, or of inferior to superior, in any
respect.

supernatural order, the sum of the end,
powers, means, and other gifts of God
which surpass the capacities and needs of
man's mere nature.

teleological order, the order of means
to due ends. See FINALITY.
REF. – *S.T.*, I, 42, a. 3.

order, *n.* 2. the allotment of each thing
to its proper place or rank. 3. the sequence
of acts, steps, events, members, etc., in a
connected series or set. 4. an ordination
or command of a superior to a subject.
ABBR. – *o., ord.*

ordered, *part. as adj.* 1. related to. 2.
directed toward (a good or end). 3. arranged in some way; organized.

ordination of reason, *phrase.* a law or command. See LAW.

orectic, *adj.* of or pertaining to the appetites or desires. ANT. – *cognitive.*

org., abbreviation for *organic, organized.*

organ, *n.* any part of an organism composed of tissues having a specialized structure and performing some definite natural function or functions.

organic, *adj.* **1.** characterized by structure, functions, unity, and differentiations, like those of an organism. ANT. – *mechanical, atomistic.* **2.** having complex relationships between parts. **3.** *chemistry, esp. of living things.* containing carbon or carbon compounds. ABBR. – *org.*

organic life, the spontaneous immanent activity in beings with specialized activities performed by special organs.

quasi-organic, similar to organisms in structure, close co-ordination, specialization, etc., but lacking an internal principle of life. It is sometimes used to describe the natural order of the universe and the scholastic concept of the state.

organism, *n.* an organized living body; a living substance having diverse (heterogeneous) organs with special structures for diverse special functions, all of which are dependent on the living whole and exist and act primarily and directly for the good of the whole.

FORMS OF OWNERSHIP AND MASTERY

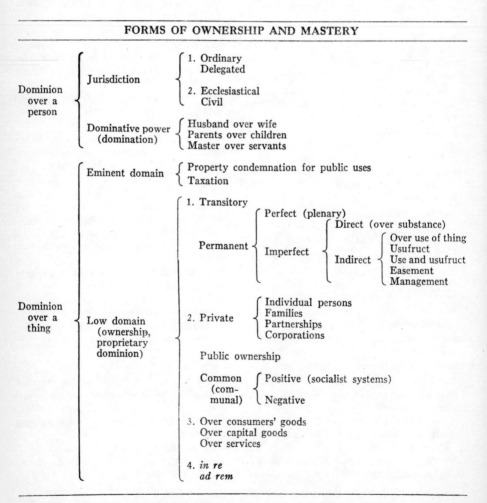

organization, *n.* 1. the arrangement, adaptation, and structure of an active being. 2. *specifically of a living being.* the organism's development of itself or its structure.

origin, *n.* procession of one from another without causal dependence on another; the principle from which such procession flows. (This theological use distinguishes it from priority of nature in a cause.) ABBR. – *orig.*

ownership, *n.* the right to control (dispose of) a material object in one's own interest in accordance with law; mastery over things.

direct ownership, *or* **dominion,** a partial ownership in which one has a right only over the substance of the thing.

indirect ownership, the right only of use, usufruct, etc., of a thing, while ownership of the substance belongs to another.

plenary ownership, the permanent right to control both the substance, use, and fruits of a material thing in one's own interest in accordance with law. Partial ownership may be shared with another in various ways.

REF. – *S.T.,* I, 96, aa. 1, 2, 4.

TITLES OF OWNERSHIP

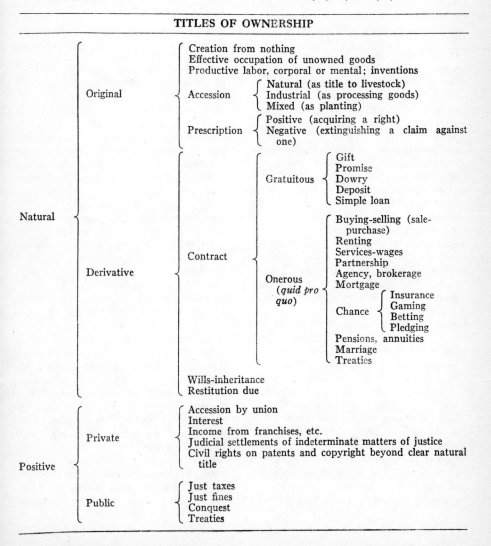

- **Natural**
  - **Original**
    - Creation from nothing
    - Effective occupation of unowned goods
    - Productive labor, corporal or mental; inventions
    - **Accession**
      - Natural (as title to livestock)
      - Industrial (as processing goods)
      - Mixed (as planting)
    - **Prescription**
      - Positive (acquiring a right)
      - Negative (extinguishing a claim against one)
  - **Derivative**
    - **Contract**
      - **Gratuitous**
        - Gift
        - Promise
        - Dowry
        - Deposit
        - Simple loan
      - **Onerous** (*quid pro quo*)
        - Buying-selling (sale-purchase)
        - Renting
        - Services-wages
        - Partnership
        - Agency, brokerage
        - Mortgage
        - **Chance**
          - Insurance
          - Gaming
          - Betting
          - Pledging
        - Pensions, annuities
        - Marriage
        - Treaties
    - Wills-inheritance
    - Restitution due
- **Positive**
  - **Private**
    - Accession by union
    - Interest
    - Income from franchises, etc.
    - Judicial settlements of indeterminate matters of justice
    - Civil rights on patents and copyright beyond clear natural title
  - **Public**
    - Just taxes
    - Just fines
    - Conquest
    - Treaties

P

p., abbreviation for *page, pages, part.*

panentheism, *n.* the opinion that the world is in God as a part, though not the whole of His being.

panpsychism, *n.* the view that all things whether individually or collectively are in some way alive, have a soul, and have psychological properties; hylozoism.

pantheism, *n.* any variation of the view that all things are divine, or that God and the universe are really identical.

parallelism, *n.* any one of several theories that physical processes and mental activities are related not as cause and effect of each other, but only as concomitant variations or occasions for each other's occurrence.

psycho-physical parallelism, any one of several theories that mental and bodily or neural states and acts occur simultaneously, but are really or only mentally separate and distinct from each other, not interacting, and not unified as acts of one substance.

paralogism, *n.* an error in syllogistic reasoning; a formal fallacy in reasoning.

part, *n.* a certain portion, piece, member, fraction, or component of a thing or composite whole. ABBR. – *p*. See chart on UNITY.

essential part, a principle necessary as a constituent of an essence; matter or form. See DEFINITION, ESSENTIAL; ESSENCE.

integral part, 1. a material part necessary to make a complete material substance of a definite nature. **2.** a piece needed to make up or belonging to a complete artefact. **3.** a part having the same nature as the original whole. **4.** an integral part of a virtue. See VIRTUE.

logical part, genus or specific difference as parts of a species or of the definition of a species.

material part, an integral part which is not contained in the definition of the whole body but which presupposes the whole essence; as fingers, feet, hands.

organic part, 1. an organ belonging to a living whole. **2.** a required member of a natural social whole.

quantitative part, integral part in sense 1 or 2.

signate part, a material part of an individual body, considered independently of form and modification by form.

substantial part, an essential part; an incomplete substance. See SUBSTANCE.
REF. – *Met.,* V. C. 25; VII, C. 10. *S.T.,* II–II, 48; III, 90, aa. 1, 2. *C.G.,* II, C. 72. *In Boeth. de Trin.,* q. 5, a. 3.

participation, *n.* **1.** sharing; communication. **2.** partial, imperfect, and analogous possession of the nature, attributes, or functions of another. **3.** an analogical likeness in the copy or the secondary analogue to the original and the cause.

participated being, 1. one whose being and perfections imperfectly imitate the perfection of its cause. **2.** hence, a member of a class of beings none of which is a pure act.
REF. – *S.T.,* I, 108, a. 5.

particular, *adj.* **1.** referring to a part of a whole. **2.** including some, not all members of a class (and these are usually indefinitely referred to). **3.** predicated of some but not all members of a class. ABBR. – *part*. USES – *particular* proposition. supposition, subaltern opposition, term.

passible quality, *phrase.* a relatively permanent disposition, excited by change in the sensitive appetite, as the disposition to worry. See chart on CATEGORIES; also PASSION; QUALITY.

passion, *n.* **1.** *the predicament or category of being.* any kind of reception of a perfection or of a privation; being, considered as acted on by another; the reception of change in the being acted upon; any passing from potency to act. **2.** *a type of quality.* a transitory sensible quality which moves or is moved by the sensitive appetite. **3.** a passive power that must be moved to act by another agent. **4.** an act of a passive power. **5.** an immanent act that has been preceded by the reception of influence or change from another being. **6.** an intense movement of the sensitive appetite accompanied by noticeable organic change, as in anger or fear. **7.** an inordinate affection or movement of the sensitive appetite connoting moral danger or the result of moral fault; e.g., uncontrolled sexual desire. **8.** the experience of the loss of a suitable form and enduring the presence of an unsuitable form; as the passion of Christ or the suffering of injustice. **9.** a property of something or an attribute that can be predicated of something, as the transcendental attributes are occasionally called passions of being.

principal passions, those movements of sensitive appetites which precede others and lead to other acts known as *consequent* passions. The principal or basic passions are love and hate, hope and fear. REF. – *S.T.,* I, 79, a. 2; 82, a. 5 ad 1; 97, a. 2; I–II, 15, a. 5, c. and ad 3; 22, aa. 1, 3; 41, a. 1; 59, aa. 2, 5. *Truth,* q. 26, aa. 1, 3, 5.

passive, *adj.* that which is in potency to be perfected or determined by some other agent or form. ABBR. – *pass.* REF. – *S.T.,* I, 79, a. 2.

patient, *n.* the subject of change; the subject acted upon or influenced by a cause; the subject of passion; the recipient of an action; material cause in the broad sense of the determinable subject of change.

peace, *n.* "the tranquillity of order" (St. Augustine); freedom from internal and external disturbance of order; well-ordered agreement or union of wills; the calm and contented order of justice.

internal peace, calm and joy of soul in its love of a possessed good without further intense effort or uncertainty.

REF. – St. Augustine, *City of God,* XIX, C. 13. *S.T.,* II–II, 29, aa. 1, 2.

per., abbreviation for *person.*

‡**per accidens,** *Latin phrase as adj. or adv.* **1.** *literally.* "by an accident," "by means of an accident." **2.** accidental or accidentally, q.v. **3.** contingently, q.v. **4.** indirect or indirectly, q.v. ANT. – *per se.* USES – *per accidens* cause, conversion, effect, intelligible, sensible, etc.

percept, *n.* **1.** the object immediately known in sense perception. **2.** a primitive (immediate, intuitive) concept. **3.** the objective concept immediately present.

perception, *n.* the power or act of immediately knowing something within us or external to us.

perfect, *adj.* **1.** complete or whole. **2.** excellent. **3.** fully in act; having all the actual qualities and good attributes that are requisite to its nature or kind. **4.** that which has attained its proper end. **5.** that which is without defects in regard to its nature, operations, or end. USES – *perfect* being, right, voluntary act, etc. See INCOMPLETE. ABBR. – *perf., pf.*

infinitely perfect, unlimited in perfection. See INFINITE.

universally perfect *or* **all-perfect,** having all real pure perfections or goods; lacking no kind of excellence. REF. – *Met.,* V, C. 16. *S.T.,* I, 5, a. 5; 6, a. 3.

perfection, *n.* **1.** any good possessed by a being; some definite actuality, reality, or good belonging to a being, suitable to it, and conceived as really or mentally distinct from other perfections present in that being. See ACT; GOOD.

first perfection, substance or form. See FIRST ACT.

mixed perfection, a reality which in nature (concept or definition) always includes potency and imperfection; as, a material or changing thing.

participated perfection, a good or actuality belonging to a thing as caused and received from another, imperfectly possessed, analogous to the highest perfection of its type, and shared with others in its genus or species. See PARTICIPATION.

pure perfection, one whose nature (concept or definition) does not state or imply any potency or imperfection.

absolutely pure perfection, one whose nature (concept or definition) completely excludes any potency or imperfection.

second perfection, perfection of the operation or of the end attained by the operation. See SECOND ACT.

simple perfection, a pure perfection. REF. – *S.T.*, I, 13; 73, a. 1.

perfection, *n.* **2.** the definite goodness or determinate actuality that a being possesses. **3.** a state in which a being completely possesses a definite kind of reality so that nothing is lacking according to its nature and the fulfillment of its natural powers and the attainment of its end. See PERFECT, sense 5.

perjury, *n.* a falsehood confirmed by oath. REF. – *S.T.*, II–II, 98.

permission, *n.* **1.** authorization to act. **2.** authorization to act in a way other than the law allows to those without the permission. **3.** foreseeing, not intending, yet not preventing the doing of something though one absolutely could prevent it.

‡**per se,** *Latin phrase as adj. or adv.* **1.** *literally.* "by itself," "through itself"; hence, by itself; because of itself; by means of itself; by reason of what it is in itself; in its own nature without reference to its relations or concomitant circumstances and associations. **2.** simply; absolutely. **3.** directly. **4.** intrinsically. **5.** essentially. **6.** by intention. ANT. – *accidentally,* "*in alio,*" "*per accidens.*"

person, *n.* an intellectual suppositum; an intellectual hypostasis; "an individual substance of a rational nature" (Boethius); an individual intellectual substance which is complete in itself, uncommunicated, and existing for itself or *sui juris.* ABBR. – *per., pers.* Compare NATURE; SUBSISTENCE; SUPPOSITUM; THING.

moral person, a society or group of persons having a common purpose, common rights and duties, and legally recognized as a moral unity.

natural person, an individual intellectual suppositum.

REF. – Boethius, *De Duabus Naturis,* III. *S.T.,* I, 29; 30, a. 3; III, 2, aa. 2, 3; 35, a. 1 and replies. *C.G.,* IV, C. 38; 43, 1st proof.

personal, *adj.* **1.** belonging to a person; special to a person and distinctive of him as an individual and intellectual being. **2.** *specifically.* belonging to the soul.

personal identity, the substantial sameness of the person, the conscious ego, or the soul with itself in the course of time and despite other changes. REF. – *C.G.,* III, C. 113, near end.

personality, *n.* **1.** *technical scholastic sense.* the subsistence proper to a person; that perfection which makes an intellectual nature to be uncommunicated or unshared by the being of another. **2.** *modern psychological senses.* **a.** the systems or psycho-physical abilities whereby man can give a unique external expression of himself. **b.** the exterior expression of one's self and one's abilities and interests and deficiencies in dealings with others. **c.** individual differences and characteristics exteriorly manifested. **3.** *accommodated scholastic sense.* the sum total of the actualities and potencies of a person.

pessimism, *n.* a view of the world or of human life which regards it as principally or wholly evil in its being, origin, and destiny; or a view that regards nature and human life as essentially purposeless, painful, and destructive.

‡**petitio principii,** *Latin phrase.* begging the question. q.v.

phantasm, *n.* see FANTASM.

phantasy, *n.* imagination.

phenomenalism, *n.* a theory that the only real things are the phenomena, and so substance, cause, form, etc., are non-existent or are mere mental constructs.

phenomenon, *n., pl.* -a. **1.** something visible or immediately observable, as distinguished from substance, form, force, or law by which or in accordance with which the phenomenon exists or is produced. **2.** *pl.* the appearances or accidents of a thing. **3.** any fact, appearance, or occurrence apprehended consciously. ANT. – TO SENSE 3 – *noumenon,* the object of thought, the thing in itself (Kant's usage).

philosophical (philosophic), *adj.* **1.** belonging to, coming from, or consistent with a philosopher or his philosophy. **2.** related to philosophy in some way. **3.** like a philosopher; expected of a philosopher; befitting a philosopher; hence, **4.** reflective and critical; reasonable; calm and contented; inquiring into and explaining by basic causes and fundamental principles; not concerned merely with phenomena, facts, temporary matters, images and feelings: as, a *philosophical* attitude towards trouble, a *philosophical* study of history.

philosophical physics, the philosophical study of change in nature; the philosophy of nature, q.v.

philosophy, *n.* **1.** *nominal definition.* the love of wisdom. **2.** the science in which natural reason seeks an understanding of all things by a knowledge of their first principles. ABBR. – *phil., philos.*

Christian philosophy, a philosophy which keeps the orders of reason and of Christ's revelation (or of nature and of grace) formally distinct, but considers the Christian revelation as an indispensable aid to reason (or nature). See LAW, CHRISTIAN NATURAL.

first philosophy, 1. *Aristotle, St. Thomas.* metaphysics, including natural theology. **2.** *Descartes.* the beginnings of philosophical certitude; hence, his methodic doubt and the foundations of the theory of knowledge.

philosophy of art, the study of the first principles of the making of things. Compare AESTHETICS.

philosophy of life, the study of the basic principles concerning the origin, nature, purpose, personal and social values of human life.

philosophy of man, the study of the first principles of the nature of man and of the unity of human nature; the philosophy of human nature; philosophical psychology inasmuch as it combines the approaches of the philosophy of nature and of metaphysics in the study of man.

philosophy of mathematics, the study of the first principles of quantity and its relations. See second degree of ABSTRACTION.

philosophy of nature, the science of the first principles of natural bodies; the science of movable beings in as far as they are movable; philosophical physics. See COSMOLOGY.

philosophy of religion, the science of reasoned truths about the origin, nature, object, and purpose of religious knowledge and religious practice; the philosophical study of religion and of the bases of revealed religion.

philosophy of science, the analysis and defense of the nature and validity of scientific knowledge and of its methods of experimenting, theorizing, and correlating findings.

practical philosophy, philosophical branches which consider the order of acts.

scholastic philosophy, scholasticism, q.v.

speculative philosophy, philosophical branches which consider beings and their order as they are in themselves, from the desire of knowing the truth about them.

systematic philosophy, an organized study of some philosopher, philosophical school, or of a branch of philosophy as presented by some philosopher or school. REF. – *Met.,* VI, C. 1. *In Boeth. de Trin.,* q. 5, a. 2. E. Gilson, *The Spirit of Mediaeval Philosophy,* C. II, "The Concept of Christian Philosophy."

BRANCHES OF SYSTEMATIC SCHOLASTIC PHILOSOPHY

A. Speculative philosophy*
  1. Philosophy of nature
  2. Philosophy of man
    (often called rational psychology)
  3. Philosophy of mathematics

  4–6. Metaphysics, first philosophy, wisdom; it includes
  4. Ontology or general metaphysics
  5. Natural theology or theodicy
  6. Epistemology

B. Practical philosophy
  7. Logic
  8. Ethics
  9. Political philosophy
  10. Philosophy of art

* See modes of ABSTRACTION.

physical, *adj.* **1.** pertaining to the material universe, bodily natures, and their order, as distinguished from mental, mathematical, moral, psychic, or spiritual. **2.** external and sensible; apparent to the senses. **3.** concrete and singular, as distinguished from abstract, metaphysical, and universal. ABBR. – *phys.*

physicist, *n.* an old term for a physical philosopher; a student of the philosophy of nature.

physics, *n.* the old term for philosophy of nature, q.v.; philosophical physics; second philosophy. ABBR. – *phys.*

‡**physis,** *n.* the Greek word for "nature."

piety, *n.* **1.** honor and reverence given to those closely related to us, as to parents (filial piety), country (patriotism), and near relatives. **2.** the gift of the Holy Spirit whereby man gives affectionate worship to God as Father. REF. – *S.T.,* II–II, 101, a. 1.

place, *n.* where a body is; the setting or position of some body in relation to surrounding place and bodies. ABBR. – *pl.*

common place, the general position of a body with respect to other bodies at some distance from it.

external place, proper place.

internal place, the space contained within the outside boundaries or surfaces of a body considered as the receptacle of the body's entire volume.

proper (special) place, the surface of the bodies surrounding an object and in immediate contact with the contained body; the surface of the containing body considered as immovable and immediately contiguous to the body located there. REF. – *Physics,* IV, CC. 4, 5. *Met.,* XI, C. 12.

plan, *n.* the deliberate scheme of order for things or actions; the foreseen program or methods of doing and acting.

divine plan, the order of the universe in the mind of God, foreseeing its members, their diversity and hierarchy, their activities, relationships, and ends. See ORDER; PROVIDENCE.

plant, *n.* **1.** a nonsentient living body. **2.** a specimen of vegetative life.

pleasure, *n.* **1.** satisfaction or gratification of senses, emotions, mind, or will having or using a good proportionate to a conscious power. **2.** a movement by which the soul as a whole is consciously brought into its normal state of being.

aesthetic pleasure, the enjoyment accompanying the perception of the beautiful. REF. – *N. Eth.,* X. CC. 4, 5. *Rhetoric,* I, C. 11. *S.T.,* I–II, 31, a. 1.

plenum, *n.* **1.** the state of the natural universe in which space is considered as fully occupied by matter (as in Greek philosophical thought). **2.** space so occupied. ANT. – *void.*

political ethics, *phrase, as distinguished from political philosophy.* principles of moral right and wrong in the actions of both rulers and subjects insofar as they are members of the state.

political philosophy, *phrase.* the science of the first principles of human organization and activity for the public temporal good; the philosophy of the state. An older term is politics. *Political science* is an empirical or descriptive science concerned chiefly with methods and means of organizing, lawmaking, governing, etc. REF. – *Politics,* III, C. 12.

polyandry, *n.* the status or institution of simultaneous marriage between one woman and more than one man.

polygamy, *n.* the status or institution of simultaneous multiple marriages by the same person. The two forms are polygyny and polyandry.

polygyny, *n.* the status or institution of simultaneous marriage between one man and more than one woman.

polysyllogism, *n.* a serial or cumulative argument in which the conclusion of one syllogism is used as the premise for a second syllogism.

polytheism, *n.* **1.** a belief in more than one god. **2.** the idolatrous practice of worshiping a plurality of gods.

posit, *v.* to lay down as a principle; to state as a fact; affirm.

position, *n.* the relative order of the integral parts in a whole. See *situs* in the chart on CATEGORIES.

positive, *adj.* **1.** factual, historical, a posteriori. ANT. – *a priori, dogmatic, essen-*

tial, theoretical. **2.** directly affirmed.
ANT. – *dubious, negative.* **3.** actual, real,
genuine. ANT. – *methodical,* as in methodical doubt; *suppositious.* **4.** explicit or
plain. ANT. – *implicit, inferred.* **5.** laid
down by or depending on authority, con-
vention, or agreement, rather than known
from nature and necessity; putting order
in the unordered. ANT. – *natural.* ABBR. –
pos.

positivism, *n.* **1.** *in general.* a view that
regards only the sensible, the singular,
and the experienced as real and holds that
only the knowledge of such facts is certain. **2.** *Comte.* the view that human
knowledge is limited to knowledge of
phenomena and their observable relations,
and is essentially relative to the knower's
ability and development.

moral positivism, the ethical opinion that
all moral values, laws, rights, etc., are
purely historical and conventional facts.
ANT. – *theories of natural law* and *of intrinsic morality.*

possession, *n.* **1.** ownership. **2.** property.
ABBR. – *pos., poss.*

possibility, *n.* **1.** capacity to be. **2.** capacity
to be true. See IMPOSSIBLE; POSSIBLE.

**metaphysical (essential, intrinsic, ab-
solute) possibility,** capacity of an essence to be since its nature is not contradictory.

moral possibility, capacity to be because the act or event is within the
ordinary normal capacities and motives
of free (moral) agents to do it.

physical possibility, capacity to be because created causes can make it or
change it.

possible, *adj. and n.* **1.** that which can be.
2. an essence conceived as non-existing;
a merely possible being. **3.** *pl.* the essences of all things considered as objects
of God's knowledge. See IDEAS, DIVINE.

extrinsically (relatively) possible,
something which can be and for which
there is a (proximate) efficient cause
capable of making it be.

intrinsically possible, that which can be
since its constituent notes are not contradictory to each other and to existence.
See chart on ACT AND POTENCY.

REF. – *Met.,* V. C. 12. *Prior Anal.,* I, C.
13. *S.T.,* I, 25, a. 3 c. and ad 4; 41, a.
4 ad 2. *Power,* q. 1, a. 3 c. and various
replies; q. 5, a. 3 c.

posterior, *adj.* in some way later, following upon, or secondary to another. ANT. –
prior.

REF. – *Met.,* V, CC. 11, 24. *Cat.,* C. 12.
S.T., I, 42, a. 2.

‡**post hoc, ergo propter hoc,** *Latin
phrase.* "after this, therefore because of
this"; the fallacy of false cause, q.v.

postpredicament, *n.* one of the classes
of terms which Aristotle discusses in his
Categories after the treatment of the
predicaments, such as opposition, privation, simultaneity, posteriority, possession,
etc.

REF. – *Cat.,* CC. 10–15.

postulate, *n.* **1.** a primary truth of a
given branch of knowledge, but derived
from another branch of knowledge. **2.** a
basic self-evident principle necessary for
the beginning or development of a given
science. **3.** an assumption or statement
used as the start of a science and conditionally true; an hypothesis.

posture, *n.* the relative position of parts
within a material being; the ninth category, as walking, sitting, prone, erect,
etc.

potency, *n.* **1.** capacity of any sort; capacity of a being or in a being to be, to
act, or to receive. **2.** capacity to be in
some way the first source of change. **3.**
perfectibility or capacity for perfection.
4. material cause. See ACT for diagram.

active potency, the principle of change
or of acting upon another inasmuch as
it is another thing; a power; the capacity
to do or make; a principle of action.

being in potency, 1. a being in some way
not actual or not fully actual. **2.** a possible being. **3.** a changeable being. **4.** a
passive potency.

in potency, in the state of receptivity;
potentially, not actually.

natural potency, a capacity in a nature
proportionate to its nature.

obediential (supernatural) potency, the
potency to receive either a miraculous

or a supernatural perfection exceeding the natural capacities of a being.

objective potency, the capacity of a mere possible to be created.

passive potency, 1. the principle which receives change from another inasmuch as it is another thing. **2.** the capacity to receive, to be acted on, to be modified. **3.** the material cause; the modifiable (determinable) principle in a being.

proximate potency, the subject or power together with the conditions proper for receiving some specified form or for performing some specified activity.

pure potency, passive potency considered without any act; prime matter.

subjective potency, a passive capacity in a subject that is already existing.
REF. – *Met.,* V, C. 12; IX, CC. 1, 2 end, 3; XI, C. 9. *S.T.,* I, 25, a. 1; 41, a. 4 ad 3; a. 5 ad 1; III, 11, a. 1. *Truth,* q. 8, a. 12 ad 4; 16, a. 1 ad 13. *Power,* q. 1, a. 1.

potential, *adj.* having a capacity or potency; possible, not actual or at least not fully actual.

potential being, see POTENCY.

potential parts of cardinal virtues, virtues cognate or related to the cardinal virtue, and somewhat like it. See chart on VIRTUES.

potentiality, *n.* abstract term for potency, especially for passive potency.

power, *n.* **1.** a principle of acting upon something else; an active potency. **2.** a faculty or immediate principle by which a nature is directly, essentially, and permanently ordered to a definite operation or a particular function. **3.** causal ability to do or to make; the principle of the effect. **4.** authority or jurisdiction.

absolute power, 1. *said of God.* mere capacity to act or to make, considering only the sovereign authority and unlimited causal efficacy of the Creator, or abstracting from God's perfections other than power and from the present order of His providence. Compare ORDINARY POWER, *below.* **2.** unlimited civil sovereignty.

active power, a faculty that immediately affects or influences its object.

all-powerful, omnipotent; causal ability to do anything good and not self-contradictory.

infinite power, unlimited and inexhaustible power to act or to make.

ordinary (ordinate) power, *said of God.* use of causal efficacy according to God's providence and in a way consistent with His other perfections of wisdom, justice, freedom, etc.

passive power, a power that is set in action by the influence received from its object.

powers of man, the specific abilities of man, regarded as distinct from his substance or his soul.

sovereign power, supreme social authority; sovereignty.

POWERS OF MAN

I. Mechanical, physical, chemical powers as material things have

II. Vegetative powers: nutrition of the living body, growth, reproduction

III. Sensory powers

  A. Of sensory knowledge
    1. The external senses: sight, hearing, taste, smell, touch (including pressure, relative warmth, kinesthetic sense, balance, sensible pleasure and sensible pain, feeling of bodily well-being and distress, etc.)
    2. The internal senses: common sense, imagination (including sense memory), cogitative power or human estimative sense, memorative power

  B. Of sensory appetency: concupiscible appetite, irascible appetite

IV. Intellectual powers

  A. The agent intellect and the possible intellect
  B. The will or rational appetite

V. Moral powers, i.e., rights

VI. Motor powers, i.e., to move one's own body in
  a) Instinctive acts, unlearned reflexes
  b) Learned but involuntary acts; acquired automatisms
  c) Voluntary acts, such as speech and use of tools

---

spiritual power, 1. a faculty that performs spiritual acts and has no bodily organ or material principle in its being. **2.** social authority in spiritual matters for spiritual ends such as the direction of consciences and the salvation and sanctification of souls.

temporal power, authority over persons in temporal matters for some common temporal good.

    directive power, a spiritual or moral power to guide consciences and to declare moral principles and issues involved in temporal matters.

    direct temporal power, immediate authority in and over matters of temporal welfare (even when no religious or moral principle is involved).

    indirect temporal power, a power which immediately is spiritual and moral, but which has secondary temporal effects resulting from the use of spiritual or directive power.
REF. – L. Sturzo, *Church and State*, p. 551.

prayer, *n*. 1. the lifting of the mind and heart to God. **2.** *specifically.* prayer of petition or request of becoming things from God or from others to be obtained from God; the unfolding of our will to God that He may fulfill it.
REF. – *S.T.*, II–II, 83, aa. 1, 2.

precept, *n*. 1. a command of a superior to a definite subject. **2.** any general rule or command of the law, as distinguished from the whole body of laws.

affirmative precept, a rule of law commanding one to act or to do something.

negative precept, a rule of law forbidding some action.

primary, secondary, tertiary precept, see LAW.

predefinition, *n*. an idea in God's mind of a thing which will be created.

predestination, *n*. the eternal fore-ordination of all temporal things by God; the decree of God in regard to what end each man will actually obtain, as known and willed by God prior to the actual activity of men. The term is principally a theological term in regard to grace and supernatural beatitude.

REF. – *S.T.*, I, 23, a. 1; III, 24, a. 1. *C.G.*, III, C. 163. *Truth*, q. 6, a. 1.

predetermination, physical, *phrase*. immediate use of power by one of the co-operating causes antecedent to any action of the secondary cause so that the secondary cause is able to act and to act only in the way in which the principal cause empowers and applies it to action. ANT. – *moral premotion, simultaneous concurrence.*

predicable, *adj*. and *n*. 1. one of the five relations in which a universal term may stand to the subject of which it is predicated. These five relations are species, genus, specific difference, property, and contingent accident. **2.** what can be predicated truly.
REF. – *Topics*, I, C. 8.

predicament, *n*. a category.

predicate, *n*. 1. *logic.* that which is affirmed or denied of a subject in a categorical proposition. **2.** *grammar.* the predicate of a sentence with all its modifiers. **3.** *metaphysics.* a quality or property or attribute inherent in or belonging to a substance. ABBR. – *pred.*

predicate, *v*. 1. to state something as belonging to something; to affirm an attribute of a subject. **2.** to use a term as a predicate.

predication, *n*. 1. the act of affirming something of a subject. **2.** the act of assigning something to a class. **3.** the act of naming something as possessing some act or perfection or as belonging to some other act or perfection.

analogous predication, attributing a perfection to an object in a sense partially the same and partially different from the attribute of the same name when applied to some other objects. See ANALOGY; CONCEPT, ANALOGOUS; and TERM.

direct predication, use of a predicate that is the same as the subject or substance. ANT. – *oblique predication.*

eminent predication, attributing a perfection to some object in a richer, fuller, superior meaning than it has in the case of other analogous objects to which the perfection is ascribed.

formal predication, attributing the perfection in its absolute nature or according to the whole of its definition.

improper predication, attributing the perfection to the subject by a figure of speech or by relation to some other attribute with which it is connected, while the subject lacks that perfection as such.

metaphorical predication, attributing the perfection to the subject by a figure of speech, especially by a metaphor.

oblique predication, attributing the predicate as a modification of the subject or as inhering in the subject; predicating a distinct accident of the subject; (sometimes) predicating a part of the whole as belonging to the whole.

substantial predication, attributing the predicate to the substantial subject by way of real identity with that substance.

univocal predication, attributing the predicate to two or more subjects in a completely similar sense.

virtual predication, attributing the predicate to a subject as to the cause which can or does produce it, but not necessarily as though the subject has the like perfection in a formal or even in a metaphorical sense.
REF. – *S.T.,* I, 13; 16, a. 6. *Being and Essence,* C. 3, near end.

premise (premiss), *n.* 1. *in general.* any previous statement that serves as a basis for argument or discussion. 2. *specifically.* one of the two propositions in a syllogism which precede the conclusion and from which the conclusion should be drawn.

major premise, 1. that which contains the major term or term of greatest extension. 2. *often.* the first premise.

minor premise, 1. that which contains the minor term or term of less extension. 2. *often.* the second premise.

premotion, *n.* causal action impelling another cause to act and exerted on that secondary cause antecedent to its own act or choice. See CO-OPERATION; PREDE-TERMINATION.

prescience, *n.* foreknowledge, particularly of free future or futurible acts and merits.

prescind, *v.* 1. formally to exclude something from the mind's attention. 2. *loosely.* to abstract. Abstraction simply attends to what it considers without explicitly excluding from a concept the other features which the concrete object of attention really possesses. Prescission is a more analytic process.

prescission, *n.* 1. the act of prescinding. 2. the objective concept resulting from prescission.

imperfect prescission, an abstraction in which one objective concept actually but only implicitly (confusedly) includes the other objective concept as being includes good. ANT. – *contraction by explicitation.*

perfect prescission, a complete distinguishing of one abstracted objective concept from another so that the one neither actually nor implicitly includes the other; e.g., the concept of the genus does not include the concept of the specific difference. ANT. – *metaphysical composition* or *contraction.*

prescription, *n.* a title to ownership of goods or to political authority acquired by long and peaceful possession.

presence, *n.* 1. to be in or near some place or person. 2. to be really united with another.

circumscriptive presence, the natural mode of presence of bodies in space whereby each part of a body occupies its own place distinct from that occupied by other parts; each part, therefore, has one restricted or circumscribed location.

definitive (diffinitive) presence, the presence of a spirit in space whereby it is active in the whole of the space occupied by the body on which it acts and is not limited to "spots" or portions of the body, and is not spread out in space, and is not measured by the space occupied; presence wholly in the whole space of the body on which it acts and wholly in each part of that space.

multiple presence (bilocation, etc.), simultaneous presence of the same substance or soul in two places distant from each other.

omnipresence, presence everywhere in space, in all bodies; unlimited presence.

It is also called *repletive* presence, or a presence filling all space.

sacramental presence, the presence of a body supernaturally after the manner of the presence of a spirit. Thus the Body of Christ in the sacrament of the Eucharist is present definitively, not circumscriptively, in the consecrated species. REF. – *Cat.,* CC. 2, 5. *Met.,* V, C. 23. *S.T.,* I, 8, a. 2; 43, a. 3; 52, a. 2; III, 76, a. 5 ad 1.

present, *adj. and n.* the current or passing instant of time; now. ABBR. – *pres.* REF. – *Physics,* VI, C. 3.

presentation, *n.* 1. the object as presented to the mind. 2. the image as presented to the memory or to the agent intellect.

preservation, *n.* conservation; maintenance in being.

preternatural, *adj.* different from and exceeding the common order of nature or the usual way that natural forces accomplish their results; intermediate between the natural and the strictly supernatural, since the preternatural result, given other conditions, forces, time, etc., is not impossible to natural bodies.

price, *n.* goods or credit asked for or given as equivalent in exchange; the valuation of goods in comparison with each other or in comparison with a monetary standard.

just price, a price in which there is such a real proportion between the goods and services exchanged that the equality of commutative justice between the seller and the buyer is maintained.

legal price, a price set up by public law as a minimum or maximum.

market (conventional) price, a price set by common estimate of the worth of goods or services so that people usually offer to sell and are ready to buy at that price.

minimum price, 1. the lowest price that will be just to the seller or to his competitors. 2. the lowest price allowed by public law.

primary, prime, *adj.* 1. in some way first, whether in being, causality, knowledge, worth, etc. 2. basic; elementary.

principiate, *n.* that which proceeds in some way from another (namely, from a principle).

principle, *n.* that from which something in some way proceeds; the starting point of being, or change, or knowledge, or discussion. ABBR. – *prin.* for singular and plural.

analytic principle, a logical principle in which the necessary connection of implication (or exclusion) of such a predicate with (or from) such a subject is or can be known by comparison of the objective concepts of predicate and subject. See JUDGMENT.

first principle, a principle not from a principle; one which does not proceed from a prior principle in its own series. An absolutely first principle has no prior principle in any series to which it belongs; as God is the absolutely first principle of being.

formal principle, 1. *logic.* one of the basic principles which justify the validity of all reasoning, such as the principle of contradiction and the *dictum de omni et nullo.* 2. *philosophy of nature.* the form in a natural unit.

logical principle, 1. a principle of knowledge; a mental principle; a truth from which other truth proceeds; a source of knowledge or of thought. 2. a rule in logic.

material principle, 1. *logic.* the premises which supply the immediate content for a given conclusion. 2. *philosophy of nature.* the matter, potency, or substratum.

ontological principle, a real principle.

principle of law, a general rule or precept of conduct. For divisions, see under LAW.

real principle, a principle of being; a being from which another being or modification of being proceeds in some way. See chart on PRINCIPLES.

self-evident principle, see AXIOM; EVIDENT, IMMEDIATELY.

seminal principle, a seed or principle hidden in the elements, implanted by God, and awaiting favorable opportunity for development. (This is an Augustinian

MAIN TYPES OF PRINCIPLES

I. Real principles

    1. Beginning and foundation
    2. Origin
    3. Occasion
    4. Condition

    5. Cause*
        Extrinsic causes
            Efficient cause (agent)
            Final cause (end)
            Exemplary cause (model)

        Intrinsic causes
            Material cause (potency)
            Formal cause (form)

    6. Elements of composition
        Potency and act
        Organic parts
        Integral (quantitative) parts

II. Logical principles

    1. Concept and definition
    2. Question and problem
    3. Sign
    4. General truths (in sciences, mathematics, philosophy, etc.)
    5. Rules and precepts of practical sciences and of arts
    6. Fonts of truth
    7. Norms and standards of measurement
    8. Starting point of an explanation
    9. Premises; logical elements of a theory, of a proof

*See separate tables for the divisions of each of the five causes.

alternative for potency and act in substantial change.)

vital principle, an intrinsic ultimate source of specific life in a living body; a soul. REF. – *Met.,* XIV, C. 1. St. Augustine, *De Trinitate,* III, C. 9. *S.T.,* I, 33, a. 1; 42, aa. 2, 3. *Power,* q. 10, a. 1, c. and ad 9, 10, 11.

prior, *adj.* preceding another in some way; hence, earlier, more basic, more original; nearer to the source or to the first member in a series; sooner; better known and known earlier than another.

logical priority, belongs to what is known before another object is known.

natural priority, belongs to those things which must be before their attributes, relations, effects, etc., can really be.

temporal priority, belongs to those things which precede others in time or in sequence of changes. REF. – *Cat.,* C. 12. *Met.,* V, C. 11. *S.T.,* I, 42, a. 3; 46, a. 1 ad 8.

privation, *n.* **1.** lack of something needed, desirable, or previously possessed; the evil. **2.** lack of form in that which has potentiality for form. **3.** lack of the full perfection proper to the nature that has the perfection incompletely. ANT. – *having.* REF. – *Met.,* V, CC. 22, 27; IX, C. 1. *Power,* q. 9, a. 7, ad 11, 15.

privilege, *n.* **1.** a right, favor, or immunity from the obligation of a law granted to a person or group, while the law remains in force for others; a private law. **2.** *modern political thought.* basic civil right immune from government interference and guaranteed by public protection. REF. – *N. Eth.,* V, C. 7. *S.T.,* I–II, 96, a. 1 ad 1.

probabilism, *n.* the doctrine that in an insoluble practical doubt concerning the lawfulness of an action that is urgent, the moral agent is free to follow any truly probable opinion on the morality of the proposed action.

probability, *n.* assent of the mind to a proposition with a motive short of evidence and with accompanying fear that the opposite may be true; a state of mind like opinion and doubt.

problem, *n.* **1.** a subject on which reasoning takes place. **2.** an unsolved philosophical question or inquiry, upon which various views are maintained, with no convincing solution as yet available. **3.** a question once disputed though now solved or disputed only by amateurs or by philosophies reputed as false.

process, *n.* **1.** a course or method or systematic series of operations. **2.** movement or advance. **3.** *in life sciences.* a projecting part or outgrowth from another structure. See ILLICIT.

procession, *n.* **1.** a coming forth. **2.** a following, as from a principle; the relation between principiate and principle. REF. – *S.T.,* I, 36, a. 2, end of c. *Power,* q. 10, a. 1.

promulgation, *n.* official notification or publication of the law made to subjects.

proof, *n.* **1.** the presentation of evidence for or against a proposition, assertion, truth, or alleged fact. Usually it refers to a convincing presentation of evidence that commands certain assent. **2.** any reason confirming what is in doubt, especially by a sensible sign. See DEMONSTRATION and chart on REASONING.

proof *quia;* **proof** *propter quid,* see DEMONSTRATION. REF. – *S.T.,* III, 55, aa. 5, 6.

prop., abbreviation for *properly, property, proposition.*

proper, *adj.* **1.** distinctive; characteristic; special; exclusive; pertaining to an attribute, accident, or object that necessarily belongs to a nature. **2.** naturally adapted to some nature. USES – *proper* accident, cause, concept, effect, knowledge, name, object, sensible, supposition, term, etc. REF. – *S.T.,* I–II, 90, a. 4.

property, *n.* **1.** *logic.* a proprium or proper difference; an attribute that does not form part of the essence of its subject, but necessarily results from that essence; a distinctive and characteristic attribute of a being. REF. – *Post. Anal.,* I, CC. 4, 6. *Topics,* I, C. 5.

property, *n.* **2.** *ethics.* **a.** things owned. **b.** the right of ownership. See OWNERSHIP. REF. – *Politics,* I, C. 4. *Rhetoric,* I, C. 5.

proportion, *n.* **1.** comparative relation between part and part in any respect, or between part and whole, or between a being and its environment. **2.** comparative share, as in distributive justice. **3.** the order of symmetry, balance, and moderation. **4.** analogy, and especially the analogy of proportionality.

moral proportion, the comparative measure of equality or inequality between two moral factors, such as that between good and evil in an act or its consequences, between deed and merit, between law and penalty, between right and obligation, etc.

proposition, *n.* a complete sentence expressing a judgment; a statement making an affirmation or negation. ABBR. – *prop.*

categorical proposition, one which makes an absolute statement about its subject.

complex proposition, one whose subject or predicate or both contain a complex term.

composite proposition, one which has a plurality of subjects or of predicates or of both or which has a qualified copula.

contingent proposition, one whose predicate is not a necessary attribute of its subject nor necessarily excluded from the subject. These are also called synthetic a posteriori judgments or judgments in contingent matter; e.g., "This auto of mine is black."

evident proposition, **1.** one whose meaning is clear. **2.** especially, one whose truth or certitude is manifest. See EVIDENT.

hypothetical proposition, one which asserts the dependence of one affirmation or negation upon another affirmation or negation, i.e., the dependence of one clause upon another clause. There are three kinds of such propositions.

DIVISIONS OF PROPOSITIONS

Basis of Division	Members
Quality of assent	1. Affirmative; negative 2. True; false 3. Certain; probable
Quantity of subject of proposition	1. Universal { Metaphysically / Physically / Morally } Usually essential judgments 2. Singular 3. Indefinite } Usually existential judgments
Structure of terms	1. Simple (single, and always categorical) 2. Composite { Categorical (assertoric) { Copulative ("and") / Adversative ("but") / Relative (degrees) / Causal ("because," "for") } Hypothetical { Conditional ("if," "unless") / Disjunctive ("either . . . or") / Conjunctive ("not both . . . and") } 3. Exponibles (hidden composites) { Exclusive ("only") / Exceptive ("all but X") / Comparative ("as . . . so") / Reduplicative / Specificative 4. Complex { Explicative clause / Restrictive clause 5. Modal { Necessary / Contingent / Possible / Impossible
Formal relations of propositions to each other	1. Opposites { Contrary / Subcontrary / Contradictory / Subaltern 2. Equivalent (equipollent, obverse) 3. Converse { Simple / Accidental (by limitation) / Contrapositive 4. Inverse
Source and motive of assent	1. Analytic a priori / Synthetic a posteriori 2. In necessary matter; in contingent matter 3. Self-evident: (in itself; to us; to the learned) / Mediately known
Special content	1. Axioms 2. Postulates 3. Statement of problem 4. Theorem 5. Thesis 6. Definition 7. Principle (esp. formal) 8. Premise 9. Conclusion, consequent 10. Corollary 11. Scholion

a. a conditional proposition is a hypothetical proposition composed of two parts so connected that the positing or negating of one is the condition on which the other part depends. (Signs: "if," "unless," etc.)
b. a conjunctive proposition asserts that two judgments contained in it cannot be simultaneously true. (Sign: "not both A and B.")
c. a disjunctive proposition connects two or more terms or propositions by the particle "or" so that not all the members are true together.
indefinite proposition, one whose universal term in the subject is of uncertain extension in its supposition.
modal proposition, one whose copula is modified by a term which shows the manner in which the predicate belongs to or is excluded from the subject. The modes are: necessity, contingency, possibility, impossibility.
necessary proposition, one in which the predicate is necessarily contained in or necessarily excluded from the nature or concept of the subject. It also states an analytic a priori judgment or is a judgment in necessary matter; e.g., "God is good"; "Man is rational."
simple proposition, one which affirms or denies one predicate of one subject.
universal proposition, one whose subject is a universal term used distributively.
REF. – *On Interpretation,* CC. 4–7. *Post. Anal.,* I, C. 2.
proprium, *n.* a property; an exclusive characteristic accident or attribute.
‡**propter se,** *Latin phrase.* by its very nature; in a necessary connection with a nature.
REF. – *Met.,* VII, C. 5.
prosperity, *n.* a condition of abundant suitable means for connatural human well-being.
protasis, *n.* condition; antecedent or introductory proposition. ANT. – *apodosis.*
providence, *n.* 1. the plan or exemplar whereby things are ordered to an end; deliberate foresight and direction to an end. 2. *loosely.* government.
divine providence, the divine plan directing all things to the end appointed by God, according to the natures of each thing.
immediate providence, foreseeing each individual being and event in itself and directing it individually to its own end and the end of the universe.
mediate providence, planning for something merely in general or through assigning the care of the thing to some intermediate agent.
moral providence, the plan for moral beings, their relations, and destinies.
natural providence, the direction of natural things to their natural ends in accordance with their natural capacities.
supernatural providence, the direction especially of intelligent creatures to an end exceeding their natures and to means proportionate to this end above their natures.
REF. – *S.T.,* I, 22; 103.
proximate, *adj.* 1. the closest to a point from which reference is made. 2. immediate or first in a series. ANT. – *remote.*
prudence, *n.* the cardinal moral virtue or habit of right reason that knows the right things to be done by men and the right way of doing them; the habit of desiring, finding, and choosing the right means for worthy human ends. See chart on VIRTUES for its parts; also see COUNSEL; PROVIDENCE.
REF. – *N. Eth.,* VI, CC. 5, 7, 9. *S.T.,* I, 22, a. 1; I–II, 57, a. 4; II–II, 47; 50. *Truth,* q. 5, a. 1.
prudential certitude, *phrase.* the certainty that a prudent man has in moral contingent matters. See CERTITUDE.
psyche, *n.* 1. the human soul. 2. the mind. 3. conscious powers. 4. *Aristotle.* the vital principle. (Note that the word has a special meaning in Freudian thought. See dictionaries.)
psycho-analysis, *n.* the diagnosis of mental and nervous disorders by careful analysis of the emotional history of the patient. It includes techniques for reviving emotional memories.
psychology, *n.* 1. the science of the human mind and its conscious acts. 2. the science of the human soul and its powers and

operations, cognitive, emotional, and voluntary. ABBR. – *psych.*, *psychol.*

general (experimental) psychology, investigation of conscious human behavior by modern scientific methods. It is an aid to philosophical psychology.

psycho-physical parallelism, see PARALLELISM.

psycho-physical problem, the philosophical problem of the existence, union, and interactions of body and mind in man.

rational psychology, see PHILOSOPHY OF MAN.

public good, *phrase.* the general welfare of the political society; the common social good of a state or civic community, especially if obtained by common means under public authority. See GOOD.

punishment, *n.* deprivation of a favor or good because of a fault. See SANCTION. REF. – *S.T.*, I–II, 87, a. 1; 88.

pure, *adj.* 1. unmixed (as with potency); free from all potency and composition in its objective concept or nature. 2. free from anything that weakens or impairs or changes its nature. 3. simple. 4. chaste.

purpose, *n.* end; final cause. See END.

Q

q., qq., qu., abbreviations for *question, questions.*

quality, *n.* **1.** *metaphysics.* an accident intrinsically completing and perfecting a substance either in its being or in its operation; an attribute of a subject and especially of a form describing what kind of thing it is. See chart on CATEGORIES.
affective quality, a quality of an object capable of producing a pleasant or unpleasant response in a perceiving subject.
passible quality, a quality of a subject by which it is easily changeable in its state, or a fleeting change of this sort; e.g., blushing.
primary quality, *used by Locke and adopted by some modern scholastics.* any one of the physical properties or sensibles which exist in the object as in our perception of them. They are all associated with quantity in the object, as extension, bulk, figure, position, number, etc.
secondary quality, *used by Locke and some later scholastics.* any of those physical properties which cause sensations that differ from the condition of the object; e.g., colors, odors, sounds, etc. They all seem to presuppose an extended object. REF. – *Cat.,* C. 8. *Met.,* V, C. 14. *S.T.,* I, 81, a. 1 ad 5; I–II, 49, a. 2.
quality, *n.* **2.** *logic.* **a.** in a categorical proposition, the affirmative or negative character of the proposition or of its copula. **b.** in a conditional proposition, the affirmative or negative connection between the condition and the conditioned.
quantified, *adj.* in the phrase, "quantified body," i.e., a body which is divisible into the parts included in it, each of which is potentially a unit and a substance.
quantifier, *n.* a term that indicates what the logical quantity or extension of the principal term is; e.g., all, each, this, etc.

quantity, *n.* **1.** *philosophy of nature.* the accident proper to a material substance in virtue of which the body must naturally have extension, i.e., possess distinct integral parts. See chart on CATEGORIES OF BEING.
contiguous quantity, a quantity whose components are in contact at their boundaries which are distinct from each other. See *adjacent* in English dictionaries.
continuous quantity, a quantity uninterrupted in its being so that its components are united by possessing common limits or boundaries.
dimensive quantity, extension or magnitude, having particular dimensions and position so that it can be measured.
discontinuous quantity, discrete; an aggregate of quantities each of which has its own complete limits or boundaries.
successive quantity, quantitative components which follow one another in place, time, movement, or series of some sort.
virtual quantity, some quantitative measure of a quality according to the objects to which a power or principle refers or to which it can or does attain, or according to the rate of action. REF. – *Cat.,* C. 6. *Physics,* V, C. 3. *Met.,* V, C. 13; XI, C. 12. *S.T.,* I, 42, a. 1 ad 1; II–II, 24, a. 4 ad 1, 3; a. 5.
quantity, *n.* **2.** *logic.* **a.** the extension of a term whether subject or predicate; **b.** the personal supposition of the subject of a proposition. See SUPPOSITION.
question, *n.* a truth or proposition under critical study for evidence or precise formulation of its truth. ABBR. – *q., qq.* (*pl.*), *qu., ques.*
disputed question, a problem; an unsettled or debated philosophical question; a proposition which is seriously affirmed and denied by opposing parties.

quiddity, *n.* essence; the answer to the question "what is it?"; the definition.

REF. – *On Being and Essence,* C. 1.

‡**quid pro quo,** *Latin phrase.* **1.** *literally.* something for something. **2.** in onerous contracts, the legal consideration or the just equivalent of the rights or goods exchanged by the contracting parties; thus, ten dollars may be the *quid* (something) paid for a pair of shoes, a *quo* (something).

R

‡**ratio,** *Latin,* *n.* 1. the essence or nature as intelligible; the intelligibility of any essence or form; the intention; the objective concept. 2. the ground, reason, or rationale of a thing; hence, form. This usage often appears in the Oxford translation of Aristotle. 3. the formal perspective under which the subject of a science is considered. See REASON, sense 2.

REF. – *In Boeth. de Trin.,* q. 5, a. 1 ad 6.

ratiocination, *n.* reasoning; drawing a conclusion from premises.

rational, *adj.* 1. possessing or using reason. 2. attained by reasoning. 3. conformed to right reason; judicious.

rationalism, *n.* 1. a view that reason is self-sufficient to know all things and need not be helped by revelation from God. 2. a view that a priori reason, independently of experience and verification of facts, can give certain knowledge of everything.

rational nature, *phrase.* the being of man considered as the principle of man's operations. See HUMAN NATURE.

reaction, *n.* the immediate response to any kind or degree of stimulation of an organism or organ or power.

real, *adj.* that to which existence belongs; that whose act is existence; anything that objectively exists and is not merely something thought about. Some scholastics would include the merely possible under the real. See BEING.

realism, *n.* any form of the philosophical position that accepts (1) the objective existence of the world and beings in it and relations between these beings, independently of human knowledge and desires; (2) the knowability of these objects as they are in themselves; and (3) the need of human conformity to objective reality in man's thought and conduct.

moderate realism, 1. the epistemological viewpoint that man's universal concepts ordinarily represent natures which are objectively real but which in themselves are singular, not universal (the universality is due to the mind's activity). 2. the general epistemological viewpoint of the origin of knowledge from sense, the dependence of knowledge on things as their measure of truth, the distinction of concept from sense image, and the superiority of intellect to sense and feeling.

REF. – John Wild, *Introduction to Realistic Philosophy,* p. 505.

reality, *n.* all existing things, including both God and the universe.

reason, *n.* 1. a. the power of reasoning; the intellect in its reasoning function. b. a name for the intellect. c. the act of reasoning or drawing conclusions from other judgments; discursive thinking. d. the entire rational nature of man. 2. a. the basis or ground or evidence presented for any opinion or conclusion. b. the explanation for something. c. the logical ground for thinking or drawing conclusions, as the premises or the causal clause in a causal proposition or enthymeme. 3. the motive for or cause of a decision or action. See chart on p. 106.

(the) higher reason, the intellect when considering divine, spiritual, and eternal things.

(the) lower reason, the intellect when considering temporal and material things.

particular reason, the cogitative power; a sensory estimate of what is good or harmful to the organism in particular situations.

right reason, 1. reason that is objectively controlled and functions according to the objective measure of truth or of conduct. 2. hence, reason conformed to evidence. 3. reason directing man according to his true end; practical wisdom; prudence. 4. what is just,

SENSES OF REASON AND "RATIO"

1. Reason as a cause	Of natural action: purpose
	Of consent of will: motive
	Of assent of mind: proof or evidence
2. Reason as a norm	Explanation, e.g., "sufficient" reason
	Of judgment, conscience, etc., e.g., "right" reason
3. Reason as the absolute nature or definition of a being	
4. Reason as cognitive power	Sensory: the particular reason or cogitative sense
	Intellectual, esp. in man — Higher / Lower
5. Reason as an act of reasoning	
6. Reason as a name for rational human nature	

sufficient reason, the adequate and necessary objective explanation of something.
Ref. – *S.T.*, I, 63, a. 1; 79, a. 9; 83, a. 4; I–II, 94, aa. 3, 4; 95, a. 2; 100, a. 1; II–II, 153. *Truth*, q. 15, a. 2. J. Peghaire, *Intellectus et Ratio selon S. Thomas d'Aquin*, p. 17.

reason, *v.* 1. to use reason. 2. to give reasons; to prove; to argue. 3. to examine by reason. Ant. – to *sense*, to *believe*, to *perceive*.

reasoning, *n.* 1. the act or process of drawing new judgments from other judgments; discursive thinking; argumentation. 2. the evidence or proofs offered in such thinking. See DEMONSTRATION; DIALECTIC; PROOF.
Ref. – *N. Eth.*, VI, CC. 1, 5. *Topics*, I, CC. 1, 10, 11. *S.T.*, I, 79, a. 9 ad 3; 85, a. 5; II–II, 8, a. 1 ad 2.

rebellion, *n.* organized resistance or use of force against authority. It is especially applied to civil rebellion.

recognition, *n.* that part of the process of memory which identifies recalled impressions as familiar or as past experiences.

rectitude. *n.* 1. *in general.* correctness; rightness. 2. *logic.* correctness in thinking; conformity to logical rules. 3. *epistemology, etc.* logical truth in the mind; right reason. 4. *ethics.* right living; due order of the will in relation to the ultimate end.

reduction, *n.* 1. the act or process of bringing something to a specified form or condition, especially to a more elementary or fundamental form. Thus, a syllogism is reduced to the first figure in order to test its validity; a composite is reduced to its parts; a false statement or false conclusion is *reduced to the impossible* by showing it implies something necessarily false or contradictory or admittedly absurd. Ant. – *eduction.* 2. the mental act of bringing something into a class or genus or within descriptive limits. Thus, substantial change is reduced to the category of substance. 3. *improperly.* to deprive of a form or restore it to the potency of matter. Abbr. – *red.*
Ref. – *Post. Anal.*, I, C. 26. *S.T.*, I, 3, a. 6.

reduplication, *n.* the significance of a term incidental to the subject of a proposition, giving the reason why the term contains the predicate. Compare SPECIFICATION.

FORMS OF REASONING, PROOF, AND REFUTATION

I. Quality of the proof

1. Demonstration (certain)

   Dialectical (probable)
   - Analogy; parable and myth
   - Sampling; statistical
   - Authority and precedent
   - Hypothesis
   - Congruence
   - Systematic explanation

2. Consistent (valid)
   Fallacious
   Irrelevant

II. Form or structure of proof

Direct
- Enthymeme
- Syllogism
  - Categorical
  - Hypothetical
    - Conditional
    - Disjunctive
    - Conjunctive
- Polysyllogism
- Epichereme
- Sorites
- Dilemma

Indirect (negative)
- Contrary instance
- Exclusion
- Reduction to the impossible
- Third alternative (escape from dilemma)

III. Method

1. A priori (which may be either *propter quid* or *quia*)
   A simultaneo (prior reason)

   A posteriori (*quia*)
   - From property to essence
   - From effect to cause

2. Deductive

   Inductive (from particulars)
   - Complete
   - Incomplete
     - Perfect
     - Imperfect

3. From the fact (*quia* proof; it is either *a posteriori* or *a priori*)
   From the reasoned fact (from the cause; *propter quid;* always *a priori*)

4. A pari
   A fortiori

---

reference, *n.* **1.** a relation. **2.** the state of being referred or related to another. ABBR. – *ref.*

referend, the second term of a relation; the signified in a logical relation; relatum.

referent, 1. the first term of a relation. **2.** the sign (of the other) in a logical relation.

reflection, *n.* the mind's attention to itself or to the cognitive or appetitive acts of the thinker; the intellect's turning back on itself or its own acts. ABBR. – *refl.*

ontological reflection, the consideration by the mind of the being or object known in a conscious act.

psychological reflection, the consideration of the conscious past acts or states of the self or the consideration of the internal psychic quality of the act of experience.

self-reflection, attention of the mind to the self as perceived in past or present experiences. REF. – *S.T.*, I, 16, a. 2 ad 1; 87, aa. 1, 3, 4. *Truth*, q. 2, a. 2 ad 2.

reflex, *adj.* **1.** reflective. See REFLECTION. **2.** pertaining to an object in its status as something already known. See CONCEPT, UNIVERSAL; INTENTION, SECOND.

reflex, *n.* an involuntary movement in response to stimulation of the nerves. Physiologically, it is an action produced by the transmission of an afferent impulse to a nerve center and its reflection thence as an efferent impulse to a muscle or gland, independently of volition. Psychologically, it may be a conscious or unconscious response to a stimulus. ABBR. – *refl.*

conditioned (conditional) reflex, a response occurring only as the result of training or acquired association.

unconditional reflex, an unlearned, inherited, or instinctive response.

refutation, *n.* **1.** the act of disproving or showing an argument to be false or wrong. **2.** the reason or evidence supporting the disproof.

rel., abbreviation for *relative, religion, religious.*

relata, *n., pl.* related things or terms.

relation, *n.* the reference of one thing to another; the order (regard, proportion, connection, allusion, etc.) of one to another. See chart on CATEGORIES.

logical relation, a reference of one to another when one or both terms (*a*) are not real, or (*b*) are not really distinct, or (*c*) are related for some non-objective reason, i.e., the foundation of the relation is not real.

mixed relation, a relation that is real considered from one term as the first related term and logical when considered from the other as the first related term; thus, the relation between knower and thing known.

moral relation, a bond between moral entities; e.g., rights.

mutual relation, a relation which is real or logical whether it is considered as existing between subject and term or between term and subject. This is not the same as an equal relation or relation of the *same denomination,* as between a brother and sister who are alike named children.

necessary relation, a transcendental relation.

predicamental (contingent) relation, a relationship that may be present in or absent from an essence without changing the essence. This is the Aristotelian category of relation.

real relation, a reference of one real thing to another really distinct from it because of an objective foundation; a relation existing in things independently of the mind knowing the relation.

transcendental relation, a relation so necessary or essential to a thing that the being cannot be without it and removal of the relation would imply a change of the essence or the destruction of the being. REF. – *Met.,* V, C. 15. *Cat.,* C. 7. *S.T.,* I, 13, a. 7, c. and ad 1; 28, aa. 1, 2, 4. *Truth,* q. 1, a. 5 ad 16. *Power,* q. 7, a. 11.

relative, *adj.* **1.** referred to another in some way; ordered to, connected with, dependent upon, limited by another in some way. **2.** considered in its relation to something else rather than absolutely in itself. **3.** unintelligible or impossible except as related to something else. ABBR. – *rel.* ANT. – *absolute.*

relative opposition, the difference between the two correlative terms; as between cause and effect or sign and signified. REF. – *Power,* q. 7, a. 8 ad 4.

relativism, *n.* **1.** *epistemology.* the view that knowledge entirely depends on and varies with the limited ability of each mind and its conditions of knowing; the denial of absolute truth and certitude. **2.** *ethics.* the view that morals are in no matters intrinsically good or evil but that all depend on variable conditions such as the will of God, customs and conventions, positive laws, degree of culture, social approval, etc.; a denial of unchanging morality and of the immutability of principles of the natural law.

relatum, *n.* the second term of a relation. See REFEREND.

religion, *n.* **1.** the sum of truths and duties binding man to God. **2.** personal belief and worship in relation to God. Religion includes creed, cult, and code. ABBR. – rel.

direct (formal) religion, beliefs concerning God and His activities and immediate personal service to God as distinguished from *indirect worship* which concerns creatures and our duties to others as willed by God.

natural religion, those truths and duties about the relations of God and man which are known or knowable by natural reason.

objective religion, the body of truths and duties binding man to God.

practical religion, 1. the practice of religion; the acts of religion as prayer, adoration, sacrifice, vows, oaths, etc. **2.** the duties of man to God.

subjective religion, personal religious belief and practice.

supernatural religion, the truths, forms of worship, and duties revealed by God to man by special supernatural signs or means.

virtue of religion, the habit or constant will to give to God the worship that is due to Him.

REF. – *S.T.*, II–II, 81, aa. 1–5. *C.G.*, III, C. 119. John Henry Cardinal Newman, *An Essay in Aid of a Grammar of Assent*, C. X.

reminiscence, *n.* that feature of memory which consists in recalling past experiences, images, etc.

remotion from matter, *phrase.* see ABSTRACTION.

remotion, way of, *phrase.* the way of negation, q.v. See NEGATION.

REF. – *C.G.*, I, C. 14.

repentance, *n.* voluntary sorrow for what has been done because it is an offense against God, together with the purpose to amend one's conduct.

representation, *n.* **1.** *in general.* a likeness, imitation, or substitution for an object. **2.** a cognitive or intentional likeness of an object, either in the senses or in the intellect. **3.** a production imitative of another object. **4.** a term or sign signifying or supposing for something else. **5.** the act of forming a likeness of

the object in the knowing power. **6.** the presentation of the retained image to the memory. **7.** the power or right to act as a substitute or authorized agent of another or of a group.

requisite, *adj.* necessary.

reservation, mental, *phrase.* use of a form of words or other signs in which the meaning is not fully expressed externally, but is at least partly ambiguous and held back in the mind.

broad mental reservation, use of an ambiguous conventional expression which reveals one's mind if properly interpreted, but does not reveal the mind clearly nor with any single definite meaning.

strict mental reservation, use of an expression which totally keeps back the meaning while pretending to reveal the mind.

resolution, *n.* analysis, q.v.

resonance, bodily, *phrase.* the bodily effects of and physiological changes accompanying emotional states, such as those of anger, fear, and love.

respect (of opposites), *phrase.* the particular detail or point in which beings or concepts are opposed.

REF. – *S.T.*, I–II, 67, a. 3.

restitution, *n.* **1.** the duty of full just repayment for injustice done to another, particularly for a violation of commutative justice. **2.** the repayment made or to be made for injustice.

REF. – *S.T.*, II–II, 62.

restriction, *n.* **1.** mental reservation. **2.** limitation.

result, *n.* effect; good produced; end achieved.

retort (*retorqueo*), *n.* a reply or refutation which turns the words of the speaker back upon himself.

revelation, *n.* **1.** the manifestation of truth; illumination. **2.** the manner or means of making a revelation. **3.** the truths or objects revealed.

divine revelation, the manifestation of truth to man by God.

natural revelation, 1. manifestation of truth by natural means concerning natural objects. **2.** the truths or objects thus revealed by nature to natural reason.

supernatural revelation, 1. manifestation of truth to man by God through formal speech or explicitly intellectual signs in a manner in which natural objects left to themselves cannot provide evidence for the knowledge communicated. **2.** truths and mysteries thus manifested to man by God.

reward, *n.* a return or repayment for work done. See MERIT; SANCTION.

right, *adj.* directed to the true end; hence, good.

right, *n.* **1.** *subjective right.* the inviolable moral power to do, hold, or claim something as one's own. **2.** *objective right.* the just thing or object over which one has an inviolable moral power. ABBR. – *rt.* See also JURISDICTION; "JUS AD REM"; "JUS IN RE"; OWNERSHIP.

acquired right, a right, natural or positive, that depends on some title obtained from some other source than the simple possession of human nature.

alienable right, a right that may be legitimately given up or exchanged.

coactive right, a perfect right.

connatural right, a natural right that belongs to man just because of his possession of living human nature.

imperfect right, a liberty to do or make or claim something, but which may not be defended by force.

inalienable right, a right so necessary to one's welfare and the performance of one's duties that a person may not give it up.

indefeasible right, a right so necessary to man's moral welfare and the attainment of man's end that he cannot give it up and it cannot be taken from him even by law for any cause whatsoever.

natural right, a right coming from the Author of nature and directly from the natural law.

perfect right, any right that is so complete that one may use proportionate force if necessary to defend the right; a right over an object that is capable of physical defense and valueless if not defended against unjust attack.

positive right, a right that belongs to a person by grant of positive law.

  civil right, a right granted by constitutional or customary or statutory law.

  divine positive right, a positive right granted by divine positive law; a supernatural right.

true right, a right granted to fulfill a moral duty or achieve a necessary end. It is contrasted with a *precarious* right or simple liberty to act in non-necessary matters and which may be restricted by positive law.

REF. – *S.T.,* II–II, 57.

rule, *n.* **1.** a principle, method, or regular procedure of action. **2.** a standard, especially an accepted or customary standard. **3.** authoritative direction or control over a subject or inferior; government. ABBR. – *r.* See NORM; DOMINATIVE POWER; JURISDICTION.

despotic rule, rule like that of a tyrant, for the sake of the ruler; the rule of force.

politic rule, rule or control for the sake of the governed, like constitutional or royal rule over free men; the rule of persuasion.

REF. – *Politics,* III, C. 6; VII, CC. 3, 14. *S.T.,* I, 81, a. 3 ad 2.

S

s., abbreviation for *series, set, society*.

sacrifice, *n.* **1.** *broad sense.* a spiritual offering of something to God, as an alms or bodily affliction. **2.** *strict sense.* the act of the virtue of religion by which an authorized person (priest) offers a precious gift to God and somehow changes the gift as a sign of God's supreme excellence and man's recognition of God's supreme dominion. A sacrifice of reparation also includes immolation of the gift. REF. – *S.T.,* II–II, 85; III, 48, a. 3. *C.G.,* III, C. 120.

sanction, *n.* **1.** *in general.* the inviolability of law. **2.** the means adopted to make the law inviolable.

imperfect sanction, one that is insufficient as a motive to obey the law or that is disproportionate to the moral value of the act sanctioned or that is both insufficient and disproportionate.

medicinal sanction, one set up as a remedy for violations of the law.

natural sanction, a sanction coming from the natural law and consisting in natural rewards and penalties. The goods and punishments may be in the order of personal or individual goods, social goods, or universal goods (namely, the gain or loss of the all-good object of beatitude, God).

perfect sanction, one that is both adequate to motivate the good deed or to deter an agent from the evil and proportionate to the value of the deed or misdeed.

positive sanctions, sanctions set up by positive law.

sanction in the active sense, the decree of the lawgiver setting up benefits for the observance and penalties for the violation of law.

sanction in the passive sense, the legally established benefits and penalties set up by the lawgiver; and especially, the penalties legally threatened for violation of the law.

temporal *or* eternal sanctions, any sanction measured by the duration of its benefits or penalties.

vindicative sanctions, penal sanctions set up for the purpose of restoring moral order and championing justice against violators of law.

scandal, *n.* **1.** *strict ethical sense.* any act or omission even if not evil in itself but which is likely to induce another to do wrong. **2.** *popularly.* a careless or malicious defamation of others. **3.** *popularly.* some disgraceful act, circumstance, or event.

active scandal, giving or causing scandal to another.

direct scandal, performing an evil act or omission with the intention of inducing another to do evil. It is called *diabolical* when the intention is malicious and not merely for selfish advantage or pleasure.

indirect scandal, performing an act when another's evil act is foreseen as likely or certain, but is permitted rather than intended.

passive scandal, taking scandal; being scandalized; falling into evil because of another's act or omission.

pharisaical scandal, insincere passive scandal taken from the good or indifferent

---

SCANDAL IN SENSE 1

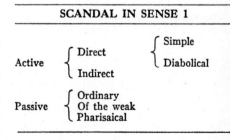

Active	{ Direct	{ Simple
	Indirect	{ Diabolical
Passive	{ Ordinary	
	Of the weak	
	Pharisaical	

---

conduct of others or such scandal that hinders spiritual good by pretense of scandal.

REF. – *S.T.*, II–II, 43, esp. aa. 1–3.

SCG; S.C.G., abbreviations for St. Thomas' *Summa contra Gentiles.*

scholasticism, *n.* **1.** the philosophy and theology of the schoolmen or of the Christian schools of the Middle Ages and of their modern successors. **2.** *specifically.* scholastic philosophy, i.e., the systematic philosophy developed in the Middle Ages from Aristotelian and Augustinian roots, highly developed by St. Thomas Aquinas, and marked by tendencies to metaphysical, theistic, and humanist interests and by conformity to Catholic orthodoxy. Three periods of scholasticism are often distinguished. (1) The medieval period from St. Anselm to Capreolus (1060–1440). The Golden Age is the latter half of the thirteenth century. (2) The second scholasticism of the Counter-Reformation period, or the Spanish-Portuguese Revival, running from about 1520–1640, and declining after the spread of Cartesianism and other troubles in the Church. (3) The modern period, sometimes known as new scholasticism, beginning in the latter half of the nineteenth century and officially recognized by Pope Leo XIII in 1879.

scholion (scholium), *n.* **1.** a marginal note or comment on a classical text. **2.** some information or discussion supplementing a thesis or proposition, such as an historical note, a textual comment, a scientific or theological item for comparison, or some practical application of the proposition.

school, *n.* a group of teachers and disciples related to each other by common traditions, teachings, methods, or interest in common problems. ABBR. – *sch., S., s.*

schoolman, *n.* a scholastic or medieval university professor of theology, philosophy, or logic.

science, *n.* **1.** *Greek and strict philosophical sense.* the certain intellectual knowledge of something in its causes; universal, demonstrated, organized knowledge of facts and truths and the reasons or causes of these. Aristotle and St. Thomas

demand necessary subject matter and demonstration as essential characteristics of science. **2.** certain, reasoned, and usually generalized knowledge of some special subject matter, such as chemistry. ABBR. – *sc., sci.*

normative science, a science leading to the discovery of rules, as ethics and optics.

practical science, a science concerned with action or practice. See KNOWLEDGE.

speculative science, a science concerned with the discovery of truth for truth's sake, i.e., for the sake of knowing. See CONTEMPLATION ; WISDOM.

subaltern (subalternated) science, 1. a science that provides material for the study of a higher science, or whose subject matter is a part of the subject matter of a more inclusive science; a specialty within a particular scientific field. **2.** a science that draws its proper principles from a higher science. **3.** a science subordinate to the purpose of a higher science. In this sense the subaltern science is also called *subordinate* or *ancillary* to the other.

subalternating science, 1. a science superior to another by including its subject matter in a fuller way and correlating that subject matter with other materials. **2.** the science that supplies the proper principles for another science. **3.** the master or *architectonic* science whose purpose governs the purpose and uses of the subordinate science.

REF. – *Post Anal.*, I, C. 2; II, C. 1. *Met.*, VI, C. 1. *N. Eth.*, VI, C. 6. *S.T.*, I–II, 57, a. 2. *C.G.*, III, CC. 78, 79, 91. *In Boeth. de Trin.*, q. 5, a. 1 ad 5.

‡**scientia media,** *Latin phrase.* **1.** *literally.* middle knowledge. **2.** that sign of God's knowledge in which He knows futuribles and free futures in their status as futuribles. Molina calls it midway or intermediate between the objects of divine vision and of simple intelligence, as well as intermediate between God's knowledge of necessary objects and of free futures. **3.** a mixed science, like astronomy, which pertains to both the first and second modes of abstraction.

‡se, *Latin pronoun, reflexive, third person, sing. or pl., in accusative or ablative case.* "self," as in *a se, in se, per se, propter se,* etc.

secret, *n.* 1. a fact, event, matter, or intention kept hidden from others or disclosed only confidentially. 2. *in the moral sense.* a hidden fact or intention which may not be revealed without harm to charity or without injustice to another.

natural secret, a fact, event, or matter which by its very nature would cause harm if disclosed to others and which natural human fellowship requires be kept secret, apart from any agreement to do so.

promised secret, a fact or intention which has been revealed to one or discovered by him but which one has promised not to make known after he came to know the secret.

secret of trust *or* professional secret, a secret which involves an agreement or implicit contract between the giver and hearer of the secret before it is communicated and which binds in justice after its communication to a privileged adviser.

‡secundum quid, *Latin phrase. literally.* "according to something"; hence, in some respect or only in the respect noted; in a qualified, restricted, or secondary sense; from a particular or limited point of view.

seek, *v.* to desire or pursue a good not yet possessed.

self, *n.* 1. a being having personality; the person considered as subject of its own acts. 2. any being considered in relation to its own identity. 3. *as a combining form.* to, for, in, toward, with one-self; denoting the agent or subject of action, the person or thing affected, the person in which the quality inheres, the beneficiary of something. 4. the reflex expression of attention to the self.

self-active, able to act or acting without external influence or stimulus. It is said of an immanent active power and also of a self-sufficient being.

self-consciousness, awareness of one's acts or of one's self. See AWARENESS; EXPERIENCE.

self-contradictory, inconsistent; having elements in a proposition, theory, or derived concept which are contradictorily opposed to each other.

self-control, interior and free command over one's self, one's actions, desires, etc., particularly when this self-mastery is according to right reason.

self-defense, the right or the act of protecting one's own rights by one's own use of physical power.

self-determination, 1. freely deciding something for one's self by one's own power; causing one's own course of action; independence. 2. the right of political independence.

self-evident, immediately evident upon inspection, without further exposition or proof. See EVIDENT.

self-existent, 1. a being that exists independently without any cause of its being or any need of any other being for its existence or activity; a being that exists by its essence or nature; a being that exists just because it is itself; *ipsum esse.* 2. hence, a being that is uncaused and completely self-sufficient and only logically related to other beings.

selfhood, the person or the personality.

self-perfective, acting in such a way that the term or fruit of action is primarily or wholly within the agent and for the good of the agent; immanent.

self-possession, independent control of one's self for one's own good under God; *sui juris.* See PERSON; PERSONALITY.

self-sufficient, independent; not needing others for one's being, or activity, or economic welfare, or happiness, or political prosperity, etc.

semantics, *n.* the science which treats of the growth of language. It is related to the logic of terms.

semasiology, *n.* the department of philology treating of the significance of words and the development of their meanings.

seminal principle, *phrase.* see PRINCIPLE.

sensa, *n., pl.* the objects of sensation, particularly those actually sensed.

sensation, *n.* 1. an act of a sense power; consciousness of singular, concrete, material objects by means of one of the sense powers and organs in a material way. **2.** cognitive representation of some material thing in a material way.

sense, *n.* **1.** any power which knows concrete material things in a material way. **2.** a collective term for sensory knowledge. **3.** the organ of sensation. **4.** the sensitive soul. See POWERS OF MAN.

central sense, the internal sense with the several functions: (*a*) of awareness of our sensations; (*b*) of unifying the cognitions of the several external senses into one image of the same material thing which the different distinct sensations represent; and (*c*) of discriminating between the various external sensations.

cogitative sense, the estimative sense as it is in man operating under the influence of reason; particular reason.

common sense, 1. the central sense as perceiving a common sensible. **2.** practical judgment or ordinary sound judgment. **3.** general convictions of most men. **4.** *some scholastics.* the immediate judgments of the first principles commonly accepted by men because of their objective self-evident nature. See CERTITUDE, NATURAL. **5.** *Reid.* general convictions of men reached by a blind intellectual instinct.

estimative sense, see COGITATIVE SENSE; INSTINCT.

external sense, any sense power which gives immediate cognition of the external material world in one of its sensible properties.

internal sense, a sense power which uses the images of the other senses as its immediate object, or which gives only mediate sensory knowledge of the external material world.

moral sense, see MORAL.

proper sense, an external sense with a special object or proper sensible.

sense memory, the imagination in its function of preserving, recalling, and concretely recognizing past images.

unifying sense, the central sense.

REF. – *On the Soul,* II, C. 12; III, CC. 2, 8. *S.T.,* I, 78, a. 4.

sense appetite, *phrase.* any animal power of seeking sensibly known goods or flee-

ing from sensibly recognized evils. See APPETITE; POWERS OF MAN.

sensible, *adj. or n.* **1.** the object of a sense, capable of being known by a sense. **2.** anything knowable by the senses either immediately or by their help.

accidental sensible (*sensibile per accidens,* **incidental sensible),** a characteristic of a being that is not known by the senses but known by the intellect with the help of sense knowledge of the sensible accidents of a thing; as substance, beauty, unity.

common sensible, something naturally perceptible by more than one external sense and primarily by none of them; as size is sensible to both the eye through color and to the hand through pressure, temperature, etc.

primary and secondary sensible, see QUALITY.

proper sensible, the object primarily and by its nature attained by each single sense; the formal object of each sense.

sensible *per se,* what is immediately perceptible by any external sense.

REF. – *On the Soul,* II, C. 6. *S.T.,* I, 17, a. 2; 78, a. 3 ad 2.

sensism, *n.* the view that reduces all cognitive and appetitive powers of man to sensory and bodily appetites. It therefore regards concepts as mere composite images, denies universals, denies any essential difference between sense and intellect and between bodily appetites and the will, and denies a substantial soul.

sensuality, *n.* the sensitive appetites.

REF. – *S.T.,* I, 81, a. 1. *Truth,* q. 25, a. 1.

sentence, *n.* **1.** *logic.* a related group of words containing a subject and a predicate with their modifiers and expressing a complete thought. **2.** *Book of Sentences.* an instructive citation from an authority.

sentient, *adj.* having the power of sensation.

sentiment, *n. strictest sense.* a conscious act of the will liking or disliking something. It is distinguished from emotion, which is purely sensible and often more intense than the mildness of a sentiment.

separation, *n.* **1.** *in general.* the act or process of dividing or disconnecting one thing, part, or member from another. **2.** the state of such division. **3.** the mental act, different from abstraction, which detaches form from matter or substance from attribute. **4.** a negative judgment. **5.** *in particular*. the third mode of abstraction which mentally frees existence from a material subject and from material conditions, preparing for the judgment of existence about such a subject. **6.** the dividing of the parties to a marriage and the release from their obligation to common life. See DIVORCE, IMPERFECT.

non-mutual separation, a real dividing of things or their parts in such a way that the first can exist without the second, but the second cannot be or act without the first.

series, *n.* an orderly arrangement of one thing after another. ABBR. – *s*.

per accidens series; *per se* series, see CAUSE, SUBORDINATE.

REF. – *Truth,* q. 2, a. 10.

sign, *n.* **1.** something which leads one to knowledge of something else. **2.** that which refers to and stands for another. **3.** a sensible manifestation of a truth; as a miracle is a proof or sign of some doctrine. **4.** an instance used as proof of a general proposition. Divisions of senses 1 and 2 follow.

arbitrary (conventional) sign, a sign which has a connection with the signified only by the agreement of men; e.g., a definite group of letters is connected by agreement with a particular object such as a fish; a flag is thus connected with a nation. See WORD.

formal (pure) sign, one which has a likeness or form common to the sign and the signified. It leads to knowledge of the signified without being itself first known; e.g., a concept thus leads to knowledge of a real object. See MEDIUM.

instrumental sign, a tool used to give meaning or understanding of another, but not based on likeness of sign and signified; e.g., spoken and written words and numerals lead to knowledge of things and mental states.

manifestative sign, one that shows the existence of something else; e.g., clue to criminal.

natural sign, something which has a natural connection with another and so leads one to a knowledge of the other with which it is connected; e.g., smoke-fire; world–God.

substitutive sign, one that takes the place of some other thing in regard to thought about or understanding of that other; e.g., words substituting for things and for concepts. See SUPPOSITION.

signate, *adj.* designated. See MATTER.

sign of knowledge, *phrase.* a conceptually distinct stage in the order of knowledge or will, though the stages are simultaneous and one in the intellect's or will's act. It is especially applied to the steps in God's knowledge and choice, where the act is all one and eternal and indivisible in God, but is virtually multiple and in a certain sequence in our way of understanding it.

signification, *n.* the capacity of a term to represent some object to the mind; the meaning of a sign; the intelligibility of a relation between two or more. See MEANING; SUPPOSITION.

similar, *adj.* nearly but not exactly the same as another. See ANALOGOUS; SAME; UNIVOCAL.

similitude, *n.* **1.** a mental form resembling the form of the object known. **2.** some likeness or resemblance of one to another. **3.** an object resembling another.

simple, *adj.* **1.** not having parts; not extended; undivided and indivisible. ANT. – *composite.* See chart on UNITY. **2.** not having potency or imperfection; pure. ANT. – *mixed.* See PERFECTION.

simple intelligence, *phrase.* simple understanding, q.v.

simplicity, *n.* absence of parts in a being.

essential simplicity, absence of constituent principles of the essence or nature.

metaphysical simplicity, having no composition of any kind.

physical simplicity, essential simplicity; no composition in the nature or essence.

quantitative (integral) simplicity, absence of material or extended parts.

simply, *adj.* **1.** absolutely; without qualification. **2.** exactly as it is in the concrete or whole.

REF. – *S.T.*, III, 50, a. 5.

simultaneous, *adj.* occurring, existing, acting at the same time or in the same species or in the same relationship.

REF. – *Cat.*, C. 13.

sin, *n.* an evil human act; "a word, deed, or desire in opposition to the eternal law" (St. Augustine); a deliberate offense by thought, word, deed, or omission against the law of God; an inordinate human act.

philosophical sin, something contrary to reason. See UNNATURAL.

theological sin, an offense regarded as against God, not merely against human nature.

REF. – St. Augustine, *Contra Faustum*, XXII, 27. *S.T.*, I–II, 71, a. 1. *C.G.*, III, C. 143.

singular, *adj.* single; individual; noting one person, thing, or class by itself. USES – *singular* concept, nature, person, proposition, substance, term, etc.

situs, *n.* the relative arrangement of the integral parts of a body in place; position; posture; the eighth category; e.g., standing, sitting, stooping. Situs now often connotes the normal location of a living organ or part in the whole body.

socialism, *n.* the economic and political theory of collective or governmental ownership and control of the essential means (capital goods) for the production and distribution of material goods.

society, *n.* the permanent moral union of two or more for a specific common good to be attained by their co-operative activity. ABBR. – *s., soc., socy.*

civil society, the state, q.v.

conjugal society, the state of marital union between husband and wife.

conventional (arbitrary, pactitious) society, one whose end and nature are determined by the free consent of its members.

corporative society, an occupational, vocational, or functional group; a freely organized, semipublic, autonomous society, intermediate between the family

and the state, and comprising all who engage in the same type of labor, trade, or profession, organized with the common economic well-being or professional excellence of all its members as the end of the society.

domestic society, 1. the family. **2.** the household.

imperfect society, 1. a society incomplete in its end, i.e., one whose purpose is not an essential human good. **2.** *especially.* a society incomplete in its possession and control of means to its end.

natural society, one whose general existence, specific end, essential nature, and essential properties are determined by the natural law because its end is a natural necessity of human nature. ANT. – *conventional society.*

perfect society, 1. a society with a complete simply human good that in its own order is not subordinate to a higher good. **2.** a society complete in its possession and right of control over all the means to attain its specific end. The first is also called *perfect in end;* the second, *perfect in means.*

REF. – *N. Eth.*, VIII, C. 9. *Politics*, I, C. 2.

sophism, *n.* a fallacious argument meant to deceive. See FALLACY.

sophistic, sophistical, *adj.* like the sophists, merely resembling philosophy; clever or plausible, but invalid and misleading.

REF. – *Met.*, IV, C. 2.

sorites, *n.* an argument consisting of an abridged series of syllogisms in which the predicate of one proposition becomes the subject of the subsequent proposition until the conclusion is reached in which the subject of the first proposition is joined with the predicate of the last premise in the series.

soul, *n.* **1.** *in general.* the ultimate intrinsic principle of life; the vital principle of a living substance; the substantial form of a living body; the first act of a physical (organic) body having life potentially. **2.** *specifically.* the human soul. **a.** *preliminary definition:* the intrinsic ultimate principle of human conscious life or of man's

knowing and willing. **b.** *in philosophy of nature:* the vital principle or substantial form of a living human being; the first act of the disposed human body with its potency for life. **c.** *in philosophy of man and metaphysics,* after proof: the spiritual and immortal substantial form of an organized human body.
REF. – *On the Soul,* II, CC. 1, 2, 4. *S.T.,* I, 75, a. 1; 76, a. 1.

source, *n.* that which furnishes a first and continuous supply of something; a constant principle in any order of causality, but especially in material and efficient causality, as a source of wealth, of knowledge, of power, or (in the order of final causality and exemplarism) a source of inspiration.

sovereignty, *n.* supreme power of ruling a perfect society.

space, *n.* three-dimensional extension conceived as abstracted from bodies and serving as a receptacle for bodies.

absolute space, the sum of all real and possible space considered as one space.

imaginary space, the container of real and possible bodies.

possible (ideal) space, space unoccupied, but occupiable.

real space, the space actually occupied by three-dimensional bodies; the container of real bodies.

species, *n.* **1.** *logic.* the predicable that designates the class to which a substance belongs; the class comprising the constituent notes of the genus and the specific difference; that concept which expresses the total and exclusive essence known to be common to many individuals; the specific essence. ABBR. – *sp., spec.* See CONCEPT, UNIVERSAL, REFLEX; DEFINITION, METAPHYSICAL; ESSENCE; PREDICABLE.

least (lowest) species, that which contains no species below it; that which is a species, but in no way a genus; the proper species; the specific essence.
REF. – *On Being and Essence,* C. 2.

species, *n.* **2.** *epistemology, philosophy of man.* a likeness or representation of the object; the cognitive form representing the object and present in the cognitive power as the intrinsic principle determin-

ing the knowing power to know actually and to know this object; the sensation or the concept. See INTENTION; REPRESENTATION.

expressed species, the completed sensation or concept as a vital likeness of the object present in the cognitive power.

impressed species, the likeness of the object as objectively caused by the object affecting the senses or by the agent intellect and the image of the object affecting the possible intellect.

intelligible species, a representation in the intellect.

sensible species, a representation in a sense faculty.

species, *n.* **3.** *metaphysics.* accidents or appearances. **4.** *debated biological sense.* a natural class in a series of living beings descended from a common stock and indefinitely fertile among themselves.

specifically, *adj.* **1.** in the same species or in the same form; according to its specific difference. **2.** definitely; concretely; as it is in concrete instances. ABBR. – *specif.*

specification, *n.* **1.** *logic.* **a.** a modification which designates definitely the note or attribute according to which the subject possesses the predicate; e.g., "Man, inasmuch as he is rational, can solve problems." **b.** that which puts something in its definite class. **2.** *metaphysics, philosophy of man.* **a.** an actualization of a potency and a removing of its indetermination. **b.** a definite actuality in a power in regard to a definite object. See FORM; SPECIES. The adjective is *specificative* or *specifying;* the verb is *to specify.*

speculation, *n.* thought for truth's sake; contemplation; theoretical study or knowledge not directed immediately to practice or action. See INTELLECT; PRINCIPLE; SCIENCE; WISDOM.

speech, *n.* **1.** formal use of signs to convey one's thoughts; deliberate use of conventional signs to communicate thought to others. **2.** any making of the unknown known to another. See TRUTH, sense 4.
REF. – *Truth,* q. 9, a. 5, a. 7 ad 4.

spirit, *n.* **1.** a positively immaterial living substance or form. **2.** *theology.* the Holy

Spirit, the third person in God. Abbr. – *sp.* See INCORPOREAL; MATTER.

pure spirit, an immaterial substance, not merely a form; a being with no intrinsic or extrinsic dependence on matter and no substantial union of nature with matter.

spiritual, *adj.* positively immaterial; intrinsically independent of matter at least in being and in some activities; not material in essence or act. See the chart s.v. *immaterial.*

S.T.; S. Th., abbreviations for *Summa Theologica* (*Theologiae*) of St. Thomas Aquinas.

state, *n.* 1. *logic.* the tenth category of habit, q.v. 2. a relatively permanent position in accordance with one's nature or permanently assumed obligations. 3. *political philosophy.* the permanent moral union of many families for obtaining perfect temporal happiness and endowed with full authority to exact co-operation of its members for that end; sovereign temporal society; the perfect civic community. See JUSTICE; SOCIETY; SOVEREIGNTY.
REF. – *N. Eth.,* VIII, C. 9. *Politics,* I, C. 2; III, C. 9; VII, C. 8.

statement, *n.* a variant of the same proposition, such as the passive voice for the active voice; e.g., "St. Thomas wrote this." "This was written by St. Thomas." See FORMULA.

sterilization, *n.* the act of rendering a man or woman infertile and incapable of generating children, but not incapable of sexual relations. The operation is referred to as vasectomy for the male and usually as salpingectomy for the female.

eugenic sterilization, infertility induced not for the good of the patient but for the supposed good of the race by preventing undesirable offspring.

punitive sterilization, infertility induced as a penalty for crime.

therapeutic sterilization, infertility induced or permitted because of some organic need of the patient's health.

stewardship, *n.* the right or the duty to take care of something whose substance belongs to another owner.

sub., abbreviation for *subaltern, subordinate, substitute(s).*

subaltern, *adj.* of inferior or lower rank. It is said in logic of the relation of species to genus, of a particular proposition to a corresponding universal proposition of the same matter and quality, and of one science to another. See SCIENCE.

subcontrary, *adj.* lower or less than contrary in difference. Subcontrary opposition exists between particular propositions which differ only in quality.

subject, *n.* 1. *logic.* a. the term signifying that about which some declaration or predication is made. b. the inferior of a universal concept or common term. 2. *metaphysics.* a. substance in relation to other predicates or attributes; as, *subject* of existence, *subject* of accidents. b. the first member of a relation; the referred. ANT. – *term.* 3. *epistemology.* a percipient or conscious being, as distinguished from other things known as the objects of which the percipient can be conscious or by which he can be affected. 4. *philosophy of nature.* the recipient of change; the substrate; the recipient of any perfection or form. 5. *philosophy of man.* a. the ego or self. b. the power or function which is controlled by a habit, as the irascible appetite is the subject of the habit of meekness. 6. *ethics.* a. the holder of a right. b. the person under the authority of a ruler or superior. ABBR. – *subj.* See chart under OBJECT.

subjective, *adj.* 1. relating to, belonging to, or emphasizing the subject of mental states; something within the mind. 2. emphasizing personal experiences, impressions, feelings, or reactions, but not adequately controlled by objective comparisons and tests. ABBR. – *subj.*

subjective parts of virtue, see VIRTUE.

subjectivism, *n.* 1. any philosophical doctrine that claims to have no direct knowledge or certitude about external objects. 2. any doctrine which admits no objective norm of truth or of morals. 3. individualism and relativism in a philosophical position. ANT. – *realism.*

subject matter, *phrase.* the object of consideration or the topic of discussion.

subject-object, *n.* the thinking subject or its acts as object of its own thought or reflection, as in self-consciousness or psychological reflection.

sublime, *adj.* grand, supreme, or overpowering in beauty.

subordination, *n.* the relation of lower to higher, or inferior to superior in any respect of excellence, authority, dependence, purpose, completeness, etc.

subsistence, *n.* **1.** the existence proper to a whole and uncommunicated substance. **2.** the formal perfection whereby a nature is completed and is uncommunicated to another. **3.** the existence of the being who exists essentially or by identity with His essence; the being who is completely self-sufficient for existence and action. See "IPSUM ESSE"; PERSONALITY.

subsistent, *adj.* having being and operation through itself, not through union with another.

subsistent form, see FORM.

substance, *n.* a being whose essence naturally requires it to exist in itself; *ens per se; ens in se;* a being that has existence in itself and by virtue of itself as an ultimate distinct subject of being. Loosely it is equivalent to essence and nature. See chart on CATEGORIES OF BEING.

complete substance, a whole substance; a natural unit.

first substance, a singular or individual substance, and usually considered as existing and not merely possible.

incomplete substance, a constituent substantial part or intrinsic substantial principle of a substance.

second substance, a species or genus of substance; some substance regarded as a universal objective concept; what is defined and has being in the primary sense.

separated substance, a created intellectual subsistent being. See SPIRIT.

substance considered as substrate, a finite substance regarded as the subject of the accidents inhering in it or of the changes occurring to it.

REF. – *Cat.,* C. 5. *Met.,* V, C. 8; VII, CC. 1, 3, 4; XII, CC. 2, 3. *S.T.,* I, 3, a. 5 ad 1; III, 77, a. 1 ad 2. *C.G.,* I, C.

25, last paragraph. *Power,* q. 7, a. 3 ad 4; 9, aa. 1, 2.

substantial, *adj.* belonging to substance rather than to accidents; reducible to the category of substance. See CHANGE, SUBSTANTIAL; FORM, SUBSTANTIAL; PART, SUBSTANTIAL; UNION. An artefact is rarely referred to as substantial.

substrate (substratum), *n.* **1.** substance considered as the subject supporting its accidents. **2.** substance considered as the subject of changes. **3.** material cause or passive subjective potency; prime matter.

subsume, *v.* **1.** to include in a class or group of some kind; to classify. **2.** to show that some fact or instance is covered by the pertinent principle or rule.

subsumption, *n.* a minor premise either in direct reasoning or in rebuttal.

sufficient reason, *phrase.* the adequate and necessary objective explanation of something. See REASON.

‡**sui juris,** *Latin genitive of possession of* suum jus, *phrase.* belonging to itself; having its own end and rights; having ontological and legal (juridical) independent existence and existing for its own good; not owned by any being (other than God).

‡**summum bonum,** *Latin phrase.* the supreme good; the object of beatitude, q.v.

‡**summum genus (supremum genus),** *Latin phrases.* the highest class; one of the ten categories.

Sum. Th., an abbreviation sometimes used for the *Summa Theologica (Theologiae)* of St. Thomas Aquinas.

superiority, *n.* higher excellence or authority than another being or class of beings.

essential superiority, greater and other excellence, not merely in degree, but in nature of its being and its activities, so that the lower nature totally lacks the perfections of the higher nature.

REF. – *S.T.,* I, 83, a. 3.

supernatural, *adj.* exceeding the powers, forces and laws, activities, course or order and end of nature or of any particular nature; caused by God alone in a natural being without the concurrent efficient causality of secondary causes (but not without the material causality of an existing subject). See BEATITUDE, SUPERNATURAL; END, SUPERNATURAL; GRACE; MIRACLE; ORDER, SUPERNATURAL; PROVIDENCE, SUPERNATURAL; VIRTUE, SUPERNATURAL.

superstition, *n.* false, base, misdirected, or excessive religious worship either in the manner of worshiping or in the object worshiped. It includes many practices, such as idolatry, spiritism, and fortune-telling.

REF. – *S.T.*, II–II, 92–96.

supposition, *n.* the use of a substantive term in context to denote a certain object or objects; the exact sense and extension of the term as a substitute for the thing or things signified. The speaker's or writer's intention, expressed in context, selects both the meaning among several which the term bears and the special object out of various possible ones to which the term's meaning is applied.

absolute supposition, use of the term for the nature as such. See DEFINITION; NATURE, ABSOLUTE.

collective supposition, use of a common term for the inferiors taken as a group but not for each of them taken separately. See CONCEPT, COLLECTIVE.

common (general) supposition, the use of a common term to signify either a common nature or the individuals possessing such a common nature. See CONCEPT, UNIVERSAL.

confused supposition, use of the common term for some undetermined members of the class possessing the common nature.

determinate (disjunctive) supposition, use of a common term for some definite members of the class possessing the common nature, so that other members of the class are excluded in the context.

distributive supposition, use of the common term for each and all of the individuals possessing the common nature.

formal supposition, use of a term as a sign of a thing or nature.

logical supposition, use of a term for an object as it is in the mind.

material supposition, use of a term to signify the term itself, such as its spelling and phonetics.

particular supposition, the limitation of a common term by a particular or indefinite pronoun.

real supposition, the use of a term as a sign of a real being, excluding beings of the mind.

singular supposition, use of a term to signify an individual actual or individual possible being.

REF. – E. Gilson, *History of Christian Philosophy in the Middle Ages,* pp. 679, 681, notes 38 and 42.

suppositum, *n., pl.* **-a.** a substance that is

MAIN DIVISIONS OF SUPPOSITION

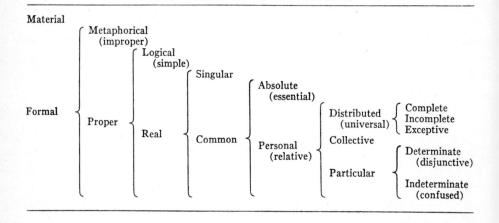

complete in itself and uncommunicated; an ultimate complete subject of its own being. Obsolete forms are *supposit, supposite*. See PERSON; SUBSISTENCE.

syllogism, *n.* **1.** an argument consisting of three propositions so connected that if the first two are posited, the third necessarily follows. **2.** a simple and complete argument. See the chart on REASONING.

complex syllogism, one that contains a complex or compound categorical proposition.

hypothetical syllogism, one that contains a hypothetical proposition as a premise, either conditional or disjunctive or conjunctive.

modal syllogism, one that contains a modal proposition.

practical syllogism, one whose conclusion is a singular proposition concerning action or choice. See CONSCIENCE; JUDGMENT, PRACTICAL.

syncategorematic, *adj.* having meaning only when used together with another word or term: as any, all, alone.

REF. – Ph. Boehner, O.F.M., *Medieval Logic: An Outline of Its Development from 1250 to circa 1400*, 19–26. E. Gilson, *History of Christian Philosophy in the Middle Ages,* pp. 678–679, notes 36 and 37.

synderesis, *n.* the natural habit of knowing the basic principles of the natural law; the knowledge of the universal first principles of the practical order.

REF. – *S.T.,* I, 79, a. 12; I–II, 94, a. 1 ad 2. *Truth,* q. 16, a. 1.

synesis, *n.* good judgment in particular moral matters.

REF. – *S.T.,* II–II, 51, aa. 3, 4.

synteresis, *n.* synderesis, q.v.

synthesis, *n.* **1.** an act of mind combining simple conceptions into more complex ones. **2.** any combining of factors, forces, ideas, etc., into something more complex; thus, a synthesis of forms, a synthesis of relations in a system. **3.** *fairly rare.* the deductive method of elaborating conclusions from a small basic set of premises.

synthetic judgment, see JUDGMENT.

system, *n.* **1.** some kind of real or logical order, especially if it is on a large and complex scale. **2.** a number of bodily organs acting together to perform one of the main bodily functions, as the nervous *system.* **3.** a coherent but unprovable explanation of reality or of history, or a certain interpretation of reality, but which is also incapable of assimilating new truths, however evident, if opposed to the system; as the Kantian *system,* the mechanistic *system,* the Marxian *system.* Scholasticism contends that it is not a philosophy in this sense of a system. For, though it is a highly complex and coherent body of truths, it is based on evident principles, and is open to constant growth and capable of assimilating new truths.

REF. – Maurice de la Taille, *The Mystery of Faith,* p. ix.

T

taste, *n.* 1. appreciation or enjoyment of an object. 2. the external sense adapted to perceive flavors.

good taste, appreciation proportionate to the intrinsic merits of an object.

teleology, *n.* finality.

temperance, *n.* 1. general moderation in conduct. 2. *specifically.* the cardinal virtue of habitual moderation in the use of sensibly pleasurable things according to the rule of reason; reason's control of the concupiscible appetite. 3. sobriety in the use of intoxicants. ABBR. – *temp.* See VIRTUE.

REF. – *N. Eth.*, III, CC. 10–12. *S.T.*, II–II, 141, aa. 3, 4; 149.

temporal, *adj.* 1. lasting only for a time; temporary. ANT. – *eternal, immortal.* 2. of this world. ANT. – *spiritual, heavenly.* 3. civil, lay. ANT. – *ecclesiastical.* 4. belonging to, limited by, characterized by time and change.

tendency, *n.* an inclination, disposition, or desire; i.e., either an attraction to move or act in a particular way to a particular good or an aversion from a particular type of evil. See APPETITE.

conscious (elicited) tendency, experienced striving or conation toward a good or away from an evil.

habitual tendency, an acquired regular tendency to seek some good or avoid some evil.

natural tendency, an inborn tendency, identical with the power of acting for a particular type of object, and not necessarily conscious in its operation.

term, *n.* 1. *metaphysics, philosophy of nature.* the first and last units, points, or terminals of any series.

formal term, the form lost in the change or the new form appearing as the result of the change.

term from which, the state or condition of a being at the start of change in it; initial term; *terminus a quo.*

term of a relation, the being to which a subject is referred. ANT. – *subject* of the relation.

term of a right, the object over which a person has a right; the objective right.

term to which, the state or condition of a being after a change or at the present moment in a still continuing change; the end term; *terminus ad quem.*

total term, the whole being before or after the change occurs.

term, *n.* 2. *logic.* a. a sensible conventional sign expressive of a concept. b. a noun or verb or phrase used in relation to other terms as a part either of a proposition or of an argument; a member or unit into which the logical analysis of a proposition or of an argument is reduced.

abstract term, one that names a subject or form which is represented as separated from the real being and existing like a substance; the sign of an abstract concept.

analogous term, one which is predicated of two or more in a sense partly the same and partly different.

categorematical term, one which has meaning when used by itself; a *syncategorematical* term has meaning only when used in combination with or as modifier of another term.

collective term, a common term which in context is applied to all the members as a unit or group, but not to them singly or separately.

common term, one which is applicable to many individuals taken individually or separately from each other.

concrete term, one which names a subject or form as it is in a subject.

distributed term, one used in distributive or explicitly universal supposition.

distributed middle term, the middle

term in the syllogism used at least once in distributive supposition.

undistributed middle term, one used more than once in particular supposition in the syllogism.

equivocal term, one which has altogether different meanings when predicated of various things, even though it has the same written or tonal symbols in its different uses.

incidental term, that part of a complex

SOME DIVISIONS OF LOGICAL SENSES OF TERM

(Basis of division after Roman numeral)

I. Significative value of the term
  1. Univocal
    Analogous
    Equivocal
  2. Absolute
    Relative
  3. Categorematical
    Syncategorematical

II. Comprehension of the signified
  4. Positive
    Negative (indefinite)
  5. Absolute (direct)
    Connoted meaning
  6. Simple

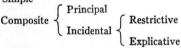

Composite $\begin{cases} \text{Principal} \\ \text{Incidental} \begin{cases} \text{Restrictive} \\ \text{Explicative} \end{cases} \end{cases}$

  7. Concrete
    Abstract
  8. Term of first intention (real term)
    Term of second intention (logical term)

III. Extension of the signified
  9. Proper

Common $\begin{cases} \text{Singular} \\ \text{Particular} \\ \text{Universal} \\ \text{Collective} \end{cases}$

  10. Distributed
    Undistributed

IV. Use in a syllogism
  11. Major
    Minor
    Middle
  12. Distributed
    Undistributed

---

or many-worded term which modifies the principal term by adding some mark of extension, quality, or clarification.

major term, the term of greatest extension of those used in the syllogism. In the first figure it is the predicate of the major premise and of the conclusion.

middle term, the term in a syllogism with which the major and minor terms are compared. In the first figure it is the subject of the major premise and the predicate of the minor premise. It never appears in the conclusion. It is called middle also in the sense of being the *medium* of proof.

minor term, the term of less extension in a syllogism. In the first figure it is the subject of the minor premise and of the conclusion.

particular term, a common term which in context or by addition of a particularizing sign applies only to some of the individuals to which the unmodified common term could apply.

principal term, that part of a complex (many-worded) term which signifies the main subject or the main predicate.

proper term, a proper noun, signifying (only) a singular object.

singular term, a common term with an incidental term that reduces its applicability to only one individual.

universal term, a common term made explicitly applicable to every member of a class by a sign of universality, as all, every, no, etc.

univocal term, one which is predicated of two or more distinct objects or natures in exactly the same sense.

term, *n.* **3.** *philosophy of man.* the mental term or the mental word. See WORD.

terminism, *n.* the Occamist form of nominalism, which makes the universal only a concept and a sign of many objects and emphasizes the study of supposition and the reality of only the individual whole.

terms, *n., pl.* the conditions of obligations, rights, duration, services, etc., which are agreed to in a contract.

testimony, *n.* **1.** the declaration or denial of a fact. **2.** evidence or proof presented, especially if it comes from a witness other than the immediately interested parties. 3. the act of testifying or manifesting to another one's own knowledge as true.

theism, *n.* the philosophical (or theological) doctrine of a personal and provident God. See ATHEISM; DEISM; NATURALISM; PANTHEISM.

theodicy, *n.* natural theology, considered especially in regard to its vindication of God's perfection and providence in spite of the evil in the universe. (Leibniz is credited with introducing this name for natural theology.)

theology, *n.* scientific inquiry, study, or teaching about God. See WISDOM. ABBR. – *theol.*

dogmatic theology, the treatment of the doctrines revealed by God as found in the authoritative sources of revelation; specifically, treatment of the content of the creed with secondary attention to moral and liturgical questions of theology.

moral theology, the theological study of human conduct according to principles of revelation.

natural theology, that portion of metaphysics which treats of the existence, attributes, and operations of God, the supreme Being; the philosophical science about God.

scholastic theology, systematic study, especially of dogmatic theology, according to the methods of the scholastics, and with only secondary emphasis on historical and textual studies.

theorem, *n.* a proposition or truth to be proved by purely deductive reasoning.

theory, *n.* 1. the body of the underlying principles of a speculative or an applied science; a complex body of knowledge integrating many facts. 2. speculative truth or contemplation, as opposed to practical wisdom or applied knowledge. 3. any hypothesis or proposed explanation, not yet established with certainty (not in common scholastic usage).

theory of knowledge, *n.* the philosophical study of the first principles of human thought and their value as knowledge. It is also called epistemology, criteriology, and even major or material logic.

thesis, *n.* 1. a proposition to be explained, proved, and defended against objections or misunderstandings. 2. a treatment of such a proposition. 3. a paper about such a proposition.
REF. – *Post. Anal.*, I, C. 2. *Topics*, I, C. 11.

thing, *n.* 1. an individual. 2. equivalent to *res;* hence, the transcendental known as essence. It is not properly an equivalent of being. 3. an object other than a person. 4. any object of thought as distinguished from words or signs of things.

Thomism, *n.* 1. any doctrine taught by St. Thomas or those respecting his ideas and guidance in philosophy or theology. 2. any doctrine of a scholastic philosopher or theologian. 3. any doctrine commonly taught by members of the Order of Preachers. 4. the body of propositions contained in the *Twenty-four Theses* approved by Pope Pius X. (This is probably the best and most accurate use of the word Thomism.) 5. Bannezian doctrines on free will, divine co-operation, grace, predestination, physical premotion, etc.

thought, *n.* 1. any mental activity or process. 2. mental activity as distinguished from feeling and intention. 3. the product of thinking, such as a concept, or judgment, or syllogism, or theory, or science.

through, *prep.* descriptive of causal action in (1) the sense of an instrumental cause through which the principal acts. (2) the form of the agent. (3) the activity of a subordinate official or agent through which a higher cause acts. (4) the authority and power of the principal agent through whom the subordinate official or delegated agent has the right to act.
REF. – *S.T.*, I, 36, a. 3 c. and ad 4; 39, a. 8 in second last paragraph; *Truth*, q. 8, a. 8 ad 13.

time, *n.* 1. "the number (measure or reckoning) of movement in respect to before and after" (Aristotle); the measure of change according to its before and after; the measure of the duration or rate of continuous successive change. 2. *the category.* position in relation to the course of events. ABBR. – *t.*
REF. – *Cat.*, C. 6. *Physics*, IV, CC. 10–14,

esp. end of C. 11. *S.T.*, I, 10, aa. 4–6; 46, a. 3, replies.

title, *n.* the concrete fact upon which a definite person's right to a definite juridical object is based. ABBR. – *tit.*

derived (secondary, subordinate) title, a title which either supplements a natural title or is acquired by way of transfer of an original title from one holder to another person.

natural title, one based immediately on the natural law.

original (primordial) title, the primary concrete fact or act by which someone first acquires a right over some juridical object previously not attached to any other person.

positive title, a title granted or recognized by positive law.

title of ownership, a definite contingent fact by which someone's right of control and disposition of some material object is established. See chart of titles under OWNERSHIP.

touch, *n.* 1. contact, q.v. 2. any one of the group of external senses whose end organs are scattered widely through the body and respond to pressure, heat, cold, pain, well-being, etc.

trace, *n.* a remote likeness to another in being or activity. It is also called a vestige. See IMAGE.
REF. – *S.T.*, I, 45, a. 7; 93, a. 6.

transcendence, *n.* surpassing excellence; existence in an order and manner above and beyond all other things. Thus, God is said to be transcendent as unlimited being, really distinct from and exalted above all things.

transcendent, *adj.* 1. supreme; of the highest excellence; distinct from and superior to. ANT. – *immanent*. 2. *in Kant.* the a priori; what is beyond or surpassing experience.

transcendental, *adj.* 1. common to all things whatsoever and to all differences between things; not restricted to any category, class, or individual. See MODES (OF BEING), COMMON. 2. necessary, essential to a being; e.g., a transcendental relation. REF. – *Truth*, q. 1, a. 1.

transeunt (transient, transitive), *adj.*

proceeding from one being or cause to another being; imparted to another. ANT. – *immanent*.

transformation, *n.* substantial change; change of substantial form or conversion. See CHANGE.

transgression, *n.* violation of a negative precept of law.

transubstantiation, *n.* 1. *theological word used at times in philosophy in comparing changes and discussing substance and accidents.* the total change of one substance, and hence of both its matter and form, into another substance. 2. *specifically.* the conversion of the whole substance of bread and wine into the Body and Blood of Christ at the consecration in the holy Sacrifice.

truth, *n.* 1. *in general.* conformity of mind and thing. 2. *principal sense.* conformity of mind with thing; adequation of mind with thing; assent to what is, denial of what is not. This is *logical truth*, truth of thought, or true knowledge. ANT. – *error*. Compare CERTITUDE. 3. *ontological* or *metaphysical truth.* conformity of thing(s) with mind; intelligibility of things. *Per se* or *essentially* the thing or its form is true according to its conformity to the idea of its maker; *per accidens* or *accidentally* it is true to anyone who can know it. 4. *moral truth.* conformity of formal speech with one's mind; truthfulness; veracity. ANT. – *falsehood, lying*.

basic truth, an immediately known proposition in a demonstration and appropriate to the topic of the demonstration. *Truths of events for purpose of analytic criticism are distinguished as:*

historical truth, the fact of the occurrence of some event, including the fact of the competence and veracity of the witnesses to it.

philosophical truth, the ultimate explanation of some event; specifically, the reason why some historical event is regarded as beyond the natural order of phenomena and beyond the power of nature.

theological truth, the reference of some event to God as its author, because it and its circumstances are worthy of God in purpose and manner of performance. REF. – *Met.*, IV, C. 7; VI, C. 4; X, C. 10. *N. Eth.*, IV, C. 7; VI, C. 2. *S.T.*, I, 16, aa. 1, 2, 4. *Truth*, q. 1, aa. 1, 2.

type, *n.* 1. the exemplary idea. See ARCHETYPE; EXEMPLAR; IDEA. 2. a genus, species, class, or group. 3. an individual, representative of the distinctive characteristics of a class of beings.

tyranny, *n.* absolutism, severity, and selfishness in ruling a state. See RULE. REF. – *Politics,* IV, C. 10.

U

ubication, *n.* the presence of a body in a definite place; the category of place. See PLACE, PROPER.

ubiquitous, *adj.* the real or seeming presence of a thing in all places at once; omnipresence.

ultimate, *adj.* 1. the last or final (member) in a set or series; first. 2. that beyond which further analysis, causation, distinction, etc., cannot be made; basic; fundamental.

ultimate, *n.* a fundamental principle, supreme cause, or very last reason.

uncommunicated, *adj.* unshared; not belonging to another as a part of it or as united with that other in one whole subject of being. See COMMUNICATION; PERSON; PERSONALITY; SUBSISTENCE.

understanding, *n.* 1. immediate, certain, undemonstrated knowledge. ANT. – *science.* 2. intimate knowledge, penetrating to the essence. 3. the intuitive habitual knowledge of the first speculative principles; *intellectus principiorum.* 4. the possible intellect; the power of knowing. 5. good judgment, especially in discovery of the equitable.

simple understanding, God's knowledge of the possibles.

REF. – *N. Eth.,* VI, CC. 10, 11. *S.T.,* I, 79, a. 8; 83, a. 4; I–II, 57, a. 2; II–II, 8, a. 1. *Truth,* q. 1, a. 12; 14, a. 4; 15, a. 1.

unessential, *adj.* 1. not pertaining to the essence or essential properties. 2. unnecessary; not required. 3. accidental; contingent.

union, *n.* 1. the act of uniting or combining the distinct or separate. 2. the state of being combined or of being constituted of distinct elements, parts, or principles. ANT. – *distinction* (but not separation). 3. the act or state of the will attaching its desires or love to the object loved. –

Forms of union mentioned are: mere co-ordination and composition; mixture; unity of parts of a body into one natural body or one artefact; substantial union of matter and form; union of substance with accidents; union or agreement of minds; union of means to an end; union of will with its object; hypostatic union.

REF. – *S.T.,* I–II, 25, a. 2 ad 2; 28, a. 1 c. and ad 3; III, 2, a. 8. *C.G.,* IV, C. 35.

unique, *adj.* 1. the only one of its kind. 2. absolutely unique or the only one of its kind that is real or possible.

unit, *n.* something that is undivided in itself and distinct from everything else; something one. See COMPOSITE; ONE; SIMPLE. See chart on p. 128.

accidental unit (*unum per accidens*), a group of units or natures related or connected together by some bond other than that of one nature or one form or a natural common purpose. Some also apply this term to the unity of substance with its accidents.

logical unit, a whole made by an act of mind or dependent purely on a mental act, as one proposition or one syllogism or logical relation.

metaphysical unit, a unit without parts; a simple being.

moral unit, a plurality of persons with one common purpose.

natural unit (*unum per se*), a thing with one nature or one form, whether it be a simple or composite nature. This is said of a natural whole, a continuum, the specific nature, and even of the undivided in general.

organic unit, something having the unity of a living organism or resembling the unity of a living organism in which specialized parts with specialized functions all act for the good of the whole.

physical unit, a composite unit or whole

which possesses one nature or one form for all its parts.

real unit, a thing which is somehow undivided.

REF. – *Met.,* V, C. 6; X, C. 1. *Politics,* III, C. 4. *Being and Essence,* C. 6. *S.T.,* I, q. 11; 30, a. 3; I–II, 17, a. 4; II–II, 49, a. 6. *C.G.,* II, C. 56.

unity, *n.* the abstract term for unit or the one; the condition or state of oneness or indivision.

universal, *adj.* 1. that which is common to many. 2. the general. 3. some one thing common to many which can be in many or be predicated of many. ABBR. – *univ.*

direct universal, see CONCEPT.

formally universal, that which is properly common to many. ANT. – *fundamentally universal.*

fundamentally universal, that which is the basis of universality in representation and predication, namely, the likeness of finite natures of the same class.

metaphysically universal, that which is common to all members of a given class of objects or objective concepts so that it is absolutely impossible that there be a single exception. See CERTITUDE; IMPOSSIBILITY; PRINCIPLE, ANALYTIC.

morally universal, that which is common and usual among moral beings, with the physical possibility that some moral being would be worse or better than the common pattern of conduct.

physically universal, common and uniform in all members of a class of natural bodies, whether in their structure, attributes, or operations, but with the possibility of miraculous exceptions. See MIRACLE; IMPOSSIBILITY.

reflex universal, see CONCEPT.

universal in causing, naming one cause which can produce many different things or many different effects, either with or without other immediate causes.

universal in essence, that which naturally can be in many things; the absolute nature. See ESSENCE, ABSOLUTE.

universal in predication, that which can be or is stated of many in a univocal and distributed sense; that which is predicated of many taken singly in exactly the same sense.

universal in representation, that which can represent many things; a universal concept; that which can represent something identically common to many things. REF. – *Interpretation,* C. 7. *Post. Anal.,* I, C. 11. *On Being and Essence,* C. 3. *S.T.,* I, 85, a. 2 ad 2; a. 3 ad 1, 2, 4. *Power,* q. 5, a. 9 ad 16.

universe, *n.* 1. all created things considered as forming a certain unity; the world as one order. 2. all natural things or creatures taken together, as distinguished from God.

universe of discourse, the restricted or fictional or hypothetical world in which certain things are said to be true or false.

univocal, *adj.* 1. that which has only one meaning. 2. that which is applied to one or to many in an identical meaning. 3. having the same nature of which an identical essential definition is truly predicable. See ANALOGICAL; EQUIVOCAL; PREDICATION. REF. – *Cat.,* C. 1. *S.T.,* I, 13, aa. 5, 10.

univocity, *n.* the state or condition of a concept or term that is identical in its reference to different concepts or objects. Compare ANALOGY.

unnatural, *adj.* that which is contrary to nature because it is contrary to the order of reason, or against the special dignity of man as man, or against the natural purpose of the kind of act performed. See CONTRACEPTION; NATURAL; VIOLENCE. REF. – *S.T.,* I–II, 71, a. 2; 94, a. 3 ad 2; II–II, 154, aa. 1, 11.

‡**unum per accidens,** *Latin phrase.* see UNIT, ACCIDENTAL.

‡**unum per se,** *Latin phrase.* see UNIT, NATURAL.

use, *n.* 1. an act of the will carrying out a command of reason in regard to the means already determined on to secure an end. 2. employment of means or exercise of power. 3. function. 4. enjoyment of property, as using a house.

improper use, some use of a thing besides the natural or normal use and imposed by the agent using it.

proper use, the use intended by nature for something or the normal purpose to

DIVISIONS OF UNITY, IDENTITY, AND DISTINCTIONS

Unity

Real

- Natural (*unum per se, natural whole*)
  - Metaphysical (simple)
    - Unique
      - In being
      - In essence
    - Common
  - Physical (composite)
    - With essential parts
    - With organic parts
    - With integral parts
- Artificial (*unum per accidens multa per se; unity of real relation*)
  - A subject united with a merely contingent attribute
  - Distinct wholes physically related by nature (called a physical system, a quasi-organic unity)
  - Principal cause with its instruments
  - Mechanical units (artificial unit in strictest sense; artefacts, especially if active)
  - Aggregations (heaps, etc.) merely related in space or in time or by chance static combination
  - Any connected series
- Moral
  - Natural
  - Conventional

Logical

- Mathematical objects
- Number as measure of multitude
- Unity of genera and of species
- Grammatical relations
- Logical relations. See *Logical Identity* below.

Identity

Real

- Absolute sameness
- Of the finite individual
  - Of the physical unit
    - Of the substance
    - Of the form only
  - Of the moral unit (a society)
- Of the nature (essence)
  - Considered absolutely (e.g., a definition)
  - Considered abstractly or reflexly

Logical

- Of signs
- Of concepts, propositions, interpretations of words and texts
- Of members of equations
- Of different systems of weights, coinage, etc.

Distinctions

Real

- Major (between two complete beings)
- Minor (between parts and co-principles, or between whole and part)
- Modal (between substance and its modes, etc.)

Formal (Scotus)

Mental (logical, conceptual, of reason)

- Nominal (verbal, purely mental, purely logical)
- Virtual
  - With a complete foundation in the thing
  - With an incomplete foundation in the thing

which an artefact is adapted. See END OF
AGENT; END OF WORK.

REF. – *Politics*, I, C. 9. *S.T.*, I–II, 16;
17, a. 3 esp. ad 1.

useful, *adj. and n.* that good which is
sought as a means to some other good,
but not for its own sake. See GOOD;
MEANS.

usury, *n. a disputed definition.* 1. any
interest or increment demanded for an
unproductive loan. 2. the act or practice
of charging interest for an unproductive
loan. 3. an excessive or illegal rate of
interest for a loan. 4. the charging of
excessive or illegal interest for a loan.

V

vacuum, *n.* a place or space not occupied by any body.
REF. – *Physics*, IV, CC. 6–9.

vainglory, *n.* see GLORY.

valid, *adj.* 1. having legal force and morally as well as legally binding. 2. sound; based on evidence and capable of withstanding criticism. 3. according to the rules of logic, as valid reasoning. 4. effective. See ILLICIT; INVALID; LICIT.

validity, *n.* the state or quality of being valid, sound, or binding.

objective validity of a concept, a concept based on objective evidence or having an objective foundation in external reality; the existence in the real world of that which is represented by the concept.

value, *n.* 1. *metaphysics.* the perfective good. 2. *ethics.* what is morally good, worthy of man, conformed to the moral standard. 3. *property, etc.* the estimated equivalent for some material good.

exchange value, the market value of an object or the aptitude of a thing for obtaining other things in exchange for it.

intrinsic value, the worth or goodness or purpose of some natural thing or activity in itself and in its natural function, independently of human esteem and compensation.

use value, suitability of a thing to serve human needs.

veneration, *n.* reverence due to someone or to something because of its connection with someone worthy of honor as one's superior.

vengeance, *n.* the infliction of a penal evil on one who has sinned.

verb, *n.* a word signifying action or passion and often modified by expressions of time. ABBR. – *v.*

verbal, *adj.* concerned with words; nominal or merely nominal.

vice, *n.* a bad operative habit contrary either to the attainment of truth or the performance of moral good.

capital vice, one from which as from a final cause other vices originate by inciting men to do other evils for its sake.
REF. – *S.T.*, I–II, 84, a. 3; II–II, 148, a. 5.

vicious circle, *phrase.* a circular argument, i.e., a fallacy in which two propositions both require proof, whereas each is proved by the other.

vindication, *n.* a defense of a right or claim, especially by public authority. Vindicative justice is retribution or penalty imposed by authority in the interest of public order because of wrong done.

violence, *n.* 1. action contrary to the nature of a thing. 2. *specifically.* force externally applied to a moral agent and tending to compel him to act against his choice or his inclination to choose in a certain way. See LIBERTY; NATURAL.

virtual, *adj.* 1. having potency, efficacy, validity, or equivalent perfection. 2. being something in effect, but not in form or appearance. The virtual is less strong than actual or formal, but much stronger than the nominal or merely apparent. USES – *virtual* contact, distinction, extension, intention, perfection, plurality, presence, etc.

virtually, *adv.* 1. by way of active potency or efficacy; after the manner of a cause. 2. not actually or formally, but equivalently and implicitly. Thus, the effect is said to be virtually in the cause; the particulars are virtually known in the universal; the conclusion is virtually in the premises; the soul by union with the body is virtually material; the whole law is virtually contained in its primary principles; the forms of lower levels of life and of the elements are virtually contained in the one form of the higher living unit; etc.

REF. – *Post. Anal.*, I, C. 1. *S.T.*, I, 76, aa. 3, 4.

virtue, *n.* a good operative habit in man; an operative habit perfecting rational powers to act according to the rule of reason; a human habit which makes its possessor good and his work also good.

cardinal virtue, one of the four principal or central moral virtues, to which the other virtues are related. Parts of the cardinal virtues:

integral parts of a cardinal virtue are such conditions, dispositions, and acts of the soul as are necessary for the perfection of a virtue, though not all of them are essential to its being. Thus, many factors are required for a very prudent man.

potential *or* **cognate parts** of cardinal virtues are virtues related to the cardinal virtue or somewhat analogous to it, but which lack the complete nature of the cardinal virtue and have a distinct formal object.

subjective parts of a cardinal virtue are complete species of a cardinal virtue, specifically distinct from each other.

Christian virtue, one specially taught by Christ, or practiced, perfected, or emphasized in a remarkable way by Christ and His followers.

infused virtue, one given to the soul by God, not acquired by the action of man; "a good quality of the mind by which we live righteously, of which no one makes bad use, which God works in us without us" (St. Augustine).

intellectual virtue, a good habit of the intellect, such as the arts and sciences.

moral virtue, a good habit of the will whose immediate object is a type of means by which the last end of man is attained.

natural virtue, one whose principles, object, and end are natural to man.

supernatural virtue, one whose principle is grace, whose end is man's supernatural destiny, whose object is a supernatural act or means or a natural means as related to the supernatural, and which man by his unassisted powers cannot acquire. See VIRTUE, INFUSED, *above.*

theological virtue, a good infused habit whose immediate object is God.

REF. – *N. Eth.*, II, CC. 1, 3, 5, 6, 9. St. Augustine, *On Free Will*, II, C. 19. *S.T.*, I–II, 55, esp. a. 4; 58, aa. 2, 3; 60, a. 5; 61, aa. 1, 2, 3; II–II, 48; 137, a. 2.

GROUPING OF SOME OF THE VIRTUES

Intellectual Virtues

Of the speculative intellect

Intuition of first principles (*intellectus principiorum*)
Mathematics
Physical sciences (physics, chemistry, geology, etc.)
Life sciences (botany, zoology, etc.)

Wisdom
- Metaphysics
- Natural theology
- Christian (revealed) theology

Philosophy of nature
Philosophy of man

Of the practical intellect

a) Liberal arts
   Servile arts
b) Practical sciences (architecture, optometry, etc.)

Practical wisdom
- Synderesis
- Ethics
- Political philosophy
- Political science
- Jurisprudence

GROUPING OF SOME OF THE VIRTUES (Continued)

Moral Virtues

Cardinal	Subjective Parts	Potential Parts (Cognate Virtues)	Integral Parts
1. Prudence	In self-direction In home-direction In statecraft and public affairs	Good counsel, both *Eubulia* and *Gnome* Ability in command Ability in execution	Memory (knowledge) Docility Sagacity Valuation Reasoning Inventiveness Foresight Circumspection Caution
2. Justice	Commutative justice Distributive justice Legal justice (social justice?)	Religion Penance Piety to parents Obedience Respect to superiors Truthfulness Liberality Fidelity Friendliness Gratitude Patriotism	a) Give rights to others b) Avoid injury to others
3. Temperance	Frugality (abstinence) Sobriety Chastity Modesty Dignity (gravity) Good temper	Continence Meekness Clemency Humility Self-respect Simplicity of life Studiousness Good manners Merriment Proper adornment	a) Sense of shame b) Sense of propriety c) Calmness (Dispositions rather than virtues)

4. Fortitude	None	Same names as integrals, but concern less difficult deeds	Concerning doing:
			  Magnanimity (natural confidence)
			  Magnificence
			  Munificence
			Concerning bearing:
			  Patience
			  Perseverance

Theological Virtues

Virtues	{ Faith Supernatural hope Charity	Gifts	{ Wisdom Understanding Knowledge Counsel Fortitude Piety Fear of the Lord

‡**vis aestimativa,** *Latin phrase.* see SENSE, ESTIMATIVE.

vision, *n.* knowledge of the existent as immediately present to the knower. Compare INTELLIGENCE, SIMPLE; UNDERSTANDING, SIMPLE.

beatific vision, the sight of God immediately present and the source of perfect happiness.

vitalism, *n.* **1.** the doctrine that living beings have a living essential constituent other than the chemical and physical constituents and properties of bodies. **2.** *specifically.* the scholastic doctrine that a vital principle is the substantial form or entelechy in any living organism, or that every living body is composed of an organic body and a vital principle or soul as its substantial form. See HYLE-MORPHISM. ANT. – *mechanism.*

vital principle, *phrase.* the substantial form of a living being; soul or psyche in the broader sense of the formal ultimate intrinsic source of all living activities. See PRINCIPLE; SOUL.
REF. – *S.T.,* I, 75, a. 1.

vocational group, *phrase.* functional or occupational group; corporative society, q.v.

void, *adj.* invalid; legally valueless; not binding.

void, *n.* empty space; a broken or disconnected matter or space; a vacuum.

volitional, *adj.* that which proceeds from deliberate reason and choice.

voluntary, *adj.* **1.** pertaining to any act or state of the will; moving one's self to act with knowledge of the action; proceeding from the will either freely or spontaneously.

deliberate voluntary act, the act of choice; volitional act.

imperfect voluntary act, any act of the will performed under conditions that limit knowledge or deliberation, and hence also limit full choice. These acts may be (*a*) semideliberate or (*b*) spontaneously follow passion and knowledge, but without any deliberation about alternatives.

perfect voluntary act, one that is performed with sufficient and unimpeded deliberation and choice.

voluntary, *adj.* **2.** any object or good which is known and willed. The *nonvoluntary,* according to Aristotle, is what an intellectual agent does in ignorance of particular circumstances of his action. The *involuntary* is what causes the agent pain or repentance; it is against his will.

conditionally voluntary object, one which the will would not choose for itself but only as an undesirable means or as a concomitant of that which it directly wills.

object directly voluntary, one which is willed or commanded in itself as the immediate object of the will.

object indirectly voluntary, one willed or permitted as a foreseen consequence or concomitant of the object directly willed; hence, it is called voluntary in cause rather than voluntary in itself.
REF. – *N. Eth.,* III, C. 1; V, C. 8. *S.T.,* II–II, 6, aa. 1, 2, 3, 6 ad 2; 20, a. 2 ad 3.

vow, *n.* a deliberate promise made to God to perform a better act.
REF. – *S.T.,* II–II, 88.

W

war, *n.* the use of armed force by a nation or part of a nation to impose its will on another nation or part of a nation.

total war, the view or practice that all persons and places in the enemy's territory are legitimate objects of attack and that all effective means may be used to win or defend one's self.

war of aggression, unjust military attack on the independence, territory, or other rights of another state.

wayfarer, *n.* a person tending to beatitude.

whereabouts, *n.* the place in or near which a body is. See PLACE; UBICATION.

whole, *n.* an entire or complete unit, containing all the parts necessary to constitute a distinct thing; something undivided (as a unit) and undiminished (lacking no part needful for its entirety). See COMPLETE; PART; UNIT.

logical whole, a class, either a species or genus; a universal whole.

moral whole, a society or moral person, i.e., a group of persons with some common intellectual purpose.

physical whole, a natural or artificial body or any natural composite unit. REF. – *Met.,* V, C. 26. *S.T.,* I, 76, a. 8; 77, a. 1 ad 1; 85, a. 3.

will, *n.* 1. the rational appetite; that power of the human soul or of a spiritual substance which tends toward a good apprehended by the intellect or away from an evil recognized by the intellect. 2. any act of this appetite, such as intention, choice, consent, use, enjoyment, love, hate, hope, desire, and joy.

antecedent will, an act of the will given before something else which would have been pertinent to the motives for acting.

commanded act of will, an act performed by some power under the direction of reason and will.

consequent will, an act of the will fol-lowing upon something else, as upon knowledge, emotion, etc., related to the will.

free will, that function of the will by which a person determines his own course of action or chooses between particular goods. See FREEDOM.

good will, an act of love in which one wishes good to another.

internal will, an act in the will itself; an immanent voluntary act; an elicited act of the will.

servile will, an act of the will based purely on motives of fear and self-interest, but not on love or principle.

will as nature, the will acting under natural necessity for happiness; the will to the necessary end of man.

will by participation, a sensitive appetite in a being who also has a will.

will as reason, the will acting with choice. REF. – *S.T.,* I, 19, a. 1; 80, a. 2; 82; 83; I–II, 8, a. 2; II–II, 27, a. 2; III, 18, a. 3.

will, *n.* 3. the act of transferring property to another upon death.

wisdom, *n.* 1. *in general.* the best form of knowledge. 2. *specifically.* the intellectual virtue or science concerning the first or supreme causes of all things.

philosophical wisdom, intuitive knowledge combined with scientific knowledge of the objects which are naturally the highest; metaphysics, including natural theology.

practical wisdom, 1. prudence. 2. any excellent form of practical knowledge, as of one of the architectonic arts.

speculative wisdom, theoretical wisdom or its pursuit for the sake of truth.

supernatural wisdom, 1. Christian theology. 2. the gift of the Holy Ghost whereby man understands and rightly judges of divine and other things by divine ultimate standards or "from God's

135

point of view" because of a connatural loving union with divine things.

REF. – *Met.*, I, CC. 1, 2. *N. Eth.*, VI, CC. 5, 7, 8. *S.T.*, II–II, 9, a. 2; 45. *C.G.*, I, C. 1; IV, C. 12.

wish, *v.* **1.** to desire or like something which is known to be not achievable. **2.** merely to wish, without effective willing.

witness, *n.* **1.** one who saw or can give a firsthand report of something; one who can give evidence based on his own immediate knowledge of a fact, event, statement, etc. **2.** evidence or testimony given by the witness.

word, *n.* an articulate sound used by human agreement as a sign of an idea and of the object of that idea. See TERM for divisions.

exterior word, the vocal or written sign of the concept of the mind.

interior (mental) word, the concept of the mind considered as an expressed likeness in the intellect and produced by the intellect in itself; the immanent term of knowledge.

REF. – *Interpretation*, C. 1. *S.T.*, I, 34,

a. 1. *Truth,* q. 4, a. 1, c. and ad 1. *Power,* q. 8, a. 1.

worship, *n.* honor and reverence due to someone. It is particularly referred to divine worship. See ADORATION; LATRIA; RELIGION; SACRIFICE.

direct *and* **indirect worship,** see RELIGION, DIRECT.

exterior (external) worship, the outward expression of internal worship, as in vocal prayers, hymns, ritual, sacrifices, etc.

interior (internal) worship, acts of the mind and will giving due honor and reverence to another, especially to God.

social worship, public honor to God, public prayer, etc., by the members of a society acting together as a moral person.

REF. – *C.G.*, III, C. 119.

written upon the mind, *metaphorical phrase.* held firmly in mind or memory. REF. – *S.T.*, I, 24, a. 1.

wrong, *adj.* **1.** *logic.* **a.** incorrect. **b.** invalid. **2.** *epistemology.* false. **3.** *ethics.* **a.** evil; not directed or leading to the end of man. **b.** sinful. **c.** unjust.

Y

Yahweh (Yahwe), *n.* the proper name of God, "I am Who am," "He Who is." God gave Himself this name when Moses spoke to Him in the burning bush. It is the same as *Ipsum Esse,* or the incommunicable divine name, or the tetragrammaton, i.e., the four consonants of the Hebrew word for this name of God. REF. – *The Holy Bible,* "Exodus," C. 3, verses 13–14. P. Parente, A. Piolanti, and S. Garofalo, *Dictionary of Dogmatic Theology,* s.v. "Tetragrammaton."

BIBLIOGRAPHY

Aristotle, *Categories; Posterior Analytics,* I, CC. 2, 11–13; *Topics,* I, CC. 5, 8; VI; VII, C. 3; *Physics,* IV, C. 2; *Parts of Animals,* I, CC. 2–4; *Metaphysics,* V, "The Metaphysical Lexikon."

Baldwin, James Mark (ed.), *Dictionary of Philosophy and Psychology* (Gloucester: Peter Smith, 1940 revision).

Bourke, Vernon J., *Thomistic Bibliography, 1920–1940* (St. Louis: The Modern Schoolman, 1945). This lists many articles and works on particular terms in scholastic philosophy.

Deferrari, Roy J., and Barry, Sister M. Inviolata, C.D.P., *A Lexicon of St. Thomas Aquinas* (Washington, D. C.: Catholic University of America Press, 1948–1949), 5 fascicles.

Eisler, Rudolf, *Wörterbuch der Philosophischen Begriffe,* 4 ed. (Berlin: Mittler, 1927–1930), 3 small volumes.

√ Garcia, F., O.F.M., *Lexikon Scholasticum Philosophico-Theologicum: Termini, Distinctiones, Effata* (Quaracchi, 1910). This gives Scotistic usage.

Geiger, L.-B., O.P., *La Participation dans la Philosophie de S. Thomas d'Aquin* (Paris: J. Vrin, 2 ed., 1953). Appendix I, "Le Vocabulaire de la Participation," pp. 457–472, studies the whole family of terms on participation, perfection, imperfection, etc., in St. Thomas' writings.

Lalande, André, *Vocabulaire Technique et Critique de la Philosophie,* 5 ed. (Paris: Presse Universitaire de Paris, 1947).

Organ, Troy Wilson, *An Index to Aristotle* (Princeton: Princeton University Press, 1949).

Parente, Pietro, Piolanti, Antonio, and Garofalo, Salvatore, *Dictionary of Dogmatic Theology* (Milwaukee: Bruce, 1951).

Peter of Bergamo, O.P., *Index Rerum Alphabeticus,* Vol. XXV of the Parma ed. of *Opera Omnia S. Thomae Aquinatis,* reprint (New York: Musurgia, 1949). It will usually be helpful to compare St. Thomas' commentaries with any text in which Aristotle presents a definition.

Runes, Dagobert (ed.), *The Dictionary of Philosophy* (New York: Philosophical Library, 1941). Definitions and discussions of many scholastic terms are contributed by scholastic philosophers. Many of the notices pertain to the history of philosophy and to philosophical systems other than scholasticism.

Schütz, Ludwig, *Thomas-Lexikon,* 2 ed. (Paderborn: Schoningh, 1895) (German).

√ Signoriello, N., *Lexicon Peripateticum Philosophico-theologicum,* 5 ed. (Rome, 1931). This gives definitions and phrases and distinctions from St. Bonaventure, St. Albert the Great, and St. Thomas.

Webster's New International Dictionary of the English Language, 2 ed., unabridged (Springfield, Mass.: Merriam, 1942).

Webster's New World Dictionary of the American Language, College Edition (Cleveland: World Publishing, 1953).

√ Wright, William Kelley, *A History of Modern Philosophy* (New York: Macmillan, 1941), pp. 617–626, "Glossary." This intelligent glossary of philosophical systems is one of the clearest for undergraduate students.